Knowledge Management

Joseph Davis
Eswaran Subrahmanian
Art Westerberg
(Editors)

Knowledge Management

Organizational and Technological Dimensions

Selected Papers from the Carnegie Bosch Institute Workshop on "Knowledge Management and the Global Firm: Organizational and Technological Dimensions" held in Sydney, Australia

With 22 Figures and 13 Tables

Physica-Verlag
A Springer Company

Professor Joseph Davis
School of Information Technologies
The University of Sydney
F09 Madsen Building
Sydney, NSW 2006
Australia
jdavis@it.usyd.edu.au

Professor
Eswaran Subrahmanian
Professor Art Westerberg
Institute for Complex
Engineered Systems
Carnegie Mellon University
1201 Hamburg Hall
Pittsburgh, PA 15213
USA
sub@cmu.edu
a.westerberg@cmu.edu

Cataloging-in-Publication Data
Library of Congress Control Number: 2004116623

ISBN 3-7908-0081-3 Physica-Verlag Heidelberg, New York

Physica is a part of Springer Science+Business Media

springeronline.com

Printed in Germany

Hardcover-Design: Erich Kirchner, Heidelberg

SPIN 10935644 88/3130-5 4 3 2 1 0 – Printed on acid-free paper

Preface

The importance and value of tracking and sharing the dispersed knowledge resources of contemporary organizations have received widespread recognition in recent years. It is widely believed that with the transition from the industrial to information-based economies, organizational knowledge has emerged as the single most critical resource at both macro- and micro-levels. A major challenge for most organizations during this transition and beyond is to learn to deal with the intricacies of discovering knowledge from the vast amounts of data being generated, identifying pockets of important knowledge in various forms, to devise strategies and techniques to formalize parts that lend themselves to codification, and to nurture technical and other solutions with which useful knowledge can be shared among relevant participants. This has the potential to produce greater knowledge utilization leading to multiplier effects in organizational performance. This calls for an approach in which both the organizational and technological dimensions of the challenge are better understood and effectively integrated.

The papers included in this volume were selected from a collection of papers presented at an invitation-only workshop entitled 'Knowledge Management (KM) and the Global Firm: Organizational and Technological Dimensions' held at the University of Sydney in Sydney, Australia in February 2003. The workshop was made possible by a generous grant from the Carnegie Bosch Institute at Carnegie Mellon University, Pittsburgh, USA. This institute is dedicated to enhancing the research into and improving the practice of knowledge-driven management of global organizations. The workshop was also supported by the School of Information Technologies at the University of Sydney and the Australian Graduate School of Management also in Sydney, Australia.

The thirty invited participants represented a broad cross section of university researchers, industry practitioners, and consultants from seven countries. Each one had either carried out significant KM-related research or was actively engaged in KM projects.

The papers presented in the workshop (nineteen in all) were organized under the following eight sections: Knowledge Management: the Landscape, Technological and Organizational Concerns in Knowledge Management, Knowledge Management and Development, Applying and Implementing Knowledge Management Solutions, Learning and Knowledge Management, Socio-Technical Networks and Knowledge Management, Externalizing and Interpreting Knowledge, and Emerging Perspectives on

Knowledge Management. The presenters were invited to submit papers to this volume after making revisions based on the lively discussions at the workshop following the presentation of each paper. After a preliminary review of the submitted papers, twelve papers were chosen for this book.

The selected papers in this book are organized under three sections: Knowledge Management: Conceptual Foundations, Empirical Perspectives, and Practitioner Perspectives. The first section is devoted to an introduction to the conceptual core of KM drawing on research and other scholarly writings from a number of disciplines. Davis, Subrahmanian, and Westerberg trace the origins of the focus on KM based on a review of this theme in fields such as Economics, Organizational Studies, Philosophy, and Information Systems and discuss the different kinds of organizational knowledge and the diverse modes of sharing. They also highlight the key role of information technology in supporting KM and enabling communities-of-practice to successfully evolve. DePaula and Fischer draw on their previous research on technology-supported learning and focus on the design and implementation of computer-based environments for the creation of new knowledge and its sharing in communities-of-interest in which the participants are drawn from diverse backgrounds. Cecez-Kecmanovic develops a novel theory of organizational knowledge (sense making theory) based on an exhaustive review and extension of Organizational Studies and related literature.

In the second section on empirical perspectives, Devinney, Midgley, and Soo present a summary of their empirical investigations into knowledge creation in contemporary organizations and report on KM's contribution to fostering innovation. Inkpen's focus is also on the creation and acquisition of knowledge but in the important context of inter-organizational alliances. Arunachalam and King present an historical analysis of industrialization in India and proceed to outline useful, KM-related policy guidelines for economic development. Lock Lee examines the functioning and contributions of social networks and communities and how they can enhance the social capital of firms.

The third and final section on practitioner perspectives includes five reflective and useful contributions from practitioners actively engaged in KM-related endeavors. Lucier and Dyer of Booz Allen Hamilton draw on their vast experience to propose and elucidate what they refer to as natural knowledge models based on the intellectual division of labor. They also tease out the implications of this highly original work. Biesner and his coauthor from Bosch explore the significance of the knowledge management approach by contrasting it with the traditional focus on basic factors of production such as capital and labor, from the vantage point of a large engineering company. Steve Denning who was responsible for initiating the knowledge management thrust at the World Bank highlights the critical role of stories and story telling in knowledge sharing and in promoting an action orientation. Kota Harinarayana who headed the strategic program which developed the highly sophisticated Light Combat Aircraft in India presents a systematic exposition of the complex and inter-connected challenges in acquiring and managing knowledge in technologically demanding and innovation-centric projects. Larry Moyer of EDS Learning Systems focuses on electronically facilitated learning and its contribution to organizational performance.

It is our conviction that the papers in this volume taken together provide a new and original perspective on organizational knowledge and knowledge management. We hope that it will be of benefit to both academics interested in improving their understanding and to professional managers seeking practical guidelines in this rapidly evolving area.

We gratefully acknowledge the financial assistance provided by the Carnegie Bosch Institute (CBI) at Carnegie Mellon University without which the Sydney workshop would not have been possible. We thank Professor Michael Trick, the President of CBI and Cathy Burstein, the CBI Coordinator whose guidance in organizing the workshop was invaluable. Richard Bailey at the University of Sydney contributed beyond the call of duty to make the workshop a success and to get this book manuscript ready. We are also thankful to Katharina Wetzel-Vandai, our editor at Springer, for her patient support.

Pittsburgh, PA.

Joseph Davis
Eswaran Subrahmanian
Art Westerberg

Contents

Part 1
Knowledge Management: Conceptual Foundations

Knowledge Management: Conceptual Foundations, Emerging Directions

Joseph Davis[1], Eswaran Subrahmanian[2] and Art Westerberg[2]

[1] School of Information Technologies, The University of Sydney, Sydney NSW 2006, Australia
[2] Dept. of Chemical Engineering and Institute for Complex Engineered Systems, Carnegie Mellon University, Pittsburgh, PA 15213, USA

Abstract

This paper traces the origins of Knowledge Management as an academic area of inquiry and as a key managerial concern in contemporary organizations. This is based on an overview of related developments in a number of fields including Economics, Organisational Studies, and Information Systems as well as some of the important developments in the business environment in recent years. We proceed to analyse and critique the status of 'organisational knowledge' from both epistemological and pragmatic standpoints and to explore the challenges in designing processes and systems for sharing such knowledge in large organizations. We also discuss technology-enabled communities-of-practice and their critical role in knowledge management.

Introduction

The notion of knowledge processing as perhaps one of the most important organizational activities has gained currency among researchers in a range of fields such as Information Systems, Organizational Studies, International Management, and Economics. This view of organizations goes beyond the more traditional information-processing perspective of organizations as being primarily engaged in the processing of large volumes of internal and external data to produce useful information to support decision making and to facilitate strategic and operational planning. It is based on the idea of organizations as knowledge producing, sharing, and disseminating entities in which there is an explicit focus on the processes and techniques for generating, selectively sharing, and utilizing knowledge. This idea is captured well in Winter's description of organizations as entities which "know how to do things" (Winter 1993). Knowledge Management as an area of academic inquiry and managerial practice is primarily concerned with a range of questions such as:

- What constitutes organizational knowledge and how is it generated and validated?
- What are the effective organizational and technological means for the sharing and transfer of organizational knowledge?
- How can organizational knowledge be measured? What are the useful metrics for quantitative assessment?
- What are the major constraints and bottlenecks that impede the effective sharing and utilization of organizational knowledge?

The important role played by the stock and application of knowledge in economic development is relatively well understood and has been addressed extensively by economists for some time (Machlup 1980, Nelson and Winter 1982, Eliasson et al, 1990). As early as 1962, Arrow had analysed the effects of *learning by doing* in firms (Arrow, 1962). However, its centrality in management of firms is a relatively recent concern. The active interest in managing knowledge as a critical organizational resource is largely a response to the challenges posed by an increasingly complex business environment characterized by intensified competition, greater globalization, compressed product life cycles, and the consequent information overload for senior management. As well, advances in information and communications technologies (ICT) in the form of internet and intranets, the World Wide Web (WWW), electronic document repositories with sophisticated search capabilities, computer-supported cooperative work (CSCW) and groupware systems, among others, promise the means for addressing the knowledge management challenge.

The issues referred to above have been faced in a more acute form by large, multinational corporations (MNCs) for which the forces of global integration, local differentiation, and worldwide innovation have become stronger and more compelling. Several scholars have argued that such firms have to devise mechanisms to enhance their global flexibility and learning levels in order to stay competitive (Bartlett and Ghoshal, 1991; Doz and Prahalad, 1991). This is increasingly achieved through the adoption of new organizational capabilities for pooling world-wide knowledge and to transfer and adapt innovative product and process technologies and project management knowhow to international markets. Several studies have investigated the organisational and technological mechanisms employed by MNCs to promote knowledge sharing and to develop and manage their intellectual resources. The implicit assumptions that underpin the category of `knowledge' in this context as reflected in the relevant literature and contemporary organizational practices have been explored and critiqued.

This paper is organised as follows: in the second section we present an overview of the antecedents of knowledge management. We briefly review developments arising from Philosophy, Economics, Organization Theory and Information Systems as they bear on KM. This is followed by a discussion of the role of information technology in supporting KM and communities-of-practice and their evolution. Section 4 includes a summary and some concluding remarks.

Organizational Knowledge

There is emerging consensus that perhaps the most important source of sustainable competitive advantage in an increasingly turbulent global business environment is knowledge. The organizational capability to create, recognize, disseminate widely, and embody knowledge in new products and technologies is critical when faced with shifting markets, rapid product obsolescence, hyper-competition, and financial upheavals (Nonaka, 1991).

However, despite extensive discussions of concepts such as 'knowledge management', 'intellectual capital' and related ones like 'organizational learning' and 'organizational memory', there appears to be a lack of conceptual clarity in the writings of many of the researchers and practising managers on their specific meanings. Davenport et al. (1998) has suggested that it is not useful to worry about the deeper ontological and epistemological dimensions of knowledge; they instead focus on specific knowledge management projects as the unit of analysis. This, in our view, is a risky strategy since it is hard to study knowledge management without a coherent conceptualisation of organizational knowledge. We present below, a review of the divergent perspectives on organizational knowledge and the latent assumptions that underpin them.

Philosophical Underpinnings

From an epistemological standpoint, most of what is characterized as organizational knowledge falls within the purview of 'weak knowledge' (Goldman, 1999). This is sharply contrasted with 'strong knowledge' which is the traditional focus of philosophical inquiry. Strong knowledge imposes very stringent criteria for the use of the term 'knowledge' which includes true belief backed up by valid justification or warrant for the belief, and the systematic exclusion of alternative possibilities. Such knowledge is rarely attainable in organizational domains. Besides, this form of skeptical rationalism bears little resemblance to the action-centered processes of generating, sharing, and utilizing knowledge (however imperfect) in organizations. It is unlikely that the 'strong knowledge' epistemology is particularly helpful in view of the inter-subjective and social nature of much of organizational knowledge. The latter tends to privilege consensus, immediacy, and perceived use value over strong-verifiability, super-objectivity, and transcendence associated with the stronger variant.

Weak knowledge implies true belief without the iron-clad backing of strong warrant or justifiability for the belief. It does, however, imply something more than just information and involves sustainable belief produced by the information that provides some kind of evidence pointing to the validity of the propositions and away from its rivals (Dretske, 1981; Goldman, 1999).

The justification for organizational knowledge is typically reliant on the following bases:

1. Coherence: knowledge fragments obtain their justification by virtue or cohering or meshing with the rest of the knowledge base so as to produce a holistic effect (Quine, 1952; Goldman, 1999).
2. Pragmatism: pragmatist epistemology emphasizes the relationship between knowledge and action. This position was initially developed by William James and subsequently expanded on by Dewey who endeavored to bridge the chasm between theory and practice, knowledge and action. The validity and use of knowledge can go only so far as it can "…..pass into actions which rearrange or reconstruct in some way, be it little or large, the world in which we live" (Dewey, 1929). Barring an extreme instrumentalist view, pragmatism attempts to develop an interactive model of knowledge based on engagement with the world through action, experimentation, and experience (Nonaka and Takeuchi, 1995).

Economics and Organizational Knowledge

Traditional microeconomic theory depicts (technical) knowledge as a quasi-public good. It is characterized by high levels of indivisibility and non-excludability. Its generation is the result of scientific research and general methodological procedures. Its transfer is largely unproblematic and is viewed as a spontaneous aspect of the economic system. The ability to appropriate the knowledge by the innovator is low even though patenting and intellectual property rights can reduce the scope for societal benefits from the knowledge (Arrow, 1969; 1994; Antonelli, 1999).

This perspective has been challenged by a number of researchers. The distinction between technological information and technological knowledge is sharply drawn with the latter conceptualised as incorporating a set of capabilities and competences needed to utilize the knowledge which in turn can be leveraged to generate new knowledge. Such knowledge is generated by a process characterized by cumulativeness and path dependence (Jorde and Teece, 1990; David, 1993, among others). Knowledge, according to this view, is highly localized and embedded in the previous background and experience of individual firms. It is the result of a learning process and involves highly specific and relatively 'tacit' knowledge processing (Antonelli, 1999). In contrast to the view of knowledge as an extraneous and exogenous input in traditional neo-classical economics, the endogenous growth model treats it like any other input such as labor and capital leading to increasing returns. In such a model, knowledge can be produced and exchanged and used in the production of other like goods, or in producing new knowledge. (Romer, 1986; 1990). Romer (1995) characterizes two of the three broad classes of inputs in the production process as being software which includes all the knowledge that has been codified and can be transmitted to others (i.e. literal computer code, blueprints, mechanical drawings, operating instructions for machines, scientific principles, folk wisdom, films, books, musical recordings, the routines followed in a firm, the literal figurative recipes we use, even the language we speak) where once the first copy of a piece of software has been produced, it can be reproduced, communicated and used simultaneously by an arbitrarily large number of people; and (3) wetware, which captures what economists call human capital and what philosophers and cognitive scientists sometimes refer to as tacit knowledge (i.e. all the things stored in the "wet" computer of a person's human brain).

Other Representations of Organizational Knowledge

The so-called knowledge-based theory of the firm is an extension of the resource-based perspective which has dominated organization theory for some time. The resource-based perspective posits that sustainable competitive advantage that a firm strives for in the marketplace is critically dependent on its key resources in the form of organizational capabilities and competencies that are difficult to replicate. Organizational knowledge is viewed as one of most significant productive resources that can contribute to competitive advantage (Kogut and Zander, 1992a; Grant, 1996). The central role of knowledge in the firm and the organizational processes and mechanisms for its integration and sharing across national borders is the primary basis of Kogut and Zander's theory of the multinational corporation. These authors have also highlighted the need for the mechanisms to be sensitive to the degree of tacitness or codifiability of the knowledge (Kogut and Zander, 1992a; 1992b)

A range of definitions and perspectives on knowledge has been presented in the organizational literature. Kerssens Van-Drongelen et al. (1996) defines knowledge primarily in the context of R&D as "… information internalized by means of research, study, or experience, that has value for the organization" (Kressens Van-Drongelen et al., 1996 p.214). Similar conceptualizations of knowledge as the result of processing and refining of information have been implicitly or explicitly employed by a number of authors. This view is an extension of the information-processing paradigm popularized by March and Simon (1959), Simon (1977), and Galbraith (1974). More recently Simon (1996) has argued that the challenge for today's managers is to filter and extract relevant knowledge from the vast amounts of potential and actual information available from internal and external sources. Effective systems need to be designed to intelligently filter information. In a similar vein, Davenport et al. describe knowledge as information combined with experience, context, interpretation, and reflection and knowledge production as comprising value addition to information (Davenport et al., 1998). Information is the flow of messages or meanings that might add to, restructure, or change knowledge according to Machlup (1980). Coyne (1997) refers to these and related representations of knowledge as the system theoretical view according to which the essential knowledge is contained in the information content and the subjective, inter-subjective, and spatial aspects are largely ignored.

An alternative view has been championed by Dretske (1981), Nonaka (1991; 1994), among others. This perspective acknowledges the importance of subjective factors such as beliefs and their links to actions as well as the relatively tacit dimension of knowledge. Knowledge is associated with beliefs produced and sustained by information (Dretske, 1981). Information represents a flow of messages but knowledge is created and organized from it, anchored by the commitments and beliefs of the concerned individuals. There is also a connection between such knowledge and the subject's ability to plan and act.

The more implicit and tacit dimension of knowledge has also been highlighted. For Polanyi (1967), explicit or codified knowledge is what is transmittable through formal and systematic languages. Tacit knowledge is more personal and subjective, making it difficult to be formalized and communicated. It tends to be deeply rooted in action, commitment, and involvement in a specific context. According to Nonaka, individuals are able to recreate their own systems of knowledge to accommodate ambiguity, noise, and randomness generated in the organization in its interaction with the external environment (Nonaka, 1994). Such knowledge resides in situated communities of interpreters rather than in texts or messages and these make sense only in particular interpretive contexts (Reddy, 1979). These communities emerge not through absorption of abstract knowledge but when members become insiders and acquire the community's shared vision and speak the same language (Brown and Duguid (1991). The notion of contextualization of knowledge and evolving communities of practice have particular resonance for MNCs given the geographic distances and cultural differences across units around the world. Following Coyne (1997), we refer to this perspective as the pragmatic view.

Table 1 presents a somewhat stylized set of distinctions between the systems-theoretic and pragmatic perspectives on organizational knowledge. It is worth noting that the dichotomy between system theoretical and pragmatic perspectives and their respective epistemological and ontological assumptions pervade most of the writings on organizational knowledge.

Table 1. Perspectives on Organizational Knowledge

	System Theoretic View	Pragmatic View
Source	documents, databases, systems, prototypes, processes and procedures, manuals etc.	People, communities
Form	Codified or codifiable; explicit	Tacit; implicit; intuitive
Transfer	Exchange of documents, electronic means, formal training	Socialization, apprenticeship, osmotic; situated learning
Organization	Relatively mechanistic	Organic
Philisophical perspective	Cartesian; separation of mind and body	More holistic; unity of mind and body

As we would expect, the fundamental differences between the system theoretical and pragmatic views in characterising organizational knowledge are reflected in the divergent approaches and perspectives on knowledge creation, sharing and management in organizations. In general, the former tends to focus on structural and systemic approaches while the latter emphasizes human-centred processes such as socialization, self-organizing teams, extended social interactions, personnel rotation etc. Besides the diverse modes of knowledge creation and transformation, the globalized firms are faced with the challenge of mobilizing and integrating fragmented forms of knowledge spread all over the world (Cohendet et al., 1999). As well, developments in information and communications technologies (ICT) are increasingly making it easier to separate, transport, and trade knowledge (Antonelli, 1996).

Nonaka has described processes for the creation and transformation of knowledge from tacit to more explicit forms. These include sharing language, experiences, mental maps and models through *socialization*, reconfiguring existing knowledge through sorting, adding, categorizing, explicit knowledge through *combination* (typically using computer technology), *externalization* of tacitly held knowledge through the use of appropriate metaphors and other triggering devices, and *internalization* of explicit knowledge by recontextualizing along the lines of double loop learning proposed by Argyris and Schon (1978). This involves the creation of new knowledge by reconstructing existing perspectives, frameworks, or premises on an ongoing basis (Nonaka, 1994, p.19). Furthermore, Nonaka presents a model of knowledge expansion and growth arising from the dynamic interplay between tacit and explicit knowledge possessed by organizations through the four processes discussed above.

While it is true that knowledge is continuously generated throughout the organization, some of the areas of critical focus have included R&D (Kerssens-van Drongelen et al., 1996; Jain and Triandis, 1990), project management, especially in distributed project management teams across multiple, geographically work sites (van Fenema, 1997; Manheim, 1993), new product develoment (Clark and Fujimoto, 1991; Wheelwright and Clark, 1992; Takeuchi and Nonaka, 1986), joint ventures (Inkpen, 1998; Culpan, 1993), technology transfer (Souder et al., 1990), and customer needs and market developments (Ashton and Stacey, 1995). A few of the arguably effective mechanisms commonly prescribed for the sharing and management of knowledge in these and other studies include:

- multifunctional project teams (Wheelwirght and Clark, 1992)
- personnel rotation (Edstrom and Galbraith, 1992; Inkpen, 1998)
- post-implementation reviews and audits (Kumar, 1990)

- best practices documentation (Davenport et al., 1997)
- structured task communication (Brown and Eisenhardt, 1995)
- learning histories (Kleiner and Roth, 1997)

A variety of IT-based systems typically involving various combinations of inter/intranet, document management and communication, knowledge discovery and data mining technologies have been proposed. Most of these provide a subset of capabilities for searching, sharing and collaborating over documents in electronic repositories and for extracting knowledge from large databases. One of the more celebrated among these is the intranet-based cooperative work and knowledge sharing system called virtual team network (VTN) developed by British Petroleum and used extensively. (Prokesch, 1997)

The ‘knowledge base’ of an organization may consist of several sources or media. Kerssens-van Drongelen et al. (1996) has classified these sources into four categories based on the work of Zeleny et al. (1990),

- brainware: knowledge in the minds of people, such as intuition, experience, specialized knowhow,
- hardware : tangible things such embodying knowledge such as material prototypes, products, R&D equipment, production processes,
- groupware: unwritten knowledge shared by people such as rules of thumb, heuristics, procedures, stories, myths,
- documentware: knowledge documented on paper or in databases/information systems such as CAD/CAM models, intranets, parts databases, patents, white paper, manuals, lab reports, hand books, project post-implementation reviews etc.

Knowledge Management and Information Technology

Developments in information and communications technologies have contributed significantly to the growing interest in the potential of knowledge management. IT-based systems can support to varying degrees the processes for the creation, storage and retrieval, sharing, and application of organizational knowledge. While some of these technologies such as databases, intelligent systems, and computer networks have been evolving for some time, the dramatic developments around the internet and the world wide web and related technologies have created considerable excitement. Part of the interest stems from the possibilities offered by the technology to effectively share explicit forms of knowledge at a low cost. It has been argued that such sharing and exchange leads to the creation of new knowledge and greater application of existing knowledge. IT is seen as an important enabler for KM initiatives in organizations with the usual caveat that the KM problem has other significant social and cultural dimensions (Davenport and Prusak, 1998). Examples of such IT-enabled applications include expertise databases, online directories, best practice databases, data warehousing systems, intrants and knowledge portals, computer supported cooperative work (CSCW) systems, and customer relationship management (CRM) systems, among others. It offers means for enabling the knowledge-intensive operations of large and small organizations to be coordinated through greater sharing and application of knowledge.

The technology-enabled approach to KM is not without problems. The expected benefits from pursuing this strategy has either not been fully realized in practice or its sustainability over time has proven to be problematic. Bonifacio and Molani (2003) attributes this failure to a basic assumption underlying most KM systems, that knowledge must somehow be standardized and centralized. Davis et al. (2004) attributes the limitations to the inevitable exacerbation of information overload arising from the use of traditional KM systems and tools. There is emerging consensus that the design of such systems need to be sensitive to the autonomy of local communities in which much of the actual knowledge processing takes place.

The foregoing suggests that the critical intersection of IT and KM is at the knowledge-based social networks which employ technology for remote coordination. These are typically communities that evolve through discovering members with similar interests and define themselves as a community-of-practice with the help of technology. They also use the technology to continually grow their skills, knowledge, and expertise (Ruggles 1998). They may use a range of technology applications such as online forums, intranets, and electronic conferencing systems to collaborate and learn in their distinctive areas of practice. Such networks and communities are less constrained by organizational hierarchies and the lateral and remote communications possibilities offered by the enabling technologies can and have played a significant role in the development of many knowledge networks. We continue with this theme in the following section

Knowledge Management and Communities-of-Practice

A number of important issues related to knowledge management have been addressed by researchers in recent years. The question of tacitness of knowledge and the whether and how this knowledge can be rendered explicit has been the focal one for a number of researchers. Tsoukas (2002) presents a detailed review of this debate. Several papers in this volume also address this important question at both conceptual and pragmatic levels. We present below a discussion of an important KM-related issue with important implications for both research and practice, that of knowledge sharing communities-of-practice and their evolution.

One of the most important contributions of KM is the recognition of the importance and economic contribution of emergent communities-of-practice (COP) and ways and means of supporting their work. These communities are distinct from groups or teams which tend to be the focus of traditional organization theory. Groups and teams are authorized and sanctioned by the organizations and generally have a relatively specific and project-related focus. They are also bounded within the organizations. In contrast, communities tend to be fluid and their membership often cuts across organizational boundaries and may include members from outside the organization. The communities tend to emerge during the course of existing or new activities and are, typically, not officially recognized. In this sense they could be said to be non-canonical and interpenetrative (Brown and Duguid, 1991)

Even though information and knowledge sharing practices in communities have been studied for a very long time, its first systematic exposition was presented in Lave and Wenger (1991). Their focus is on the acquisition of knowledge as a social phenomenon through participation in a communal process. The level of participation varies depending on the individual member's status, level of authority, or seniority in the community, all of which are continually renegotiated. A newcomer's initiation into the COP is by means of a process that Lave and Wenger describe as 'legitimate peripheral participation' in which legitimacy relates to evolving authority relations in the community, peripherality to the social standing of the newcomer, and participation to the fact that much of the learning is by participative 'doing' and interacting with the community. They have examined a number of case studies based on this model of community initiation in the context of apprenticeship training even though its applicability is more general. Wenger (1998) has suggested that COPs' strengths include the shared repertoire of resources they are able to build over time and the implicit or explicit policies, procedures, rituals, and even shared language they evolve which can facilitate knowledge sharing. It is important to note that the community-oriented perspective on KM represents knowledge-as-object and knowledge-as-action views as mutually constituting and that the knowledge in its holistic form is a property of the community.

A number of case studies of the functioning of both co-located and distributed, knowledge sharing, communities-of-practice has appeared in the literature. One of the most comprehensive accounts of the practice of community knowledge sharing supported by a bottom-up community-based knowledge system is the 'Eureka Story' from Xerox Corporation (Bobrow and Whalen 2002). The basic premise of this work is that some of the more useful organizational knowledge is deeply embedded in the insights and experiences of employees and the culture of work communities. Consistent with Brown and Duguid (1991; 2000), such knowledge originates in the form of practical solutions to difficult problems encountered in everyday work. These solutions constitute critical knowledge resource for ordinary work practices. Much of this knowledge remains embodied in work practices and are often shared and reified through conversations and stories among colleagues and work groups. Such knowledge could remain localized within small groups unless the organizations can intervene effectively through appropriate policies and creative application of information technology.

Bobrow and Whelan present a detailed account of the their experiences over seven years in the design, development, deployment, and evaluation of the Eureka system intended to support Xerox customer service engineer (who repair the copiers and printers) community to learn and share the useful field experiences and practices. The main goal of the system seems to be to enrich and amplify the creativity and innovativeness of the knowledge workers who are closest to the problem and to enable the sharing of the resulting knowledge among a wider community of over 20,000 such technicians worldwide. The authors candidly describe their early failures in applying artificial intelligence (AI) techniques primarily arising from the porousness and incompleteness of the knowledge bases. An important breakthrough arose when the company started deploying anthropologists to employ ethnographic methods to study how the field engineers actually worked; not how they said they worked. The company recognized the importance of non-canonical knowledge in the form of repositories of real solutions to difficult and not infrequent problems that the filed engineers encountered in their day-to-day work. The groups in which such knowledge was shared were localized and the challenge of the Eureka system was to make the knowledge more portable so that it can travel beyond the local work group and to extend the community's reach. The software development was based on the principle of co-design with the user community by responding to and making changes based on the suggestions and criticisms provided by the key community informants. The Eureka system was initially introduced in France where it was a big initial success. Contributions to the system in the form of new tips and system use by the community grew steadily and the KM system was generally recognized as a success in the French phase of the implementation riding on the French

Minitel system for the distribution of information (in the early days of the internet).

The next phase of the implementation was to extend it to Canada. Even though the community involved was similar to the one in France, some of the technical difficulties proved to be daunting. The distribution was handled through a client-server computer system in which the server database provided quick access to the knowledge tips. The communication between the users and the server was through a dial-in connection from the community members' laptops to a community bulletin board service with an efficient search facility to find the information needed. The infrastructure was not the most ideal but the community was still able to overcome many of these problems and Eureka evolved into a useful tool for the community of product engineers and technicians.

The migration of Eureka to the United States was much more of a challenge. To begin with, the sheer size of the community with over 10,000 technicians spread out over a vast area meant that there was no real community-of-practice in the sense that most KM writers understand it. Even without additional technical challenges, the participative co-design of the system with the community was virtually impossible. The inevitable bureaucratic interventions that come with the size and scale of such operations diluted the community-oriented aspects of knowledge sharing with Eureka. Despite this, the system was eventually widely accepted and evolved into a mainline program. The Eureka experiment is one of the largest reported experiments in community-based knowledge capture, validation and sharing and offers a number of interesting insights into nurturing communities-of-practice and supporting them with computer systems.

An important and relatively successful example of knowledge sharing communities is the ones behind the development of open source software (OSS). Open source movement has attracted significant attention in recent years mainly because it offers a robust and viable model for the production of scalable and secure software. The source code of the software is non-proprietary and is freely available and not subject to any constraints on modification or distribution. The main idea behind OSS is that good software evolves when a dedicated community of developers, programmers, and users can read, modify, and redistribute the source code. There are strong claims that this community-oriented evolutionary process produces better quality software than the traditional hierarchical and closed source software (CSS) development model.

There are currently tens of thousands of OSS projects at various stages of development. Each project is undertaken by a virtual community of dozens or hundreds of developers who are geographically distributed and coordinate their activities through the internet. The community members bring a variety of expertise and skills and contribute at varying levels of intensity. According to Raymond (2001), the key principles of the 'bazaar' model of community-based software development are the early and frequent releases of code and intense communication among the developers and with the customers/users and the taming of complexity and early and effective detection of most defects made possible by the large body of developers and users. Von Hippel (2001) offers qualified support for the strength of OSS development model based on the power and usefulness of the extended communities involved.

From the KM perspective it is important to recognize the knowledge creation and sharing activities of the communities behind these OSS projects, many of which are able to make useful contributions in the form of innovative software processes and products. The voluntary nature of the participation implies that these communities are in a continual flux with members taking on varying roles and the new members being inducted while others withdraw for short or long periods. However, members do take on specialised roles such as core members, active developers, peripheral members, bug reporters, bug fixers, readers, passive users etc. (Nakakoji et al 2002). Individual members graduate to more responsible roles typically based on the degree of competence they demonstrate as evidenced by the quality and maturity of the contributions they make. The transparency of individual contributions is facilitated by an electronic shared memory of all the activities and communications in the form of bug trackers, new feature trackers, concurrent version system (CVS) for managing code contributions, message boards, discussion forums which are typically aggregated at sites like Sourceforge (www.sourceforge.com). OSS communities are excellent exemplars of technology-enabled knowledge sharing communities in action. It has been suggested that the virtual organizations behind the OSS communities with their knowledge sharing practices, multiple interacting governance mechanisms, and reputation systems offer a viable, alternative model for traditional commercial and other organizations (Markus et al 2000).

Even though the significance of communities-of-practice in knowledge creation and sharing is clearly recognized, the level of sophistication of the IT tools and systems to enable the communities to evolve and grow can only be described as primitive. The Eureka case study discussed above highlights some of the challenges in providing computer support for such emerging communities. The experiences of the open source communities on IT support seem to be better but there is still scope for improvement. Another aspect of COPs that need greater research attention is that of knowledge sharing beyond the individual communities. In many situations, there is a need for part of the knowledge generated by COPs to be filtered and made available to people outside the communities and to other communities.

Conclusion

This paper has sketched the antecedents and the evolution of knowledge management as both an academic focus of research and scholarship as well as an important managerial preoccupation in contemporary organizations. We have traced the origins and development of KM from an interdisciplinary perspective drawing on developments in a range of fields including philosophy, economics, organization theory, and information systems. We have highlighted the differences between qualitatively diverse forms of organizational knowledge and their implications for KM. We have also outlined some of the challenges for designing and deploying information technology-based solutions for supporting effective KM. We also make a strong case for a focus on the critical role of communities-of-practice and their evolution based on the premise that understanding, nurturing, and supporting them presents one of the most significant KM challenges.

References

Antonelli, C. (1996), "Localized Knowledge Production Processes and Information Networks", Journal of Evolutionary Economics, 6, pp. 281-296

Antonelli, C. (1999), "The Evolution of the Industrial Organization of the Production of Knowledge", Cambridge Journal of Economics, 23, pp. 243-260

Argyris, A. and Schon, D. (1978), Organizational Learning, Reading, MA: Addison-Wesley

Arrow, K. (1962), "The Economic Implications of Learning-by-Doing" , Review of Economic Studies, 29, June, pp.155=173

Arrow, K. (1969), "Classificatory Notes on the Production and Transmission of Technical Knowledge", American Economic Review, 59, pp. 29-35

Arrow, K. (1994), "Methodological Individualism and Social Knowledge", American Economic Review, 84, pp. 1-9

Ashton, W.B. and Stacey G.S.(1995), "Technical Intelligence in Business : Understanding Technology Threats and Opportunities", Int. J. of Technology Management, 10(1)

Bartlett, A.B. and Ghoshal, S. (1989), Managing Across Borders: The Transnational Solution, Boston, MA : Harvard Business School Press

Bobrow, D.G. and Whelan, J. (2002), Community Knowledge Sharing in Practice: the Eureka Story, Journal of the Society of Organizational Learning, MIT Press, 4(2), Winter

Bonifacio, M. and Molani, A. (2003), The Richness and Diversity in Knowledge Creation: An Interdisciplinary Overview, Journal of Universal Computer Science, 9(6), pp. 491-500

Brown, J.S. (1991), "Research that Reinvents the Corporation", Harvard Business Review, Jan.-Feb

Brown J.S. and Duguid, P. (1991), "Organizational Learning and Communities of Practice: Toward a Unified View of Working, Learning, and Organization", Organization Science, 2(1), pp. 40-57

Brown S.L. and Eisenhardt K.M. (1995), "Product Development : Past Research, Present Findings, and Future Directions", Academy of Management Review, 20(2), pp. 343-378.

Clark, K.B. and Fujimoto, T. (1991), Product Development Performance, Boston, MA: Harvard Business School Press

Cohendet, P., Kern, F., Mehmanpazir, B. and Munier, F. (1999), "Knowledge Coordination, Competence Creation, and Integrated Networks in Globalized Firms", Cambridge Journal of Economics, 23, pp. 223-241

Coyne, R. (1997), "Language, Space, and Information", In Droege, P. (ed.), Intelligent Environments, Amsterdam: Elsevier, pp. 495-516

Culpan, R. (1983), Multinational Strategic Alliances, Binghampton, NY: Howarth Press Inc.

David, P.A. (1993), "Knowledge Property and the System Dynamics of Technological Change", Proceedings of the World Bank Annual Conference on Development Economics, Washington DC: The World Bank

Davis, J., Subrahmanian, E. and Westerberg, A. (2004) The Global and the Local in Knowledge Management, Journal of Knowledge Management, Special Issue on Technology, to appear

Davenport, T.H., De Long D.H. and Beers, M.C. (1998), "Successful Knowledge Management Projects", Sloan Management Review, 39(2), pp. 43-57

Davenport, T.H. and Prusak, L. (1998), Working Knowledge, Cambridge, MA: Harvard Business Review Press

Dewey, J. (1929), The Quest for Certainty, New York: G. P. Putnam

Doz, Y. and Prahalad, C.K.(1991), "Managing MNCs: A Search for a New Paradigm", Strategic Management Journal, 12(5), pp. 145-164

Dretske, F. (1981), Knowledge and the Flow of Information, Cambridge, MA: MIT Press

Edstrom, A. and Galbraith, J. (1977), "Transfer of Managers as a Coordination and Control Strategy in Multinational Organizations", ASQ, 22(2), pp. 248-263

Eliasson, G., Foster, S., Lindberg, T., Pousette, T. and Taymaz, E. (1990), The Knowledge Based Information Economy, Stockholm : The Industrial Institute for Economic and Social Research

Galbraith, J.R. (1974), "Organization Design: An Information Processing View", Interfaces, 4(3), pp. 30-36

Goldman, A.I. (1999), Knowledge in a Social World, Oxford : Oxford University Press

Grant, R.M. (1996), Toward a Knowledge-Based Theory of the Firm, Strategic management Journal, 17, pp. 109-122

Jain,R.K. and Triandis, H.C. (1990), Management of R&D Organizations : Managing the Unmanageable, New York: Wiley and Sons

Jorde, T.M. and Teece, D.J. (1990), "Innovation and Cooperation: Implications for Anti-Trust", Journal of Economic Perspectives, 4, pp. 75-96

Inkpen, A.C. (1998), "The Management of Knowledge in International Alliances: The Role of Collaborative Process", Carnegie Bosch Institute Working Paper, available at http://cbi.gsia.cmu.edu/work/inkpen.htm

Kerssens-Van Drongelen, I.C., de Weerde-Nederhof, P.C., Fissher, O.A.M. (1996), "Describing the Issues of Knowledge Management in R&D: Toward a Communications and Analysis Tool", R&D Management, 26(3), pp. 213-230

Kleiner, A. and Roth, G. (1997), "How to Make Experience Your Company's Best Teacher", HBR, Sept-Oct., p. 172-178

Kogut, B. and Zander, U. (1992a), Knowledge of the Firm, Combinative Capabilities, and the Replication of Technology, Organizational Science, (3), pp. 383-397

Kogut, B. and Zander, U. (1992b), Knowledge of the Firm, Technology Transfer, and the Theory of the Multinational Corporation, Working Paper, Institute of International Business, Stockholm School of Economics, December

Kumar, K. (1990), "Post-Implementation Evaluation of Computer-Based Information Systems: Current Practices", Communications of the ACM, 34(2)

Lave, J. and Wenger, E. (1991), Situated Learning: Legitimate Peripheral Participation, Cambridge: Cambridge University Press

Machlup, F. (1980), Knowledge: Its Creation, Distribution, and Economic Significance, Princeton, NJ: Princeton University Press

Manheim, M.L. (1992), "Global Information Technology: Issues and Opportunities", International Information Systems, 1: pp. 38-67

March, J.G. and Simon, H.A. (1959), Organizations, New York: John Wiley

Markus, M.L., Manville, B. and Agres, E.C. (2000), "What Makes Virtual Organizations Work"? Sloan Management Review, 42(1), pp. 13-26

Nakakoji, K, Yamamoto, Y, Nishinaka, Y, Kishida, K. and Ye, Y. (2002) Evolution Patterns of Open Source Software Systems and Communities, Proceedings of the ACM IWPSE Conference, Orlando FL, pp. 76-85

Nelson R.R. and Winter S.G. (1982), An Evolutionary Theory of Economic Change, Cambridge, MA: Harvard University Press

Nonaka, I. (1991), "The Knowledge Creating Company", HBR, Nov-Dec., pp. 96-104

Nonaka, I. (1994), "Dynamic Theory of Organizational Knowledge Creation", Organization Science, 5(1), pp. 14-35

Nonaka, I. and Takeuchi, H. (1995), The Knowledge Creating Company, New York: Oxford University Press

Polanyi, M. (1967), The Tacit Dimension, Garden City, NY: Doubleday Anchor

Prokesch, S.E., "Unleashing the Power of Learning: An Interview with British Petroleum's John Browne", HBR, Sept-Oct., pp. 146-172
Quine, W.O. (1953), "Two Dogmas of Empiricism", in, From a Logical Point of View, Cambridge, MA: Harvard University Press
Raymond, E.S. (2001), The Cathdral and the Bazaar: Musings on Linux and Open Source by an Accidental Revolutionary, 2nd ed. Sebastopol, CA: O'Reilly
Reddy, M. (1979), "The Conduit Metaphor: A Case of Frame Conflict in our Language About Language", In Ortony, A.(ed.), Metaphor and Thought, Cambridge, UK: Cambridge University Press, pp. 284-324
Romer, P. (1986), Increasing Returns and Long Run Growth, Journal of Political Economy, Vol.94, pp. 1002-1037
Romer, P. (1990), Endogenous Technological Change, Journal of Political Economy, Vol.98, pp. S71-S112
Romer, P. (1995), Beyond the Knowledge Worker, World Link, Jan-Feb
Ruggles, R. (1998), "The State of the Notion: Knowledge Management in Practice", California Management Review, 40(3),pp. 80-89
Simon, H.A. (1977), The New Science of Management Decision (Revised ed.), Englewood Cliffs, NJ: Prentice Hall
Simon, H.A. (1996), "Knowledge and the Time to Attend to it", Paper presented at the Carnegie Bosch Institute International Conference on High Performance Global Companies, April 21, 1996, Boca Raton, FL, available at http://cbi.gsia.cmu.edu/work/96-2.htm
Souder, W.E., Nashar, A.S. and Padmanabhan, V. (1990), 'A Guide to the Best Technology Transfer Practices", Technology Transfer, Winter-Spring
Takeuchi, H. and Nonaka, I. (1996), "The New Product Development Game", HBR, Jan-Feb
Tsoukas, H. (2002), Do we Really Understand Tacit Knowledge? Paper presented to Knowledge Economy and Society Seminar, London School of Economics, 14 June 2002
van Fenema , P. (1997), "Management of Globally Distributed Projects: Experiences form the GOLDD Team", Proceedings of the International Conference on Information Systems, Atlanta, GA, pp. 474-475
von Hippel, E. (2001), Innovation by User Communities: Learning from Open Source Software, Sloan Management Review, 42(4), pp. 82-86
Wenger, E. (1998), Communities of Practice: Learning, Meaning, and Identity, Cambridge: Cambridge University Press
Wheelwright S.C. and Clark, K.B. (1992), Revolutionizing Product Development, New York: Free Press
Winter, S.G. (1993), On Coase, Competence, and the Corporation, The Nature of the Firm,Oxford University Press, Oxford, UK
Zeleny, M., Cornet, R.J. and Stoner, J.A.F. (1990), "Moving form the Age of Specialization to the Era of Integration", Human Systems Management, Vol.9, pp. 153-170

Knowledge Management: Why Learning from the Past Is Not Enough!

Rogério dePaula and Gerhard Fischer

Center for LifeLong Learning & Design (L3D)
http://www.cs.colorado.edu/~l3d
Department of Computer Science and Institute of Cognitive Science
University of Colorado, Boulder, CO, USA

Abstract

Traditional knowledge management (KM) approaches aim to archive information from the past so lessons will not be forgotten, implying that the information needs of the future are expected to be the same as they were in the past. The basic assumption underlying our approach is that knowledge is not a commodity to be consumed but is collaboratively designed and constructed, emphasizing innovation, continuous learning, and collaboration as important processes.

Our approach to KM focuses on a *design perspective* in which workers as stakeholders create new knowledge as they carry out their work practices. Our goal is to enable innovative practices at a social level by supporting collaboration and communication. We see knowledge as an intrinsic aspect of collaborative design practices, in which stakeholders are integrating the knowledge they collaboratively construct into the (re)design of solutions and the practices themselves.

Exploring this approach, our research has studied the design and deployment of a collaborative KM system, Web2gether, which was developed to facilitate the creation and development of social networks among special education professionals. This effort has set the stage for a more systematic and thorough study of the integration of this technology into these professionals' day-to-day work practices. It has enhanced our understanding concerning the issues pertaining to the adoption of Web2 gether as a KM system and its effectiveness in addressing its users' real information and support needs.

Introduction

The traditional approach for knowledge management (KM) often considers knowledge as a commodity (Murray, 2000). An alternative view of KM oriented toward design communities focuses on support for collaboration, communication, and development of social networks (SNs) among stakeholders in design activities.

A discussion on KM cannot be restricted to the epistemological analysis of knowledge or the technical evaluation of a KM system. It has to address the various scales of interaction that impact the work practices of those involved in the processes of introducing and employing new KM practices and systems. Although the underlying definition of knowledge, either as a commodity or as the outcome of a design practice, will influence the design approach for KM practices and systems (see Table 1), a more thorough guideline for design needs to be complemented with a deeper understanding of social, technical, and organizational aspects of the context in which KM is to be employed. These aspects will help in unveiling the opportunities and challenges of the approach.

Toward this end, we have devised a more complete framework for KM based on the *design perspective*. In this framework, knowledge is regarded as being distributed among stakeholders and artifacts, being enacted while they carry out design activities within communities of practices and/or interests. As such, this framework draws on the concepts of distributed cognition, social networks, and information ecologies. A KM system to support this perspective should be based on the design of living organizational memories, which are evolving and collaborative repositories of information. This design approach draws on a process model for evolving and collaborative systems – namely, the seeding, evolutionary growth, reseeding model.

In this chapter, we describe and contrast the two conceptual foundations for KM to set the stage for an empirical study in which the *design perspective* was employed to support the complex and distributed work of special education professionals. This study has helped us further understand the opportunities and challenges in employing such a perspective in a real context. A successful integration of novel KM practices and systems into the work setting required major organizational and social changes, which can be facilitated or hindered by existing organizational structures (such as work, social, and incentive structures). Only through the balance between "the traditions and the transcendences" (Ehn, 1988) will KM approaches be able to respect these existing structures and at the same time help to enhance these practices with innovations.

The two perspectives outlined in Table 1 serve as the focus of the approach put forth later in this chapter. We start our discussion by describing and comparing the *commodity perspective* and the *design perspective*. Next, we describe our effort to apply the *design perspective* to a major project in which we created a collaborative KM system, Web2gether, to serve the needs of the special education professionals for people with disabilities. Our research has shown the opportunities and pointed to some of the benefits in utilizing this system to support the work of these professionals. We focused on providing them with professional and personal support through the development of social networks. To this end, we designed Web2gether to support the distributed and situated work of special education professionals, by implementing the notion of social network in the core of the system. The *design perspective* is not without challenges. We discuss the lessons learned from our research and development effort, including some challenges in deploying Web2gether.

Table 1. Two Perspectives of KM (Fischer and Ostwald, 2001)

	Commodity Perspective	Design Perspective
Nature of Knowledge	Object	Enacted
Creation	Specialists	Stakeholders
Integration	Design time	Use time
Tasks	System-driven	User-driven
Learning	Transferred	Constructed
Dissemination	Broadcasting	On-demand
Technologies	Closed, static	Open, dynamic
Work Style	Standardized	Improvised
Social Structures	Top-down	Peer-to-peer
Work Structures	Hierarchical	CoP and CoI
Incentive Structures	Job assignments	Direct involvement
Breakdowns	Errors to be avoided	Opportunities

Two Perspectives on KM

In the traditional views of KM, knowledge is regarded as a commodity that needs to be captured, stored, and indexed to allow efficient retrievals in the future. The underlying assumption is that future needs are most likely to be the same as those of today. The responsibility for creating adequate "knowledge structures" to enable future retrievals from the shared repository of "knowledge objects" is delegated to specialists (e.g., knowledge engineers), who at *design time* (when a KM system is designed and developed) create such structures.

Our work is grounded on a design perspective of KM that supports a design culture in which collaborating, working, learning, and creating knowledge are complementary aspects of the same social practice. From this perspective, knowledge does not reside inside one's head, but is distributed in a network of stakeholders and artifacts, and collaboratively constructed and enacted as work situations unfold. Stakeholders are reflective practitioners (Schön, 1983), who struggle to understand and solve ill-defined problems. Learning is intrinsic to problem solving because problems are not given but must be framed and solved as unique instances. Knowing in action provides a rich interpretive framework for individuals to cope with these new situations. As Schön put it, "our knowing is in our actions" (ibid, p. 49).

This perspective has two essential aspects. First, stakeholders, not specialists, create knowledge. Knowledge is an intrinsic aspect of acting in practice and is created by those who own the problems as they emerge (Fischer, 1994). Second, knowledge is a collaborative by-product of work. By actively participating, stakeholders become "knowers," and by collaborating, they construct knowledge. These aspects are summarized in Table 1, which contrasts the traditional "commodity perspective" of KM with the "design perspective."

From our perspective knowledge should not be treated as an object created, integrated, and stored by knowledge specialists at *design time*, to be later manipulated, transferred, and retrieved by users at *use time* (when the KM system is deployed and used), when they encounter problems and knowledge becomes necessary. It is instead one of the by-products of getting work accomplished, as enacted in collaborative practices by a network of stakeholders. In this network, these stakeholders, such as engineers, architects, government representatives, and local citizens, engage in the design of a joint solution to a common problem, and collaboratively constructing the knowledge necessary to address the problem at hand.

Knowledge is integrated into potential solutions at *use time* by means of user-driven tasks, rather than being predefined at *design time* through a series of canonical (system-driven) tasks. In light of that, the design process considers learning as a process of knowledge construction acquired as stakeholders act and improvise while carrying out their activities. In contrast, the commodity perspective regards learning as the transfer of knowledge from the "knowers" to the "learners." Knowledge is *broadcast* to an audience through standardized tasks, rather than being activated *on-demand.*

These two perspectives emerge from and support two distinct organizational structures. Knowledge as a commodity rests on top-down social structures in which there is a clear distinction between those who create the knowledge and those who need and use it. From the design perspective, no clear line exists between these two groups in that those who own the problem and need the knowledge are the ones who help to create it and later integrate it into the solutions. The top-down structure often reflects the hierarchical structures of roles and power of work structures, whereas the peer-to-peer structure reflects the types of work structures that take place in communities of practice (CoPs) (Wenger, 1998) and communities of interest (CoIs) (Fischer, 2001).

Another relevant implication of a top-down approach pertains to the incentive structures required to maintain the ongoing processes of creating and integrating knowledge as practices distinct from problem solving. This approach thus fosters a discrepancy between who does the work and who benefits (Grudin, 1988). This requires formal reward systems in organizations to motivate the process, such as mandatory and/or paid job assignments. In contrast, in a bottom-up approach, the incentive structures are often inherent from the collaborative structures of CoP and CoI. Stakeholders in this approach are more likely to actively participate due to their direct involvement with and ownership of the problems at hand.

The design of a technology to support either perspective carries with it certain implications. The commodity perspective rests on the premise that knowledge will be acquired, indexed, and stored at *design time* to address problems at *use time*. This implies the design of a closed system whereby information is preprocessed by knowledge engineers before the users of the system can make use of it. In contrast, the *design perspective* is grounded on the premise that knowledge is enacted in practice, and that stakeholders will activate the necessary other networks, information sources, and technologies so they can address their situated needs.

Traditional Views of Knowledge

In the 1990s, a major strategic shift took place in organizations with the acceleration of the rate of political, economic, and technical changes as well as the increasing worldwide use of information and communication technologies. At the same time that such changes were paving the road for a global market, globalization reciprocally helped to accelerate them. The new tendencies of this "information economy" required organizations to shift from simply thinking about products and marketplaces to focusing on resources, human capacities, and core competencies. The ability to outperform the marketplace rested on continuous generation of human capital, "generation and synthesis of collective, and organizational knowledge" (Brown and Duguid, 1998, p. 91). Particular attention was given to the challenges and opportunities of sharing and transferring knowledge within and across organizations. This became the major tenet and driving force of the traditional KM paradigm, which assumes that experiences lived in the past should not be forgotten in order to inform future experiences. Knowledge required and created thereof is deemed as a stock or resource to be captured, codified, archived, transferred, and disseminated, i.e. as currency.

The major approaches to address the challenges posed by this view take a "taxonomic" (Tsoukas, 1996) perspective. Such a perspective attempts to classify different "types of knowledge" in different organizations, which supposedly would create effective means for generating, sharing, and managing knowledge (Orlikowski, 2002). Many classifications stem from and elaborate on the distinction made by Polanyi (Polanyi, 1966) between tacit knowledge and explicit knowledge. Other dichotomies associated with knowledge were thereafter elaborated, such as codified versus noncodified knowledge (Hansen, 2002); "know-how" versus "know-what" (Brown and Duguid, 1998); and procedural versus declarative knowledge. They represent important, yet limited attempts to explain how *knowers* know (or learn) what they know (or need to know) to accomplish their tasks.

Explicit knowledge is commonly portrayed as simply codified or codifiable knowledge. As such, knowledge is treated as information, or "know-what," which can be reified and thereby captured, codified, and archived for future reference, and often is removed from the context in which it was generated. In contrast, *tacit knowledge* is usually discussed as personal, non-articulated, experience-based, and skill-type bodily knowledge (Polanyi, 1966). It can be thought of as a latent ability, often acquired through experience that can be enacted and activated in the context of work practices. As such, tacit knowledge contains subjective elements that make it more difficult to articulate, and it embeds elements of a particular practice that makes it difficult to transfer from one practice to another, thus making it "sticky." It is distributed among stakeholders, artifacts, and the social environment, which together with norms, division of labor, and motives constitute the activities of a CoP or a CoI.

A purely taxonomic view of knowledge poses intractable difficulties to the design of KM systems. The articulation and (de)contextualization of tacit knowledge are widely debated, yet unsolved problems. Due to the nature of *tacit knowledge*, namely being based on experiences derived from actions and interactions in a context, it emerges from a practice and can not be always associated with a specific element that constitutes it. Because *tacit* and *explicit knowledge* are mutually constituted and thereby are *sui generis* (Brown and Duguid, 1998), the transferring of knowledge from one practice to another becomes inherently problematic. There is a need for KM researchers and practitioners to go beyond the dichotomies. Knowledge should instead be seen as the ability to enact knowledgeably in practice (Orlikowski, 2002), as "know-how" integrated with "know-what" in practice, and as an emerging, often distributed, property of these practices.

These dichotomies have led to a narrow view of knowledge, organizational knowledge, and knowledge management. Knowledge has been regarded as a stock or a thing that somehow needs to become explicit so that it can be shared among stakeholders within and across organization boundaries. It fails to recognize that *tacit* and *explicit knowledge* are mutually constituted (Tsoukas, 1996) and cannot (and should not) be detangled from the practice from which they emerged. In particular, this view has led to two problematic notions of knowledge and the approaches to knowledge, namely, *knowledge of the past* and *knowledge as commodity*.

Knowledge of the Past

"Those who cannot remember the past are condemned to repeat it."
(George Santayana)

The quote from George Santayana reflects the underlying assumptions pertaining to the traditional approaches for KM. The major goal is to archive "knowledge" from the past so that lessons will not be forgotten. This is a rather limiting view of KM because it implies that the information needs of the future will necessarily be the same as they were in the past. Subsequently, those who need information for the problem at hand are treated as simply passive consumers of information (Fischer, 2002).

Knowledge of the past represents an attempt to articulate knowledge gained from previous experiences in order to anticipate future problems and to inform future actions. In organizations, it takes the form of best practices, scenarios, technical and directive documents, and reports that are generated by specialists based on previous experiences as well as anticipated and interpreted future needs. The goal is to provide efficient ways for users to access and share such explicit knowledge, although it alone is most likely to be insufficient to help in solving the problem at hand. Two distinct problems thus arise from this view. One is the assumption that this static and somewhat limited notion of knowledge can handle the complex and dynamic nature of real-life problems. The other is that it relies on existing understandings of the work practices it intends to support (Orr, 1990) and on imaginative limits of those who create it (Snowden, 1998).

In analyzing the effectiveness of formal documents in supporting everyday practices, Orr (1990) asserts that directive documentations are "designed not to enable deduction but to direct technicians to the solution through a minimal decision tree" (p.171). The premise is that the most effective sequence of actions can be determined at *design time* by developers and knowledge engineers who have a strong understanding of the technologies they develop but are likely to have a limited understanding of the context wherein such technologies are used. Not only do they have to anticipate possible problems with the technology, possible diagnoses, and efficient paths to the solution, but they also assume that the problems technicians will face in the field and the instructions to solve them are context-free, due exclusively to technical mishaps. Orr shows the extent to which this approach alone has been elusive and ineffective. He argues instead that users' most important goal is not necessarily to "fix a machine," but rather the relationship between the clients and their machines, and their relationships with the clients – in other words, "to keep clients happy" (ibid, p. 172).

Knowledge of the past is thus useful to the extent that it can anticipate future needs and be transferred across different contexts. It involves the articulation and organization of possible states and needs that can be anticipated at *design time* to address problems at *use time*. Hence, it constitutes a closed system. The "closedness" refers to the fact that the underlying sociotechnical structures of such systems are determined at *design time* and are unlikely to be modified at *use time* by the users. *Closed systems* do not give ownership to those who own the problem, but to a selected group of designers whose major challenge is to foresee all possible tasks and breakdowns in order to store answers to questions that might arise thereafter. These systems are likely to contain information that is chronically out of date and reflects an outsider's view of the work (Brown and Duguid, 2000).

Closed systems often limit the communication channels between those who own (or have mastered) the (sociotechnical) artifacts and those who own the problem (Fischer, 1994). In real work settings, stakeholders may not restrict their actions to those anticipated by a directive documentation (Orr, 1990), but their achievements and their innovative actions would unlikely be shared with other members of their work community via the "official channels." Innovation will likely happen outside the system. The sharing of innovations, "know-how," and successful work experiences – war stories – often takes unexpected pathways. Orr (Orr, 1996) revealed that, due to the absence of information or difficulties in interpreting the directives in the documentations, technicians expect to learn from one another, and, despite the individual character of their work, they make the effort to meet each other and to share their "war stories."

Knowledge as Commodity

"Knowledge is presented as a commodity to be acquired, never as a human struggle to understand, to overcome falsity, to stumble towards the truth." (Postman, 1995, p.116)

From an economic standpoint, the simple idea of being able to stock knowledge as a disembodied asset belonging to the organization was compelling enough for managers to open-heartedly embrace the KM vogue of the 1990s. From a technical perspective, the idea of manipulating knowledge as information was embraced as the solution for the challenges posed by the information economy in the information age. The emphasis on knowledge in organization has encouraged studies on the nature of knowledge that yielded the re-conceptualization of the firm as a dynamic knowledge-based activity system (Spender, 1996). The superficial and naïve implementation of KM approaches, resting on knowledge as a commodity, resulted in a blind emphasis on knowledge-based systems at the cost of deemphasizing knowledge as an attribute of people (Brown and Duguid, 2000).

The commodity perspective reifies "knowledge as a stock or set of discrete elements" (Orlikowski, 2002, p. 250). Studies based on the distinction between codified and noncodified knowledge (Hansen, 2002) exploit the underlying assumption that the major difficulty of transferring knowledge hinges on the difficulty of representing it. They show that the strength of the relations between knowledge seekers and knowledge providers affects the likelihood of "noncodified" knowledge being transferred. Although these studies have offered this important insight concerning the importance of *social ties* (both weak and strong) between those who own the problem and those who have the knowledge, they failed to provide a richer account for the nature of knowledge. They basically treated knowledge as information.

The Fallacies of Traditional Knowledge Management

The traditional approaches for KM, which have mistaken knowledge for information and a commodity, can be costly. Brown and Duguid (2000) tell a story of a firm that spent a generous amount to take over a rival, primarily in order to capture this firm's impressive intellectual capital, only to finally realize that its real competitive advantage had "lain in the operating knowledge of its line employees, all of whom had been let go" (p. 122). Similarly, the somewhat blind notion that KM would allow firms to downsize their "expensive" staff by process reengineering, which has instead caused them to lose human capital and its collective knowledge, instrumental for their operations. As John Thomas (Thomas, 2001) put it:

"It is a myth that we can simply "capture" the knowledge of a thirty-year expert in explicit form so we can fire the expert and hire someone with no relevant skills off the street, who can now use the "knowledge base" to perform like an expert"

At the surface, it seems natural to use knowledge and information interchangeably, but there are significant social and technical implications in doing so. Information can be treated as a self-contained element that can be manipulated, stored, and retrieved, whereas knowledge entails a knower (Brown and Duguid, 2000) knowledgeably acting in practice (Orlikowski, 2002). The focus shifts from studying only "what" people hold and share and the suitable technologies for doing so toward studying of the processes whereby *motivated* actors become knowledgeable and share their "knowing how" in practice and the suitable social and technical contexts for doing so.

Simply designing so that experiences of the past will not be forgotten in the future is insufficient to adequately address the current (and future) challenges of our society. Such an approach emphasizes information needs, although the major challenge nowadays can be characterized as *information overload*. Designing for "anytime and anywhere" is not as relevant as designing to "say the right thing at the right time in the right way" (Fischer and Ostwald, 2002a). KM should be designed to support evolution and implement *meta-design* principles (Fischer and Scharff, 2000) to support a design culture.

Design Perspective: Social and Situated Views of KM

The greatest contribution of the Internet was not necessarily to facilitate *reach* (easy access to information) but to facilitate *reciprocity* (social exchange worldwide) (Brown and Duguid, 1998). Similarly, the *design perspective* for KM goes beyond *reach* to allow *reciprocity*. It recognizes the key role of human agency in knowledgeable performances (Orlikowski, 2002), which are processes by which stakeholders are capable of knowledgeably acting in practices and thereby making appropriate and informed decisions concerning a problem at hand.

Knowledge is often portrayed as a possession that people carry around in their heads and transfer to each other, despite the fact that work is unlikely to be carried out in isolation, let alone without the aid of external artifacts. In contrast, we see *knowing* as mediated by artifacts situated, and often distributed, in the social environment (Salomon, 1993). Knowledge then becomes people's ability to act, participate, and make appropriate and informed decisions. Knowledge thus emerges from the synergy (rather than the synthesis) of distributed social networks of stakeholders and artifacts, operating in concert to help each other accomplish a common goal. It is no longer held or possessed, but fluid, distributed, and "activated." It focuses on the role of human agency in enabling the work to get accomplished in the context of a *design practice* within a CoP or CoI.

Due to the complex nature of social settings in which knowledge is enacted, it is critical to understand the various aspects that contribute to the formation of the *sociotechnical conditions* for stakeholders to accomplish their work, instead of focusing solely on the knowledge-transferring problem. To this end, we propose a conceptual framework to understand the sociotechnical conditions at *design time* as well as at *use time*. This framework attempts to guide the design of KM systems by highlighting the distributed and collaborative nature of design practices, and to help in the analyses of organizational issues that may facilitate or hinder the use of such systems. This framework draws on the following concepts:

- **Communities of Practice and Interest**: Design contexts in which the design perspective on KM emerges.
- **Distributed Cognition**: Knowledge distributed in the environment.

- **Social Networks**: Knowledge as a property of the interactions and relationships among stakeholders and artifacts.
- **Information Ecologies**: Complex, coordinated, dynamic, and dependable relationships among actors and information sources.
- **Living Organizational Memories**: Design rationale for the evolving KM system to support social networks.

Communities of Practice

The inherently social and situated nature of knowing invites us to consider a meaningful social structure in which knowledge is enacted, created, and shared among stakeholders. Such a structure should represent the social and historical contexts in which they are capable of acting, participating, and making appropriate and informed decisions. Social practice represents an important sociocultural structure that embraces most of these aspects. Through practice, members of a sociocultural community develop a shared understanding of what they do, how they do it, and how they are related to each other and to other communities and their practices.

Because individuals often work in collective settings, and knowledge is distributed among practitioners and their social environments, social practice was broadened to account for the relationships among these individuals within their working communities. Lave and Wenger (1991) define a CoP as a social structure that captures the interdependence and relationship among individuals, (legitimate) participation, communities, and sociocultural practices. A CoP creates the conditions for its members to exercise their ability to put their knowledge into practice (Wenger, 1998).

The ability to knowledgeably act in practice often is different from the "official knowledge" specified in manuals, directive documentations, and best practices. It emerges from experience and, more important, active participation in CoPs. For example, Orr (1996) shows that technicians must first learn about the work and the social settings, including the technology, in which services occur so as to tackle the actual sources of the problems, which in most cases are not necessarily technical. Such knowledge to act in practice can be acquired only through participation and experience, and mostly shared among members of the same community of practice.

Despite the informal aspect in most of organizations, CoPs are often very stable social structures. CoPs have histories, cultural identities, interdependences among members, and mechanisms for reproduction (Lave and Wenger, 1991). Such stability enables the development of trust, shared language, strong social ties, and common values, which facilitate the creation and dissemination of knowledge among the members of CoPs. Although CoPs are a powerful source of knowledge, they can easily be restricted by the limitations of their own world-view, that is, the risk of *group-think*.

Communities of Interest

Working on complex problems usually requires the collaboration and coordination of stakeholders from different CoPs. We define a CoI (Fischer, 2001) as a group of stakeholders brought together from different CoP, on the basis of a common concern or interest, to solve a particular complex design problem. They can be thought of as "communities-of-communities" that help CoPs to overcome the problems they create for themselves. In contrast to project teams, wherein employees are held together by a formal contract such as a business project, CoI stakeholders are held together by a shared interest. There are fundamental differences in their goals and motivations.

CoIs are often more temporary than CoPs and do not establish a social practice. They are characterized by a shared interest in the framing and resolution of a design problem and can be more innovative and more transforming than CoPs if they can leverage on the "symmetry of ignorance" (Rittel, 1984) as a source of collective creative innovations. Challenges facing CoIs are in building a shared understanding of the problem at hand, which often does not exist at the beginning but evolves incrementally and collaboratively. Members of CoIs must learn to communicate with and learn from each other (Engeström, 2001), although they may have different perspectives and perhaps different vocabularies for describing their ideas. Learning within CoIs is more complex and multi-faceted than *legitimate peripheral participation* (Lave and Wenger, 1991) in CoPs, which assumes that there is a single knowledge system within which newcomers move toward the center over time.

Because CoPs hold a single knowledge system, acting knowledgeably is often unproblematic and relatively easy compared to the challenges of operating within CoIs, which often do not share a common language and practice. Various social strategies have been proposed to mitigate these challenges and facilitate the sharing of knowledge and allowing knowledgeable performances within CoIs, such as: developing *boundary objects* (Bowker and Star, 2000), supporting *knowledge brokers* (Barbara and Clifton, 1992), fomenting the use of electronic communication systems, and disseminating "useful-practices" (in contrast to best-practices) (Orlikowski, 2002). These strategies are important as attempts to circumvent the social and technical obstacles that often impede an effective exchange of information within CoIs.

Distributed Cognition

The *design perspective* requires a framework for studying the distributed nature of KM. Resting on a distributed and coordinated notion of knowledge, such a framework should account for the complex, distributed, and sociohistorical nature of human actions in the world. In our research, we have employed distributed cognition (Hollan, et al., 2001, Salomon, 1993) as such a framework.

Distributed cognition holds that knowledge does not necessarily reside solely in a person's head, but is often created by and revealed in social practices, and mediated by sociotechnical artifacts situated in a social environment. One major contribution of this framework is to expand the unit of analysis for cognition from merely focusing on cognitive processes in an individual's head toward a systemic view of cognition delimited by functional relationships of the elements that participate in a task situated in a sociohistorical context. Another important contribution is to bring culture, context, and history back to the study of cognition. According to distributed cognition, all human activities are embedded in sociohistorical contexts, which are not solely created by local cultural and historical practices, but also co-created by each participant's own history and life-experience.

Social Networks

Social networks (SNs) offer a way to understand the complex dynamics of communities (Hillary, 1955), and how people exchange support, by shifting away from a sociogeographic structure toward a structure of interpersonal relationships (Wellman and Gulia, 1999). SNs help us understand how individuals share information, experiences, and support, and how they accomplish their tasks (Nardi, et al., 2000). Sns are source of human capital (Coleman, 1988) that allow stakeholders to engage in socially meaningful collaborative activities, helping them recognize the importance of their cohort in the building of knowledge. The strength of interpersonal ties (weak or strong) is instrumental to community organization, the diffusion of influence, information and innovation, social cohesion, and emotional and professional support (Granovetter, 1973, Rogers, 1995).

The SN view of exclusively linking people needs to be extended to include information, resources, and artifacts. A knowledge level perspective is required to extend the traditional view of an SN (Carley and Hill, 2001).

Traditionally, an SN refers to "the who" in the organization, which refers to the active agents who possess the knowledge to get the work done. "The who" is capable of knowing some of "the what" or "who else to ask," and thereby capable of taking knowledgeable actions. "The what" is essentially information (i.e., resources, personal and professional support, and related personal experiences and stories) that is traditionally not an element of an SN. From the *design perspective* of KM there is a need to integrate "the who" and "the what," and, more important, to support the synergy between them so as to allow knowledge to be enacted in practice. SNs in organizations thus become distributed cognition systems, the existence of which can be often attributed to balanced information ecologies.

Information Ecologies

The distribution of cognition in an SN creates the need for the orchestration of human actions to allow common goals to be achieved. Such orchestrated actions, as Hutchins describes in his account of ship navigation (Hutchins, 1993), can be achieved only through learning-by-doing-in-practice and, more important, through learning to become an active and responsible member of a CoP or CoI. The last construct of our framework concerns the nature of the relationships among all elements that participate in creating the contexts in which knowledgeable actors knowledgeably act. Its major focus is not on the synthesis of such elements, but on their synergy. Ecology can be thought of as a cognitive architecture – complex networks of stakeholders interacting, and thereby enabling information flow among them – and as a sociotechnical system.

The notion of ecology represents synergy among heterogeneous elements, and also alerts for the danger of ecological failure due to environmental imbalance (Nardi and O'Day, 1999). Ecology implies a focus on evolution, and the need to constantly nurture the relationships among its members. Hence, it should be given the time to grow, but not without its members' active efforts to direct and shape it so as to create adequate (social and technical) environments that in turn enable synergy among its elements. For instance, Nardi and O'Day (1999) describe the important, yet often unaccounted, work of librarians in corporate libraries. Librarians and clients often work together repeatedly and get to know each other. This allows librarians to better understand their clients' actual information needs, allowing them to offer information that their clients would otherwise be unable to find. Conversely, clients know when and how to appropriately place their requests by knowing what to expect from the librarians.

As sociotechnical systems, these *information ecologies* cannot be completely understood by the study of its parts, but by the relationships among them, that is, the complexity of integrating technology into the environment as well as its use and its reciprocal impact on the practices and the technology itself. Such interrelationships highlight the importance of active participation of those whose work practices and everyday lives will be affected by the technology, the long-term co-evolution of activities and technologies, and the "keystone species" – individuals with skills, experiences, and motivations without which an ecological system cannot adequately function.

Living Organizational Memories for KM

Based on the message of this chapter of that learning from the past is not enough, we need collaborative KM systems in which participants can go beyond the information given (Bruner, 1973) by creating new understandings and by learning from their peers. Informed participation (Brown, et al., 1994), which transcends the simple access to existing information sources (Fischer and Ostwald, 2002b), requires social changes as well as new interactive systems that provide the opportunity and resources for social debate and discussion rather than merely delivering predigested information to participants. Systems that attempt to capture "all possible information" are closed systems, and they are most likely to fail in supporting all needs from real-world problems without being constantly reinvented.

To change KM systems from closed to living organizational memories (Terveen, et al., 1995), we have developed a process model, *the seeding, evolutionary growth, and reseeding (SER) model* (Fischer, et al., 2001), that supports the design and deployment of evolving and sustainable systems. The SER model describes three phases of evolution in terms of the stakeholders involved and their activities. The *seeding* phase creates the initial conditions for the adoption and initial use of a system. The *evolutionary growth* phase is characterized by a series of "creation, integration, and dissemination" cycles (Fischer and Ostwald, 2001), whereby relevant information that emerges from work activities is created, integrated, and disseminated by those who own the problem. Finally, *reseeding* is a stage wherein the system is reorganized to address future needs.

The *SER* model is supported in turn by *meta-design*. *Meta-design* is a design approach that attempts to create technologies that support content changes as well as structural changes at *use time*. It supports processes for creating new media and environments that allow users to act as designers.

It enables structural changes at technical, social, and content levels, and it attempts to create a new mindset wherein users are no longer simply consumers of information, but are active co-designers (Fischer, 2002).

Web2gether: KM Support for Special Education

The Web2gether project is a multi-year-long effort embedded in the larger research project "CLever: Cognitive Levers – Helping People Help Themselves" (CLever, 2003) to understand and provide social and technical means for supporting the use of technologies in special education. Early in our investigation (Kintsch and DePaula, 2002), we found that one of the major barriers to the adequate use of technologies in this environment was the lack of professional as well as social support. We shifted then our approach from simply offering a technical solution to facilitate the access to these educational resources toward a sociotechnical approach to offer means for participants to reach each other, and thereby create and develop SNs. Web2gether was designed aiming at this goal by helping caregivers not only find resources, but form SNs and share their experiences. Sharing experiences has been shown to be an effective design approach for KM systems in the context of distributed and complex work practices (Bobrow and Whalen, 2002). It aims to go beyond the mere access model of technology (Arias, et al., 1999) by following the *SER* model. It is a collaborative KM system, which instantiates the conceptual framework presented in this chapter.

In our research, we were able to identify a series of conflicts and contradictions that emerged from special education practices, and opportunities to overcome some of these limitations with the support of the use of a collaborative KM system. The support for SNs is an important step toward the development of communities (of practice and interest). Our attempt to deploy and implement Web2gether in the schools has raised numerous concerns regarding its use and adoption. These concerns are presented here along with the lessons learned.

A Brief History of Web2gether

This project began when an assistive technology specialist from the BVSD created and distributed a CD-ROM with a large number of programs that were potentially beneficial for the education of students with special needs. The failure to see widespread use of the CD initiated our current research program and resulted in a conceptual framework for understanding the low adoption and the high abandonment rates of technologies in special education (Kintsch and DePaula, 2002).

To address this problem, the CD-ROM was improved with *meta-data* to support the location of the available educational resources suited for particular needs. This extension was still limiting to the extent that it could not support the "creation-integration-dissemination" cycles (Fischer and Ostwald, 2001) that are necessary to support adequate sharing of information among and across social practices.

We extended this approach by developing Web2gether. During the last few years, we have built a close relationship with the special education community, which has allowed us to collaborate on the design, development, and deployment of Web2gether. The information space of Web2gether was initially "seeded" with the software applications from the CD-ROM. This initial seed was considered to be a necessary condition to motivate users' active participation and thereby foster new contributions.

Table 2. Development Phases of Web2gether

	CD-ROM	Web2gether	
Development	Phase 1	Phase 2	Phase 3
Data Structures	Categories	Meta-data	Personal experiences
Information Access	Browsing	Searching	Recommendation
Design Approach	Access	Access	Informed participation
Goal	Facilitate access to the resource by making them readily available	Facilitate the discovery of the resource by implementing searching mechanisms	Development of SN among caregivers to facilitate support to the use of technology in schools

The system underwent three major design and development phases during this time.
Table 2 shows the phases that have been implemented and assessed. It highlights the major design orientations in each phase, namely underlying data structures, major information access mechanisms, design approaches,

and design goals. Aiming at providing support for the *design perspective* of KM and addressing some of the concerns from our fieldwork, Web2gether evolved to becoming a *living organizational memory*.

The design focused on the following considerations (see Fig. 1 for more details on the implementation of this considerations):

- Ongoing support for the professional development process;
- Equal access to the professional development opportunities;
- Safe environment for sharing experiences and ideas in that participants have their privacy and confidentiality assured;
- Recognition and reward mechanisms for achievement and participation;
- Support for both institutional as well as individual requirements (i.e., a resource shared through the technology should address the particular needs of a student with disabilities and his or her particular educational goals based on the curriculum);
- Help for users to find others with similar interests, needs, and experiences, and to effectively enable them to find information/resources relevant to the task at hand;
- Support for managing personal contact in order to facilitate communication and overcome the sense of isolation.

Web2gether allows users to share stories and personal experiences (Denning, 2001, Thomas, 2001) regarding unique cases in which users came up with effective solutions to address their unique needs. For example, In the *Café* (see Fig. 1) users may share experiences regarding unique behavior challenges in trying to facilitate inclusion of students in the general education classrooms; adaptations made on existing technologies for unusual situations not anticipated by technology designers (e.g., computer games originally designed for entertainment being utilized to help a student with severe cognitive disability to learn cause-and-effect concepts); and accommodations and modifications of curricular materials to meet the unique needs of students with multiple disabilities (see Area 5 in Fig. 1).

By making the accumulated experiences of individuals in an organization publicly available to each other, and in particular to newcomers, we hypothesized that Web2gether can help in establishing connections among weakly bonded individuals (see Area 1, 2, and 6 in Fig. 1). Information sharing thereby facilitates the development of stronger social bonds among like-minded individuals facing similar experiences, thereby enabling the exchange of professional and personal support. Web2gether can enhance the practices in special education by helping these professionals connect with one another and get the support they need to cope with their day-to-day challenges (see Area 1 in Fig. 1).

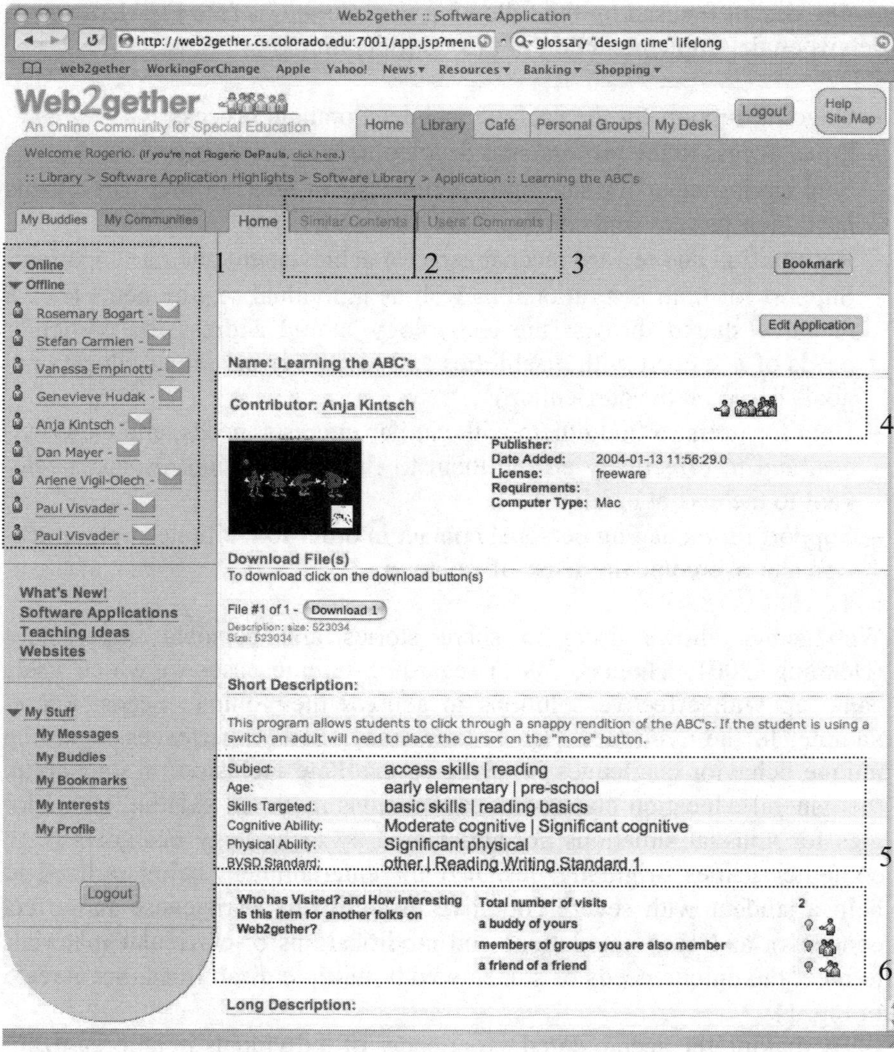

Fig. 1. Web2gether Screenshot – This figure highlights six major areas of the Web2gether system that address some of the design consideration presented in this chapter: 1) Management of personal contact information; 2) Support for finding resources relevant to the problem at hand (Similar Contents); 3) Collaboration and professional support (Users' Comments); 4) User's relationship with the contributor; 5) Support for institutional requirements and individual needs; and 6) Who is accessing?– social awareness based on social networks.

The goal of Web2gether was not only to enable users to access information relevant to their problems at hand, but also to turn these resources into *objects-to-think-with* as well as *objects-to-talk-about* (i.e., to provide means whereby users can interactively rethink their problems, re-conceptualize information needs, and share their problems and ideas). For instance, in reading others' personal experiences and stories, a user could learn how to approach a given problem and identify unique modifications in existing technologies to support it. Web2gether makes use of stories as means for fostering the creation and dissemination of personal experiences by continuous learning to replenish and renew the existing stock of life-experiences and educational resources. These experiences not only provide situated information regarding the context in which the technology and education materials were previously utilized, but also provide means for users to identify other users with similar experiences to ask for support. By doing so, they become means for the creation and development of an SN among those involved with special education.

Research Setting and Methods

The design, development, use, and assessment of Web2gether took place at various schools in the Boulder Valley School District (BVSD) – a school districted in Colorado, in which our research center is located. In the BVSD, special education services are available to all students whose disabilities interfere with their ability to receive reasonable benefit from general education instruction alone. Currently, the district offers special education support to more than 3400 students, ranging from students with mild learning or emotional disabilities to students with severe multiple disabilities. Approximately 165 special education teachers, 300 teacher aides, 15 occupational and physical therapists, and 30 speech language pathologists work with these students.

We collected data through participant observation, semi-structured interviews, and informal open-ended interviews. We conducted a series of site-visits at different schools in the BVSD, where we observed and followed the work of special education professionals, and we carried out a series of semi-structured and informal interviews with special education teachers and related service providers, namely occupational and physical therapists, speech language pathologists, social workers, and psychologists, to understand the issues pertaining to the use of technologies in the support of their students. We observed the work of several of these professionals working directly with students with disabilities, and participated in a few technology-training meetings.

Lessons Learned

Table 3 summarizes the lessons learned from our research. It highlights the major opportunities as well as challenges to the use of Web2gether by special education professionals in schools. Our fieldwork has revealed a great opportunity to apply the *design perspective* to support special education information and support needs. In contrast to the traditional views of education and classrooms, special education is a unique and complex work environment that involves not only the education of students with disabilities, but also continuous time, people, and resource management, not unlike a traditional office environment.

Opportunities for Web2gether

Special education teachers (hereinafter referred to as teachers) are frequently physically, professionally, and socially isolated from their peers and other professionals. Limited time for extra-curricular activities and the state of being constantly overworked (Barab, et al., 2001) contribute to the lack of opportunities for sharing and for building relationships with other professionals. They have been unable to establish connections that would facilitate the sharing of "know-how," information, and support important to their day-to-day challenges in dealing with the unique needs of their students, namely *universe-of-one*. Experiences to help other teachers cope with emerging problems are seldom shared. Teachers often find themselves unable to deal with issues that peers may have already experienced and for which they found solutions. Not knowing "who to ask, and who to tell" (Kass and Stadnyk, 1992, Nardi, et al., 2000) becomes a major problem in coping with the *universe-of-one* nature of special education. *Learning from the past* is unable to fully address these issues. One example is the traditional teacher professional development method that hinges on training programs and the development of best practices or training is inadequate to provide the ongoing and long-lasting support necessary for a sustainable education of these professionals (Barab, et al., 2001, Schlager, et al., 2002). Being isolated and having to deal with very unique problems are great challenges in special education work practices, but they also offer great opportunities to the use of Web2gether.

Benefiting from Existing Information Ecologies. Special education is a complex environment in which one finds a few cohesive information ecologies. Within these ecologies, information, support, activities, and technologies necessary for the adequate support of the needs of students with disabilities synergistically flow among special education professionals and through their artifacts and social practices. They are, however, the exception rather than the rule – islands of success stories made possible by the dedication and hard work of individual persons. We saw an opportunity in Web2gether to provide a means whereby teachers can bridge these ecologies, find the professional and personal support they need, and share their experiences.

Important *key species* in these ecologies are the assistive technology specialists. They play a critical role in fostering the use of technology and the dissemination of information across schools. The use of technologies hinges on the active involvement and ability of these professionals not only to find the appropriate technologies, but also to collaborate with teachers and parents in accommodating, modifying, and learning how to use them. These specialists act as "knowledge brokers," bridging the gap between those who need support and the potential solutions. In realizing the role played by these professionals, a great deal of design effort was put on supporting their work. Not only are they likely to benefit the most from a broader adoption of Web2gether, but they experience a lower entrance cost (or threshold) to use it because their practices are more closely related to the use of such technology from the beginning. There is a higher value in using the system as well as motivating others to use it. In this regard, they play a critical role in disseminating the use of the system throughout the district because one important aspect of their work is to provide these professionals with new technologies.

Learning by Sharing Experiences. The exchange of stories is an important aspect of learning among special education professionals. They often share stories and life experiences as a means to give and receive technical, professional, and social support. Stories set the stage for discussions as well as create the necessary common ground for helping and learning to take place. They help these professionals learn from each other and understand the context in which solutions to the problems are employed so they can attempt to carry them over to their specific situations and needs. We observed in our fieldwork that stories provide more situated and contextual information regarding the experience, allowing specialists to contrast the current situation with their previous experiences, and thereby come up with more effective solutions to the problem at hand. This is often the case among collocated professionals or those working in teams within schools, but it is seldom the reality across schools. The only opportunities take place in training sessions or in-services offered by the district. Web2gether attempts to help teachers overcome these physical barriers, allowing them to reach out to one another and exchange their experiences.

Table 3. The Opportunities and Challenges to the Use of Web2gether

	Opportunities	Challenges
Nature of Knowledge	Universe-of-one	Highly situated in time and students' day-to-day needs
Creation	Teachers dealing with unique cases, create situated solutions to these problem	Time constraints, and motivating active participation
Integration	Matching solutions of unique cases with the problem at hand, and matching unique uses of technologies with the curriculum	Time and knowledge for doing the matches
Tasks	Find resources and support from others to help educate their students	Constant management of resources, and paperwork – impediments to the use of innovation
Learning	From each other's experiences and stories	Costs of actively participating and taking the time to learn
Dissemination	Reducing the costs by connecting individuals facing similar experiences	Time constraints, privacy, and lack of a culture of sharing
Technologies	Living OM and recommender system	Costs of learning to use innovations, acceptance of innovations and changes
Work Style	Constant needs for adaptations and modifications to match the educational needs and abilities of students – highly improvised	Overworked, and under constant time pressure
Social Structures	Overcoming the physical isolation or classroom limitations and constraints	Top-down (or institutionalized), lack of a sharing culture, and isolated
Work Structures	Reaching those facing similar challenges	Hierarchical, highly regulated
Incentive Structures	Personal initiatives	Difficulties to motivate risk-taking or learning
Breakdowns	Learning from experience, and improving existing practices	Lack of resources and time to cope with the costs of failures

Much of the reality concerning the actual use of Web2gether was unveiled when we attempted to introduce it into the work practices. This has helped us further understand the barriers for change in the school environment, which hinders attempts to introduce Web2gether into its practices. We observed that these barriers for change became a major impediment in the adoption of the system. Not being able to change existing practices and norms directly affected the use and adoption of the system. We next describe some of these barriers when we introduced Web2gether into special education work environments. They highlight the major challenges special education professionals face in using the system to support their work practices (see Table 3).

Barriers for Change: Challenges in Introducing Web2gether

> *"This book is not so much about stories to preserve organizations: it's about using stories to change them." (Denning, 2001, p xviii)*

Technological innovation is only one side of the solution for the challenges teachers face in their daily practices. For Web2gether to add any value to their practices, it needs to be meaningfully integrated into the overall organizational structures (i.e., social, work, and incentive structures). This requires changes in both technology and organization.

Changes are often subject to conflicts and resistances. The complex interrelation between technical and organizational changes is seldom reported in the KM literature. In our research, despite all the efforts to seed the information spaces with appropriate contents and despite the support from the department of special education in the district to facilitate the introduction of Web2gether into the classrooms, we faced many challenges to overcome the barriers to organizational changes.

Lack of Incentive Structures. The school system offers little incentive for promoting changes, taking risks, and adopting innovative ideas. The only reward for changing and trying to improve the education of their students is the teachers' personal satisfaction and the sense of self-fulfillment. Schools often do not reward their employees for achievements, but are likely to punish them for failures (Hodas, 1996). Teachers rarely take risks in implementing innovations whose benefits are not directly associated with the institutional interests.

Lack of Time. Time pressure often hinders any attempt or willingness to find, learn, and use new technologies. Due to ongoing time pressures, teachers are more likely to see high costs in the use of a technology. They then face the dilemma of the active user (Carroll and Rosson, 1987): how to balance time to get the work done and to learn to use an innovation. The dilemma of the active user is related to the rational choices workers make while facing competing or conflicting situations, such as the trade-offs between dealing with pressing problems and investing in long-term solutions (such as learning to use a new technology). Overcoming this situation does not necessarily reside on learning outweighing work, or vice versa, but rather on the integration of both. Learning and working should become the same aspect of carrying out any activity in a work practice. Toward this end, innovations in the workplace have to be meaningfully integrated into practices, so that learning and use become the same activity through which users can see tangible benefits and long-term impact in their work practices and careers.

Tangible Rewards and Long-term Investments. In normal situations, special education professionals are likely to take a more conservative position and carry out activities that are likely to have a clear and short-term impact on their work as well as their careers. For example, special education teachers are likely to spend a great deal of their time teaching their students to take the standardized tests because these tests have a direct and obvious impact on their work, as opposed to spending time engaging in activities to learn how to use Web2gether so that they can obtain support from other professionals. In this kind of situation, institutional pressures that clearly impact their careers eclipse any benefit from the long-term investments of using Web2gether.

Merging Existing with New Structures. In order to understand the challenges to change is critical to first understand the relationship between social and technical structures existing in the environment and the social and technical structures embedded in the design of a technology. The introduction of a technology often requires institutional and social changes to accommodate the new structures engendered in its use. If these new structures conflict with the existing ones in some respects, a barrier to change will ensue, and innovations likely will not be adopted. The reconciliation of these two structures can be facilitated by the use of participatory design activities as well as *meta-design* approaches to allow users to make appropriate modifications and accommodations in the structures embedded in the technology as the need for changes unfold through its design and use.

"Build It and No One Comes:" Challenges in the Seeding Process

One major challenge in the design and deployment of Web2gether was that "*we build it, and no one came*" (Smith and Farquhar, 2000). Collaborative and evolving systems are of no value or use without users' active and informed participation and contributions. To help overcome this "cold-start" problem, the information space on Web2gether was initially seeded (Fischer, et al., 2001) with the software applications from the CD. We hypothesized that this initial seed was argued to be a necessary condition to motivate teachers' active participation and thereby foster new contributions.

Despite the seeding process, no major use of Web2gether was observed early in the project. Ever during the design of Web2gether, we were not convinced that "if we build it, they would come."

Creating meaningful seeds is the first step toward this goal. The seed was originally regarded to be the technical infrastructures and the initial contents implemented on Web2gether. This notion had to be extended to include social infrastructures to support the use of the system in its users' everyday work activities. We concluded that a meaningful seed for a KM system necessarily has to address the existing information and support needs, but it should not be limited to technical functionalities and content. In our research it was fundamental to provide social infrastructures that permit users to integrate the innovations and changes promoted by the use the system into their everyday work practices.

A seed should be a bridge between existing practices (and the sociotechnical structures embedded in them) and the innovations (and the sociotechnical structures embedded in the design of the system):

- It should provide social structures that promote collaboration and connections between users;
- It should set the tone of the discussions and interactions to help them understand the possibilities offered by the system; and
- It should also be built on structured activities that help integrate the use of the system and their everyday activities, thereby facilitating its adoption.

A seed is a *boundary object* that, while helping users make sense of the sociotechnical system by linking innovation and existing practices, creates opportunities for them to rethink and improve these practices in this new context. It is the first step to facilitate a meaningful integration between "traditions and transcendences."

From "Knowledge of the Past" to "Informed Participation"

The "knowledge of the past" approach for the design of KM systems reinforces a passive notion of information sharing, in which users are supposed to act as consumers of information previously digested by content designers or knowledge engineers. It encourages forms of participation that are primarily motivated by an individual's interest in self-benefit ("what is there for me now?"), which is generally not conducive to a more sustainable participation, and thereby to the development of a living organizational memory. In contrast, the *design perspective* puts forth the notion of "knowledge as enacted in practice," emphasizing that knowledge is constantly evolving as a by-product of "knowers'" interactions with one another and acting in the context of their social practices. Knowledge requirements and workers' participations are not static – everyone is a potential knowledgeable contributor.

It is critical that users abandon a purely "consumer" mindset, and take on a more *designer mindset* (Fischer, 2002). This is a cultural change whereby users learn to take an active as well as informed role in the processes that directly impact their own work practices and social environments. Moving from the mere passive attitude of expecting to be able to access all possible resources toward a more active attitude of becoming informed participants represents a major cultural shift not only in the ways people make use of collaborative KM systems, but in the ways they do their work, interact with others, and see their roles in the society. It does not mean that users need to be active all the time, but to be willing to take risks, learn, and do things in ways that have not been imagined before in order to contribute to their personal development as well as the development of their social practices, and helping them to do the same. Only with this progressive attitude can collaborative KM systems such as Web2gether be of value to its users and to society in general.

Conclusion

In this chapter, we have proposed the *design perspective* of KM. It supports the concept of social networks in which communities of practices and interests work collaboratively produce solutions to complex design problems. Knowledge is viewed as distributed and synergistically enacted by a network of actors when they carry out their design practices.

Special education is a complex environment that benefits from this KM perspective. Teachers face everyday unique challenges that require the expertise of a team of dedicated professionals working synergistically and collaboratively to help those with disabilities accomplish their daily tasks. In this environment, the *knowledge of the past* perspective is not enough. Instead, our fieldwork has shown the opportunities and benefits in introducing a KM system based on the *design perspective* into special education as a means for continuous learning. We have designed and implemented Web2gether to help special education professionals obtain ongoing and sustainable professional and personal support and to have access to education resources they need to help their students with disabilities.

These benefits are not likely to be realized without the co-evolution of practices and technology. Technology alone will not solve the institutional and cultural challenges necessary for the implementation of the *design perspective* on KM. Major institutional and technical barriers for change need to be overcome. Changes will take place only if those involved in the design and development of innovations come to appreciate the delicate balance between existing cultural practices and innovations. Without a seamless integration of these two "worlds," we will not be able to create the necessary sociotechnical conditions for a new synergy between existing structures and new structures to emerge. Only through a careful balance between "tradition and the transcendence" will KM solutions be able to augment existing norms, values, and cultures with innovations.

Our research in this context supports the argument why *learning from the past is not enough* to help stakeholders accomplish their tasks practices. Knowledge is not a commodity to be consumed but is collaboratively designed and constructed in the *doing of work*. Our fieldwork has unveiled the opportunities as well as the challenges of implementing an alternative perspective for KM, *the design perspective*, which addresses this complex and situated nature of work. A complete discussion on KM cannot be limited to an epistemological analysis of knowledge or a technical evaluation of KM systems. It has to address the social, political, and technical issues of existing practices to guide the design as well as the introduction of KM innovations into the practices of those will be directly affected by them.

Acknowledgments

The authors thank the members of the Center for LifeLong Learning & Design (L^3D) at the University of Colorado, in particular the members of the CLever Project funded by the Coleman Institute, who have made major contributions to the conceptual framework described in this chapter. The research was supported in part by (1) the *Coleman Institute*, University of Colorado at Boulder; (2) the *National Science Foundation*, Grants (a)

REC-0106976 “Social Creativity and Meta-Design in Lifelong Learning Communities,” and (b) CCR-0204277 “A Social-Technical Approach to the Evolutionary Construction of Reusable Software Component Repositories”; and (3) *SRA Key Technology Laboratory*, Inc., Tokyo, Japan.

References

Arias, E. G., Eden, H., Fischer, G., Gorman, A. and Scharff, E. (1999), Beyond Access: Informed Participation and Empowerment. In C. Hoadley (Ed.), Proceedings of the Computer Supported Collaborative Learning (CSCL '99) Conference, Stanford, pp. 20-32

Barab, S. A., Makinster, J. G., Moore, J. A., Cunningham, D. J. and Team, T. I. D. (2001), Designing and Building an On-line Community: The Struggle to Support Sociability in the Inquiry Learning Forum. Educational Technology Research & Development (ETR&D), 49 (4), pp. 71-96

Barbara, D. and Clifton, C. (1992), Information brokers: Sharing knowledge in a heterogeneous distributed system (Techincal Report No. MITL-TR-31-92). Princeton, NJ: Matsushita Information Technology Laboratory

Bobrow, D. G. and Whalen, J. (2002), Community Knowledge Sharing in Practice: The Eureka Story. Journal of the Society for Organizational Learning, 4 (2)

Bowker, G. C. and Star, S. L. (2000), Sorting Things Out — Classification and Its Consequences. Cambridge, MA: MIT Press

Brown, J. S. and Duguid, P. (1998). Organizing Knowledge. California Management Review, 40 (3), pp. 90-111

Brown, J. S. and Duguid, P. (2000), The Social Life of Information. Boston, MA: Harvard Business School Press

Brown, J. S., Duguid, P. and Haviland, S. (1994), Toward Informed Participation: Six Scenarios in Search of Democracy in the Information Age. The Aspen Institute Quarterly, 6 (4), pp. 49-73

Bruner, J. (1973), Beyond the Information Given. New York: W.W. Norton and Company

Carley, K. M. and Hill, V. (2001), Structural Change and Learning within Organizations. In A. Lomi (Ed.), Dynamics of Organizational Societies: Models, Theories and Methods. Cambridge, MA: MIT Press/AAAI Press/Live Oak

Carroll, J. M. and Rosson, M. B. (1987), Paradox of the Active User. In J. M. Carroll (Ed.), Interfacing Thought: Cognitive Aspects of Human-Computer Interaction. Cambridge, MA: The MIT Press, pp. 80-111

CLever. (2003), CLever: Cognitive Levers -- Helping People Help Themselves, at http://www.cs.colorado.edu/~l3d/clever

Coleman, J. S. (1988). Social Capital in the Creation of Human Capital. American Journal of Sociology, 94, pp. S95-S120

Denning, S. (2001), The Springboard: How Storytelling Ignites Action in Knowledge-Era Organizations. Woburn, MA: Butterworth-Heinemann

Ehn, P. (1988), Work-Oriented Design of Computer Artifacts (second ed.). Stockholm: Arbetslivscentrum

Engeström, Y. (2001), Expansive Learning at Work: Toward an Activity Theoretical Reconceptualization. Journal of Education and Work, 14 (1), pp. 133-156

Fischer, G. (1994), Putting the Owners of Problems in Charge with Domain-Oriented Design Environments. In D. Gilmore, R. Winder and F. Detienne (Eds.), User-Centered Requirements for Software Engineering Environments. Heidelberg: Springer Verlag, pp. 297-306

Fischer, G. (2001), Communities of Interest: Learning through the Interaction of Multiple Knowledge Systems. In S. Bjornestad, R. Moe, A. Morch and A. Opdahl (Ed.), 24th Annual Information Systems Research Seminar In Scandinavia (IRIS'24), Ulvik, Norway, pp. 1-14

Fischer, G. (2002), Beyond 'Couch Potatoes': From Consumers to Designers and Active Contributors. FirstMonday: Peer-Reviewed Journal on the Internet, 7 (12), at http://firstmonday.org/issues/issue7_12/fischer/

Fischer, G., Grudin, J., McCall, R., Ostwald, J., Redmiles, D., Reeves, B. and Shipman, F. (2001), Seeding, Evolutionary Growth and Reseeding: The Incremental Development of Collaborative Design Environments. In G. M. Olson, T. W. Malone and J. B. Smith (Eds.), Coordination Theory and Collaboration Technology. Mahwah, NJ: Lawrence Erlbaum Associates, pp. 447-472.

Fischer, G. and Ostwald, J. (2001), Knowledge Management – Problems, Promises, Realities, and Challenges. IEEE Intelligent Systems, January/February 2001, pp. 60-72

Fischer, G. and Ostwald, J. (2002a), Seeding, Evolutionary Growth, and Reseeding: Enriching Participatory Design with Informed Participation. In T. Binder, J. Gregory and I. Wagner (Ed.), Proceedings of the Participatory Design Conference (PDC'02), Malmö University, Sweden, pp. 135-143

Fischer, G. and Ostwald, J. (2002b), Transcending the Information Given: Designing Learning Environments for Informed Participation. In e. a. Kinshuk (Ed.), Proceedings of International Conference on Computers in Education (ICCE 2002), Auckland, New Zealand, pp. 378-381

Fischer, G. and Scharff, E. (2000), Meta-Design – Design for Designers. In D. Boyarski and W. Kellogg (Ed.), 3rd International Conference on Designing Interactive Systems (DIS 2000), New York, pp. 396-405

Granovetter, M. (1973). The Strength of Weak Ties. American Journal of Sociology, 78, pp. 1360-1380

Grudin, J. (1988), Why CSCW Applications Fail: Problems in the Design and Evaluation of Organizational Interfaces. In L. Suchman (Ed.), Proceedings of ACM CSCW'88 Conference on Computer-Supported Cooperative Work. New York: ACM, pp. 85-93

Hansen, M. T. (2002), Knowledge Networks: Explaining Effective Knowledge Sharing in Multiunit Companies. Organization Science, 13 (3), pp. 232-248.

Hillary, G. A. (1955), Definitions of Community: Areas of Agreement. Rural Society, 20, pp. 111-1122

Hodas, S. (1996), Technology Refusal and the Organizational Culture of Schools. In R. Kling (Ed.), Computerization and Controversy: Value Conflicts and Social Choices (Second ed., Vol.). San Diego, CA: Academic Press, Inc.

Hollan, J., Hutchins, E. and Kirsch, D. (2001), Distributed Cognition: Toward a New Foundation for Human-Computer Interaction Research. In J. M. Carroll (Ed.), Human-Computer Interaction in the New Millennium. New York: ACM Press, pp. 75-94

Hutchins, E. L. (1993), Learning to Navigate. In S. Chaiklin and J. Lave (Eds.), Understanding Practice. Cambridge, UK: Cambridge University Press, pp. 35-63

Kass, R. and Stadnyk, I. (1992), Using User Models to Improve Organizational Communication. In Proceedings of 3rd International Workshop on User Modeling (UM'92). Dagstuhl, Germany: The German Research Center for Artificial Intelligence, pp. 135-147

Kintsch, A. and DePaula, R. (2002), A Framework for the Adoption and Abandonment of Assistive Technology. In (Ed.), SWAAACK Conference, Breckenridge, CO

Lave, J. and Wenger, E. (1991), Situated Learning: Legitimate Peripheral Participation. New York: Cambridge University Press

Murray, P. (2000), Designing Busineess Benefits from Knowledge Management. In C. Despres and D. Chauvel (Eds.), Knowledge Horizons: The Present and the Promise of Knowledge Management. Boston, MA: Butterworth-Heinemann, pp. 171-194

Nardi, B. A. and O'Day, V. L. (1999), Information Ecologies: Using Technology with Heart (First ed.). Cambridge, Massachusetts: The MIT Press

Nardi, B. A., Whittaker, S. and Schwarz, H. (2000), It's Not What You Know, It's Who You Know: Work in the Information Age. FirstMonday: Peer-reviewed Journal on the Internet, 5 (5), at http://www.firstmonday.dk/issues/issue5_5/nardi/

Orlikowski, W. J. (2002), Knowing in Practice: Entacting a Collective Capability in Distributed Organizing. Organization Science, 13 (3), pp. 249-273

Orr, J. (1990), Sharing Knowledge, Celebrating Identity: War Stories and Community Memory in a Service Culture. In D. S. Middleton and D. Edwards (Eds.), Collective Remembering: Memory in Society. Beverly Hills, CA: SAGE Publications, pp. 169-189

Orr, J. (1996), Talking about Machines – An Ethnography of a Modern Job. Ithaca: ILR Press/Cornell University Press

Polanyi, M. (1966), The Tacit Dimension. Garden City, NY: Doubleday.

Postman, N. (1995), The End of Education – Redefining the Value of School. New York: Alfred A. Knopf

Rittel, H. (1984), Second-Generation Design Methods. In N. Cross (Ed.), Developments in Design Methodology. New York: John Wiley & Sons, pp. 317-327

Rogers, E. M. (1995), Diffusion of Innovations (Fourth ed.). New York, NY: The Free Press of Glencoe

Salomon, G. (Ed.). (1993), Distributed Cognitions: Psychological and Educational Considerations. Cambridge, United Kingdom: Cambridge University Press

Schlager, M. S., Fusco, F. and Schank, P. (2002), Evolution of an On-line Education Community of Practices. In K. A. Renninger and W. Shumar (Eds.), Building Virtual Communities: Learning and Change in Cyberspace. Cambridge, MA: Cambridge University Press, pp. 129-158

Schön, D. A. (1983), The Reflective Practitioner: How Professionals Think in Action. New York: Basic Books

Smith, R. G. and Farquhar, A. (2000), The Road Ahead for Knowledge Management – An AI Perspective. AI Magazine, 21 (4), pp. 17-40

Snowden, D. J. (1998), The Paradox of Story: Simplicity and Complexity in Strategy. The Journal of Strategy & Scenario Planning (Nov 1998), pp. 1-8

Spender, J. C. (1996), Making Knowledge the Basis of a Dynamic Theory of the Firm. Strategic Management Journal, 17 (Winter Special Issue), pp. 45-62

Terveen, L. G., Selfridge, P. G. and Long, M. D. (1995), Living Design Memory: Framework, Implementation, Lessons Learned. Human-Computer Interaction, 10 (1), pp. 1-37

Thomas, J. (2001), Information about Knowledge Management, at http://www.truthtable.com/know.html

Tsoukas, H. (1996), The Firm as a Distributed Knowledge System: A Constructionist Approach. Strategic Management Journal, 17 (Winter Special Issue), pp. 11-25

Wellman, B. and Gulia, M. (1999), Net Surfers Don't Ride Alone: Virtual Community as Community. In B. Wellman (Ed.), Networks in the Global Village. Boulder, CO: Westview Press, pp. 331-367

Wenger, E. (1998), Communities of Practice – Learning, Meaning, and Identity. Cambridge, UK: Cambridge University Press

A Sensemaking Theory of Knowledge in Organizations and Its Application

Dubravka Cecez-Kecmanovic

School of Information Systems, Technology and Management
Faculty of Commerce and Economics, UNSW
Sydney, NSW 2052, Australia
E-mail: dubravka@unsw.edu.au

Introduction

To create and provide products and services, organizations utilize their various resources. Different organizations use their resources differently, with varying market success and economic and social outcomes, depending on the knowledge they draw upon. A view of *organizations as knowledge systems* focuses on the ways organizations draw upon their knowledge and create new knowledge so as to best utilize their resources in providing distinctive products and services (Penrose, 1959; Nonaka and Takeuchi, 1995; Spender, 1996). The most interesting insight from such a view is that there is no limit in an organization's utilization of its knowledge resources: "the more practitioners *invent* new ways of using their resources (themselves included), the more services they can potentially derive" (Tsoukas, 1996, p. 13; emphasis in the original). The key difference that makes a difference is the *knowledge* organizations draw upon and their knowledge generating capacity.

That knowledge makes a difference to performance has been realized by many organizations worldwide. In order to 'manage knowledge' better organizations undertake various knowledge management programs, appoint chief knowledge officers (CKO), and implement Knowledge Management Systems (KMS) (Alavi and Leidner, 2001). Managing knowledge is considered to be of critical importance for sustained competitive advantage (Nonaka, 1994; Grant, 1996; Earl, 2001). However, despite the abundance of literature on knowledge management in Information Systems (IS), organization studies, management, cognitive science, sociology, and other disciplines, practitioners do not find many applicable or useful concepts, frameworks and models (Earl, 2001). Interestingly enough there are no sat-isfactory answers to fundamental questions: What is the nature of knowledge that organizations try so hard to manage and what does it actually mean 'to manage' knowledge?

This paper addresses these questions by exploring knowledge in organizations from a sensemaking perspective (Weick, 1995) assuming that knowledge is both an input to and a product of sensemaking. By investigating distinct kinds of sensemaking proposed by Weick (1995) and inspired by Wiley's (1988, 1994) semiotic theory of self, the paper identifies distinct types of knowledge that organizations draw from. Identifying different types of knowledge and understanding their individual nature and their mutual relationships are important both theoretically and practically, if we are to understand how organizations create and use their knowledge and in what ways they can improve managing it.

The objective of the paper is to present a Sensemaking Theory of Knowledge in Organizations and demonstrate its applicability and value in studying knowledge management practices (including those supported by IT) and in explaining their organizational implications. To achieve this objective, the paper:

1. describes a Sensemaking Model of Knowledge in Organizations that identifies different types of knowledge at four distinct sensemaking levels: the *individual knowledge* at the intra-subjective sensemaking level, the *collective knowledge* at the inter-subjective level, the *organizational knowledge* at the generic-subjective level, and the *cultural knowledge* at the extra-subjective level, including the interrelationships between the knowledge types;
2. discusses characteristics of knowledge types and the dynamics of knowledge creation, sharing and deployment in organizational processes at each level and between levels, and then
3. illustrates how the theory can be applied to better understand knowledge management processes (using examples from three field studies) and to gain new insights into organizational implications of knowledge management (whether explicit and intentional or assumed and unintentional).

In such a way the paper seeks to contribute to the understanding of a firm as a distributed knowledge system.

The paper is organized in six sections. The next section briefly discusses knowledge-based approaches to organizations. This is followed by a presentation of the assumptions and basic concepts of a sensemaking view of organizations in section three, and a Sensemaking Theory of Knowledge in organizations in section four. In section five the applications of the theory and its contribution to understanding and explanation of knowledge management phenomena are illustrated by examples drawn from recent field studies. In the concluding section, the paper reflects on some concerns regarding the future development of knowledge management field raised in the Workshop.

Organizations as Knowledge Systems

Knowledge-based approaches to organizations seek, on one hand, to classify the different types of organizational knowledge and, on the other, to explain the nature of knowledge in organizations (Tsoukas, 1996). Several taxonomies of knowledge have been proposed out of which we will mention only two most prominent ones. Spender (1996) classifies knowledge along two dimensions: a) knowledge held by an individual or by a collective; and b) knowledge articulated explicitly or manifested implicitly. As a result, according to Spender, knowledge can be i) *conscious* (explicit, held by the individual); ii) *objectified* (explicit, held by the organization); iii) *automatic* (preconscious, individual) or iv) *collective* (manifested in organization practices). Tsoukas (1996) rightly questions the rigid and artificial distinction between individual and social knowledge implied by this taxonomy.

Another quite influential taxonomy was proposed by Nonaka (1994) and Nonaka and Takeuchi (1995). They also start from a distinction between explicit and tacit knowledge, based on their interpretation of Polanyi's work (1962, 1966). They propose that translations and conversions that take place between explicit and tacit knowledge are essential for knowledge creation and use in a company. They identify four types of knowledge conversion (explicit-to-explicit, tacit-to-explicit, explicit-to-tacit and tacit-to-tacit) based on which they propose a spiral model of knowledge creation in a company. While Nonaka and Takeuchi's theory has been widely used and cited, its assumptions regarding the nature of tacit knowledge have been called into question. Namely, Tsoukas and Vladimirou (2001) and Tsoukas (1996) criticized Nonaka and Takeuchi's adoption of Polanyi's theory (1962, 1966) and demonstrated that their interpretation of Polanyi's notion of tacit knowledge was erroneous. Tacit and explicit are not two separate types of knowledge, but are mutually constituted. Explicit knowledge is always grounded in a tacit dimension, (Polanyi, 1966). Tacit knowledge, as Tsoukas explains, "is the necessary component of *all* knowledge; it is not made up of discrete beans which can be grounded, lost or reconstituted" (1996, p. 14).

A good example of a study seeking an explanation of the nature of knowledge in firms is one by Tsoukas (1996). He extends the view of organizations as knowledge systems (Grant, 1996) and examines a concept of a firm as *a distributed knowledge system*. Inspired by Hayek's (1945) (re)formulation of economic problem of society, Tsoukas argues that firms are inherently decentered systems and that the knowledge they need to draw upon is indeterminate and emerging, and cannot be known by a single mind. He also provides a well-grounded explanation of a distributed nature of a firm's knowledge. Tsoukas (1996) explains social practices as consisting of three dimensions: role-related normative expectations, dispositions (formed in past socializations), and interactive situations (involving local knowledge of particular circumstances, time and space). While firms may have more or less control over normative expectations, they have no control over its members' dispositions nor could they determine the use and creation of knowledge in social interactions in which members' normative expectations and individual dispositions are instantiated.

The approach adopted in this paper draws from both streams of research in that it aims to classify types of knowledge and also contribute to the understanding of knowledge in organizations. The theoretical foundation of the work presented here, however, is different from approaches in either of the streams: it originates from the sensemaking perspective of knowledge in organizational context.

A Sensemaking View of Knowledge in Organizations

Sensemaking is an everyday activity, briefly described as "the reciprocal interaction of information seeking, meaning ascription, and action" (Thomas, Clark, and Gioia, 1993, p. 240). Whenever we encounter an event that is surprising, puzzling, troubling, or incomprehensible, we try, more or less consciously, to interpret it, and to assign meaning to it, that is, to make sense of it. In the process of interpretation and explanation we typically draw from our experience and from our background knowledge of a context within which the event occurred. We also often talk to colleagues (workers, citizens, friends), share our experiences, test and co-create our assumptions and beliefs in an attempt to 'structure the unknown' and assign the meaning to the surprising event. The interpretation and understanding of the event, achieved either individually or collectively, is an outcome of the sensemaking process (Louis, 1980, p. 241) the importance of which is usually more appreciated if it triggers or enables an action.

Several aspects of sensemaking are relevant for exploration of knowledge in organizational contexts. First, an individual makes sense of her/his work environment, tasks and activities, and also more broadly of organizational processes and events. In this process, the individual both uses and re-creates her/his personal knowledge. Second, members of an organization interact, informally and formally, to explore problematic situations, share their assumptions and experiences, and co-create inter-subjective meanings. In this collective sensemaking process problematic situations are named and framed, the boundaries of intervention are set, and a coherent 'structure' imposed allowing an intelligible action (Schon, 1983). Key components of this process – knowledge sharing, achieving mutual understanding, inter-subjective meaning making and knowledge co-creation, as well as taking action – are all entangled in social interaction in an undistinguishable manner. Only by engaging in and observing social interaction, can we as researchers make sense of them and learn about collective knowledge, its formation and use.

Third, in any organization there are commonly accepted norms and rules for seeing and doing things. An organization is characterized by its processes, structures, and roles, the meaning of which is shared among its members without them participating in their creation. The meanings ascribed to organizational roles (normative expectations), organizational processes and structures persist while individuals performing them may change. Sensemaking involved in creating and maintaining such generic meanings is called 'generic subjective'. This is the so-called social structure level at which "concrete human beings, subjects, are no longer present. Selves are left behind at the interactive level. Social structure implies a generic self, an interchangeable part – as filler of roles and follower of rules – but not concrete, individualized selves" (Wiley, 1988, p. 258). While inter-subjective meaning making through social interaction is a source of innovation, encouraging change, generic subjectivity enforces control, securing stability.

Fourth, involved in all sensemaking processes described above, are customs, norms, habitual behavior, rituals, myths, metaphors and other language forms, etc., that fall under the general rubric of culture. This realm of abstract symbolic reality underpins all other sensemaking levels. Referring to Wiley (1988), Weick calls culture an 'extra-subjective' level of sensemaking which provides a reservoir of background knowledge allowing and constraining meanings at other levels.

Organizations can thus be viewed as a dynamic web of sensemaking processes. They are created and recreated by continuous and simultaneous interplay between all types of sensemaking: intra-subjectivity of its members, their inter-subjective and generic subjective (social structure) sensemaking, all embedded in organizational culture (that is in extra-subjective sensemaking). The three levels of sensemaking above the level of individual should be understood, not in a hierarchical sense, but as different generalisations of social reality, each more distant from the individual.

The Sensemaking Theory of Knowledge in Organizations

By taking this four-level sensemaking view of organizations as my point of departure, I explore the nature of knowledge at each level and processes by which such knowledge is created and managed. I begin with the level of individual sensemaking, where knowledge belongs to an individual and is thus called the individual knowledge. I then identify and describe the inter-subjectively created or collective knowledge, the generic, social structure or organizational knowledge, and knowledge embedded in culture, at the three levels of sensemaking beyond an individual. Studying the nature of sensemaking processes at each level should help us understand not only the nature of knowledge and how knowledge is created, maintained and used at these levels, but also the continuous interplay and knowledge dynamics between the levels.

Individual knowledge is acquired through personal experience and reflects education, work experiences and past socialisations. It involves a person's values, beliefs, assumptions, experiences, skills, expertise, etc. that enable the person to interpret and make sense of the environment, perform tasks and take actions. In other words, individual knowledge is created, maintained, used and recreated through intra-subjective sensemaking. By being involved in particular organizational processes and work practices, by interacting with other members, an individual gains new experiences, faces problems and makes sense of them, which frequently triggers revisiting and updating his/her personal knowledge. This results from the intra-subjective sensemaking (and by implication individual knowledge) being intertwined with and influenced by other sensemaking processes.

Individuals who work together and complete tasks jointly (eg. as a project team or a strategic planning group) often learn to cooperate with one another, interpret situations inter-subjectively and undertake joint or coordinated actions. What makes a group of individuals act as a *collective,* capable of completing complex tasks that no single individual would be able to complete, is their *collective knowledge*. The nature of collective knowledge (derived from the concept of *collective mind* by Weick and Roberts, 1993) is essentially different from individual knowledge in that it does not reside within but between and among individuals. To understand collective knowledge we need to understand social interaction and patterns of interlocking behaviours among the individuals that lead to joint or coordinated actions. Collective knowledge, defined as an emergent capacity to act collectively, involves continuous co-creation of inter-subjective meanings and mutual understanding through 'heedful interrelating' (as defined by Weick and Roberts, 1993, following Ryle, 1949). Weick and Roberts (1993, p. 362) warned that heedful performance should not be mistaken for habitual performance. "In habitual action – they explained – each performance is a replica of its predecessor, whereas in heedful performance, each action is modified by its predecessor (Ryle, 1949, p. 42)."

Social interactions and collective knowledge also create and maintain a particular level of social reality. Through inter-subjective meaning making and heedful interrelating individual selves get transformed from 'I' into 'we' (Weick, 1995). In any social setting, these processes are ongoing within groups and among groups, leading to a multiplicity of pockets of collective knowledge that are in a state of flux, with shifting focus and indeterminable boundaries.

Unlike collective knowledge, organizational knowledge has more visible forms, is typically subject to legitimation and is thus more easily identifiable. Organizational knowledge involves generic meanings and social structures shared by and transmitted to organizational members irrespective of their participation in their creation. Typically it includes notions of organizational structure, roles, policies, norms, rules and control mechanisms, social networks, scripts or patterns of activities and actions. Tsoukas and Vladimirou (2001) call it 'organizational knowledge in a strong sense'. Generic meanings may emerge through different processes. On one hand, generic meanings may be created through sensemaking processes involving institutional role-holders (typically top managers), following the norms and rules that prescribe how organizational knowledge is legitimated (a due process etc.). In such a process, which is a kind of a top-down process, organizational knowledge is assumed to flow to and be shared and used by organizational members in their everyday activities. On the other hand, generic knowledge may emerge through a continuing transition from inter-subjective meanings to generic-subjective meanings, that is, through a bottom-up process. These two processes are in fact operating simultaneously. In their dialectic relationship Weick (1995, p. 71) sees the essence of organising.

The fourth type of knowledge defined by the Sensemaking Model is *knowledge embedded in culture* which assumes a stock of tacit, taken-for-granted convictions, beliefs, assumptions, values, norms and tradition that members of an organization draw upon in order to make sense of a situation and create meanings at all other levels. As part of a symbolic reality, cultural knowledge is *extra-subjective*. As such knowledge embedded in culture serves as a reservoir from which they derive their meanings and thereby get to understand each other. In other words, knowledge embedded in culture determines the horizon of possible understanding among the members of an organization. Moreover, common beliefs and values are said to be the 'glue' that holds communities together (Blumer, 1969). People are usually not consciously aware of their cultural knowledge. Such knowledge is transmitted through language, symbols, metaphors, rituals and stories. Only when an element of this knowledge is explicated and brought into a situation can it be thematised, contested, and justified. Only then does it become criticisable knowledge that is part of an explicit stock of knowledge resulting from interpretive accomplishments of actors at other levels.

The Sensemaking Model of Knowledge in organizations that identifies the four knowledge types – the individual, collective, organizational and culture knowledge – is graphically presented in Figure 1. It should be noted here that while the four types of knowledge identified by the model reflect the different nature of knowledge and knowing in organizational context (resulting from the different nature of sensemaking) they are not, and cannot be separated. These four types of knowledge are mutually constituting. They are intertwined in such a way that they continuously influence and recreate each other. In order to understand the nature of knowledge in organizations, it is obviously important to identify and analyse different types of knowledge at each sensemaking level, but it is equally important to investigate how knowledge at one level affects the other, and how tensions between them arise.

The Sensemaking Model portrays an anatomy of knowledge in organizations. It explicitly describes the distributed character of knowledge in organizational context thus contributing to the understanding of organizations as distributed knowledge systems (Tsoukas, 1996). The model also enables decomposition of 'knowledge management' into specific types of knowledge management tasks. At each level of sensemaking, knowledge is emerging: it is continually created, recreated, maintained, shared and applied. At each level, sensemaking is affected by knowledge emerging at all other levels.

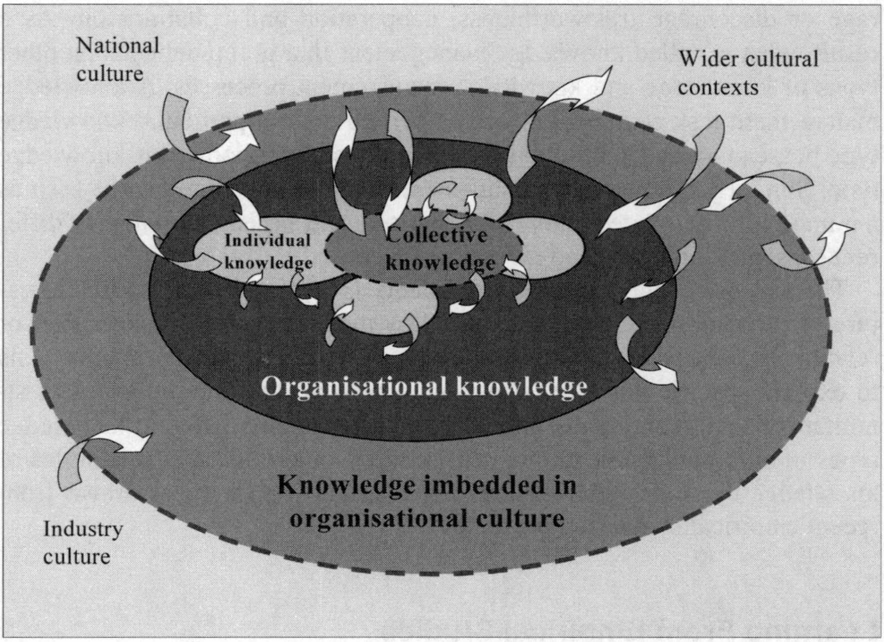

Fig. 1. The Sensemaking Model of Knowledge Management in Organizations

For instance, the emergence of collective knowledge – creation of shared understanding as a basis for cooperative action by a group of individuals engaged in a project, policy decision-making, or IS development – is the process inherent to the group but is influenced by i) each individual's knowledge, ii) organizational structure knowledge (norms, rules, normative expectations) and iii) organizational culture. These influences may be more or less obvious, intentional and forceful. Firstly, when individuals participate in a group activity they bring into this activity their individual knowledge, their experiences from past socialisations, their schemes of perception, thought and action, or in Bourdieau's (1990) words their 'habitus'. Each individual may be more or less open to argumentation and more or less capable and willing to develop mutual understanding of a situation and engage in 'heedful interrelating' with others. Secondly, the normative context and structures determined by knowledge management at the organizational level may be more or less conducive to knowledge sharing and cooperation at a group level. In addition, organizational knowledge may impose strict rules, incentives or limitations for both the intra-group or inter-group cooperation and knowledge sharing. Thirdly, organizational culture and the embedded knowledge which is the least amenable to being managed, provide a broad social and historical context, a value system, language, and tacit background assumptions and beliefs which may encourage or discourage trustworthiness, cooperation and collaboration. As a result, what is called knowledge management in a group depends on other types of knowledge and knowledge management processes. A knowledge management task can thus be seen as pertaining to a particular knowledge type but, cannot and should not be limited to studying only this knowledge type. Similarly, knowledge management in an organization can be seen as a number of interrelated knowledge management tasks undertaken at different sensemaking levels and across the levels.

The purpose of the Sensemaking Theory is to describe the particular nature of each knowledge type identified by the model and characteristics of relationships between the knowledge types. Furthermore, the theory aims to explain specific knowledge management tasks and the dynamics of simultaneous and continuous mutual influences among different knowledge types in an organization. In the next section some illustrative examples of knowledge dynamics and tensions between knowledge types drawn from recent empirical studies are presented.

Learning From Empirical Studies

The Sensemaking Theory of Knowledge has been applied and developed further in field studies of knowledge management processes in three different organizations. The first was the field study of a university restructure process in which a large three-member Federated University (distributed on seven campuses) transformed into a unitary university, including transformation of all academic, administrative, and management structures and processes, as well as Information Technology (IT) services (Cecez-Kecmanovic and Jerram, 2001, 2002; Jerram, et al., 2002). The second was the field study of an Investment Banking Company and continuous development of its core Information System (Cecez-Kecmanovic and Key, 2001, 2002). And the third was the longitudinal case study of a retail company (Colruyt, Belgium), its decision-making practices and the use of a groupware system (Cecez-Kecmanovic and Janson, 2000). By drawing from these field studies I will illustrate how the Sensemaking Theory of Knowledge informed the interpretation of findings and how in turn learning from these studies contributed to further theory development.

Organizational Knowledge vs Collective Knowledge

Organizational knowledge generally tends to persist and resist change, thus ensuring organizational stability. On the other hand, inter-subjectively created collective knowledge is just the opposite: it is a permanent source of creativity and innovation that emerges from social interaction. Even in relatively stable environments, inter-subjectively created knowledge tends to challenge generic meanings, established practices and norms (or other aspects of organizational knowledge), thus undermining social structure stability. There is, as Weick (1995) points out, an inherent tension between inter-subjectively created, collective knowledge, on one hand, and the generic, organizational knowledge, on the other. Managing this tension is one of the key knowledge management issues with large ramifications for organizational performance, which often remains unrecognised and poorly understood. How is the tension between inter-subjective knowledge and organizational knowledge managed in the observed organizations?

In the Colruyt Company decision-making is highly distributed. Employees interested in a problem and those having expertise to solve it, self-nominate to initiate and participate in problem resolution. The philosophy of the Colruyt Company is continuous innovation and development through employees' participation and workplace democracy. The development of the Company has to a large degree depended on bottom-up initiatives and innovations and broad cooperation within groups and between groups across the Company. Creation of collective, intra-subjective knowledge through social interaction (face-to-face and via the in-house developed groupware system ISID) is promoted and highly valued. The Company is managed less by control and more by providing participatory social framework, and by nurturing cooperation and trust (Janson and Cecez-Kecmanovic, 2003). When inter-subjectively created knowledge challenges established organizational knowledge (eg. a discount policy, norms regarding customer services, confidentiality rules), a public debate via ISID is instigated and all interested or affected members are typically invited to self-nominate and take part in a task force. The Company culture implies that the force of the better argument should determine the outcome.

Here we see that the tensions between collective knowledge (which emerges from social interaction) and organizational knowledge do arise and that the Company has well-established norms and processes to deal with them and to learn from them. Furthermore, embedded into these processes is the groupware system ISID which assists and enables Company-wide debate and a broad access to organizational decision-making (Cecez-Kecmanovic and Janson, 2001). An interesting lesson to be learned from the Colruyt Company is how to harmonise inherent tensions between organizational knowledge and collective knowledge emerging through numerous and on-going social interactions. While the Colruyt Company encourages knowledge co-creation and sharing through social interaction, it also carefully maintains its organizational knowledge. However, it does so in a harmonious way. The distinguishing features of the Colruyt Company are its culture of cooperation, collaboration, and solidarity, its participatory ethos and its reflective practice. In particular, their use of ISID in everyday communications facilitates the emergence of collective understandings and at the same time enables a constructive questioning of the established organizational knowledge (norms, rules, policies). In summary, the emergence of collective knowledge through social interaction is stimulated, enabled and guided by organizational and cultural knowledge. At the same time, organizational and cultural knowledge are reproduced, challenged and recreated through reflective organizational practices.

In the case of the University restructure, one of the major objectives was to establish a single academic structure and a unique set of educational programs, policies and procedures for the whole, united University. While in the past, there were attempts to unify educational programs across member-Universities, its was never fully achieved (eg. students enrolled in one member-University needed a special permission to take subjects from other members). In the restructure the old organizational knowledge of member-Universities was officially abandoned and new organizational knowledge of the unitary University had to be created and legitimised. The University Executive understood well the immensity and complexity of the task. They also rightly worried that the restructure of such a scale might instigate disintegrative forces and chaos. Therefore they felt responsible to carefully manage change and control the restructuring process. To prevent chaos and ensure the least disruptive transition from the old to the new University, the Executive designed a one-year restructure process driven by the guidelines and various policy documents (available on the intranet). The guidelines, proposed by the Executive, specified principles, norms and rules for the new academic structure. While the formation of four Colleges was determined by the Executive, the schools within these colleges were first to be proposed by academics themselves, in a so-called bottom-up process, following the rules in the guidelines, and then decided by the Executive.

The guidelines represented the first evidence of the new organizational knowledge formulated by the Executive. It was tacitly assumed that academic staff would understand the meanings in this document and that they would be able to apply it 'correctly' in their particular circumstances. Circumstances, though, were very different across disciplines and across member-Universities. For instance, academics from various psychology units in the old University structure did not have problems in proposing the new School of Psychology. Their discipline was well defined and the expected number of staff in the proposed School of Psychology was within the prescribed range, so they easily fitted within the guidelines' criteria and received approval from the Executive. Academics in some other fields, though, did not sail through that easily. Some academic groups experienced huge problems and were not able to agree on a school proposal that would satisfy the guidelines. In the field of management, for instance, three school proposals were initially submitted. The differences could have been resolved had some rigid criteria for school formation in the guidelines been changed. As a result, academics from the management group submitted a request for change which the Executive rejected. The final decision by the Executive to accept one proposal and reject others disappointed many and greatly discouraged them from further active participation.

This example illustrates how the Executive took control of the new organizational knowledge creation processes. Being convinced in the legitimacy of their objectives – unification of the University – the Executive believed it was their duty to establish new organizational knowledge to replace the old member-Universities' knowledge. They also expected different academic groups from the three former member-Universities (each having different organizational culture, different teaching approaches and attitudes towards academic disciplines) to appreciate their intentions, to understand the new organizational knowledge, and more importantly, to apply it without having a chance to adapt it to their specific circumstances. The Executive did not expect nor did they understand why some academic groups had different views regarding the new academic structure and how it should be formed. Tension between the new organizational knowledge (as expressed in Guidelines) and collective knowledge, inter-subjectively created by academic groups (related to individual school proposals) grew. This tension was never resolved and ramifications were still felt after the new academic structure took place.

The task of changing organizational knowledge was not recognized as such, but was nevertheless among the key issues that determined the outcomes of the restructure. The analysis of the restructure processes, and especially the inauguration and implementation of guidelines, informed by the Sensemaking Theory of Knowledge, clearly indicated why the problems occurred and how the tension could have been attenuated. Had it been understood beforehand that organizational knowledge could not simply be re-shelved (by top management or anybody else), but that it had instead to emerge through reflective organizational practices and continuous interchange with similarly emerging collective understanding, many problems and conflicts could have been avoided.

The Use of Email as an Enabler of Staff-Executive Communication

Another interesting insight came from the analysis of the use of email to communicate ideas, suggestions and concerns by staff (academics and general) to the President of the University during the restructuring process. The idea was that an open communication channel between all interested staff and the President would democratise the restructure process and help staff contribute to the decision-making. While this was technically feasible, and many academics and administrative staff, including the President, took it seriously, such use of email failed to achieve the objectives. The President was flooded with emails and made an honest effort to read them all and responded to as many as possible. Interviews with staff who sent these emails showed that they considered this whole exercise 'futile' and 'misleading'. They felt their emails 'went into a big hole' without making any impact. The President, on the other hand, was convinced that many good ideas and proposals were actually taken into account. Looking through the lens of the Sensemaking Model, we see that individuals assumed that by sending emails with their views and proposals to the President, they would participate in the formation of the new organizational knowledge. As they did not get feedback and did not engage in any shape or form in the organizational knowledge formation process, they felt misled and denied their legitimate rights. On the contrary, the President believed that by acquiring, sorting and summarising ideas and proposals from several thousand staff emails to inform the organizational knowledge re-creation (at the Executive level), individual staff knowledge was in fact taken into account. The President and other members of the Executive were hence convinced that the use of email did democratise the restructure process. Informed by the Sensemaking Model of Knowledge, we found out that the both sides, the staff and the Executive, had unrealistic expectations due to the lack of understanding of the nature of organizational knowledge and the process of its re-creation (Jerram, et al., 2002).

The lessons learned from this case study contributed to further theoretical development of the Sensemaking Model of Knowledge Management in organizations. The nature of organizational knowledge is such that it needs to be widely shared by all members of an organization. Only then will it help individuals and groups to coordinate their actions and contribute to an organization's capacity to act. Successful re-creation or transformation of organizational knowledge cannot be achieved by concentrating all meaning making at the social structure level irrespective of 'quantity' of the individual members' input. Knowledge in an organization is inherently distributed and discursive. No matter how well intentioned, concentration of knowledge creation and maintenance at the social structure level to bear on all local circumstances, especially in large organizations, is problematic and unsustainable. The lessons from this study confirmed that "the key to achieving coordinated action does not so much depend on those 'higher up' collecting more and more knowledge, as on those 'lower down' finding more and more ways of getting connected and interrelating the knowledge each one has" (Tsoukas, 1996, p. 22).

Inter-group Relations and Knowledge Sharing

In the Investment Banking Company case the major issue was how to improve services to clients and increase competitive advantage. Analysts' knowledge was considered a key Company resource that determined the quality of services and ultimately its competitive advantage. By developing an Information System (IS) that captured analysts' spreadsheet models (representing their knowledge about listed companies) in the Company database and thereby providing much bigger range and higher quality of financial reports to clients, the Company achieved its objectives. After initial resistance, analysts learned to use the IS and to appreciate its value for their job. The Company attracted a significant number of new large clients who used the IS directly. The philosophy of the IS team was continual IS development and co-evolution with the Company (Cecez-Kecmanovic and Key, 2001, 2002).

The analysis of knowledge management issues behind the successful development and use of the IS revealed productive interactions between the IS team and the analysts as well as between the IS team and the clients. The IS team gradually developed mutual understanding with analysts which enabled productive social interaction, knowledge sharing and co-creation. Having such experience, the IS team knew how to approach external clients and establish mutual understanding and trust with them as well. Lessons learned from this case study pertain to inter-group relationships, collective knowledge creation and coordination of actions.

Knowledge sharing and co-creation emerged through recurrent interactions between members of these groups driven by collectively shared aims to excel in their individual jobs and, in the case of the IS team, in their group task – IS development. The history of joint accomplishments enabled heedful interrelating between IS team members and analysts and later on between IS team members and clients. This in turn improved mutual understanding and trust. As a result individuals felt that they improved their individual knowledge and they were more efficient and effective in completing their complex tasks. What we observed in addition was that they also developed their collective knowledge, which was demonstrated in patterns of heedful interrelating and patterns of coordinated actions. Whilst it is widely believed that the culture in investment banking is highly individualistic, and that company performance essentially depends on analysts' expertise, we found that company performance can be enhanced further through the emerging collective knowledge built around the IS development and use, which is thoroughly social. Whereas one might think that 'capturing' analysts' knowledge in the database was a key to the IS and the Company success, the researchers found that it was actually knowledge sharing among the three groups (analysts, IS team and clients) and the emergence of their collective knowledge that made the IS and the Company successful (Cecez-Kecmanovic and Key, 2001, 2002). These findings confirm Weick and Robert's (1993) proposition that notion of collective mind, "conceptualised as a pattern of heedful interrelations of actions in a social system" (p. 357), can explain organizational performance and their capacity (or lack of it) to act in complex and turbulent environments.

Conclusion

This paper addressed the question of the nature of knowledge in organizations and what managing knowledge actually entails. The Sensemaking Theory of Knowledge, outlined briefly in the paper, identifies and describes different types of knowledge in organizations – individual, collective, organizational, and cultural – that are in permanent flux, influencing and re-constituting each other. The Sensemaking Theory of Knowledge is consistent with and contributes to the view of the firm as a *distributed* knowledge system "which is not, and cannot be, known in its totality by a single mind" (Tsoukas, 1996, p. 22; Hayek, 1945, 1982). This theory describes several ways and levels of knowledge distribution in an organization: from individual knowledge of organizational members, to collective knowledge of groups, to organizational knowledge and knowledge embedded in culture. Through the emergence within and dynamic interchange between these types of knowledge, knowledge in an organization is continually transformed and re-constituted. By drawing from the three field studies of knowledge management, the paper illustrates the applicability and usefulness of the Sensemaking Theory of Knowledge in investigating these simultaneous knowledge creation processes and the dynamics of knowledge transformation in practice.

The outline of the Sensemaking Theory of Knowledge and illustrations of its application, while brief and cursory at times, indicate that there is a wealth of knowledge and theoretical concepts created in disciplines such as psychology, social psychology, sociology, organization theory, economics, and communication, to mention just a few, that pertain to knowledge in organizations and could be useful for understanding specific aspects of its creation, transformation and use. Why such sources of valuable knowledge and theory have not been more widely used in knowledge management practice? – is a question raised at the Workshop quite rightly. While the reasons are various, it can be argued that among the key obstacles is the complexity of these concepts and theories that makes their interpretation and application in knowledge management practices quite difficult. Due to their complexity, concepts and theories from different disciplines are typically not quite understood (discussed, applied, criticized) outside limited professional circles. To understand them and interpret them in the specific context of knowledge management is not straightforward and often requires considerable background disciplinary knowledge.

When some of these theories, though, do cross over disciplinary boundaries, such as, for instance, concepts of 'tacit' and 'explicit knowledge or theories of group behavior (brought from social psychology), they run the risk of being oversimplified and applied as easy-to-do recipes. This is exactly what happened when Nonaka and Takeuchi (1995) adopted concepts of tacit and explicit knowledge from Polanyi's work (1962, 1966). They interpreted tacit and explicit knowledge as two mutually exclusive types each of which can be transformed into the other. Taken as unambiguous and clear-cut concepts, tacit and explicit knowledge form the basis for their model of knowledge transformation, that became hugely popular in knowledge management literature and practice. A contrary example is the notion of collective mind (Weick and Roberts, 1993) that draws from several complex theories and is itself a complex concept, which has not made it into the knowledge management literature, despite its demonstrated explanatory power and high potential value in understanding knowledge sharing and conditions for coordinated action. One is tempted to conclude that the wealth of knowledge and theories from other disciplines have been imported and applied to knowledge management problems only when heavily simplified and presented in an easy digestible form. It is arguable, however, that this should not necessarily be so.

If we, practitioners and researchers in knowledge management, realize that the problems we face and questions we ask are not entirely new and that we may in fact be asking old questions using a different language, perhaps with different purposes in mind, we may appreciate the wealth of knowledge created before we came to the scene. Furthermore, when dealing with any specific issue – be it the nature of personal versus the collective knowing and acting, or the problems of knowledge sharing and transfer within or between organizations – we need to investigate what has been done in relevant disciplines so far, and whether and how an existing body of knowledge can be applied to our specific problems. Such investigations would require collaboration with researchers and professionals from relevant disciplines (eg. psychologists, anthropologists, sociologists) to ensure 'proper' interpretation and mindful appropriation of concepts and theories from these disciplines for specific purposes of knowledge management. Proper interpretation here means deep understanding and critical assessment of various concepts and theoretical foundations and their specific meaning within the context of knowledge creation, transformation and use in organizations. Mindful appropriation means the adoption of concepts and theories that takes into account background knowledge from originating discipline(s) and preserves their authentic meaning and richness while being re-interpreted and re-defined for knowledge management.

Finally and more broadly, the reluctance of knowledge management professionals to embrace the new worldviews, new paradigms, and new dimensions of problems at hand may be seen as another obstacle to fruitful adoption of concepts and theories from other disciplines and their integration into knowledge management field. The Workshop like this one, that brings together both practitioners and researchers with different backgrounds and professional affiliations, is an excellent example how this obstacle can be overcome. As we have experienced in this Workshop, opening up to the new worldviews, new paradigms, and new dimensions of problems is not really threatening or arduous but can indeed be challenging and hugely exciting.

References

Alavi, M. and D.E. Leidner (2001), "Knowledge Management and Knowledge Management Systems: Conceptual Foundations and Research Issues". MISQ, 25, 1, 107-136

Blumer, H. (1969), Symbolic Interactionizm: Perspectives and Method. Englewood Cliffs, NJ: Prentice Hall

Bourdieau, P. (1990), The Logic of Practice. Cambridge, UK: Polity Press

Cecez-Kecmanovic, D. and M. Janson, (2000), "The Rationality Potential of Information Systems: A Critical Approach". In Proceedings of the Eleventh Australasian Conference on Information Systems ACIS 2000, Brisbane, 6-8 December, (CD-ROM)

Cecez-Kecmanovic, D. and Janson, M. (2001), "Electronic Discourses and Rationalisation of Organizations", Proceedings of the Americas Conference on Information Systems AMCIS 2001, Boston, MA, USA , August 3-5, (CD-ROM)

Cecez-Kecmanovic, D. and C. Jerram (2001), "Understanding Crisis from a Sense-Making Perspective: An IS Operation Change". In Proceedings of The Twelfth Australasian Conference on Information Systems ACIS 2001, Coffs Harbour, NSW, Australia, 103-112

Cecez-Kecmanovic, D. and C. Jerram (2002), "A Sensemaking Model of Knowledge Management in Organizations". In Proceedings of the European Conference on Information Systems ECIS 2002, Gdansk, Poland, 894-904

Cecez-Kecmanovic, D. and R. Kay (2001), "IS – Organization Coevolution: The Future of IS". In Proceedings of the 22nd International Conference on Information Systems ICIS 2001, New Orleans, US, 363-372

Cecez-Kecmanovic D. and R. Kay, (2002), "Enabling Knowledge Sharing: New Challenges for Information Systems". In Proceedings of the Thirteenth Australasian Conference on Information Systems ACIS 2002, Melbourne, Australia, Vol. 1, 61-73

Earl, M. (2001), "Knowledge Management Strategies: Toward a Taxonomy". JMIS, 18, 1, 215-233

Grant, R.M. (1996), "Prospering in Dynamically-Competitive Environments: Organizational Capability as Knowledge Integration". Organization Science, 7, 375-387

Hayek, F.A. (1945), "The Use of Knowledge in Society". American Economic Review, 35, 519-530

Hayek, F.A. (1989), The Pretence of Knowledge. American Economic Review, 79, 3-7

Janson, M. and D. Cecez-Kecmanovic (2003), "Information Systems and the Participatory Ethos", The European Conference on Information Systems ECIS 2003, Naples, Italy, 18-22 June

Jerram, C., Cecez-Kecmanovic, D., Treleaven, L. and C. Sykes (2002), "Email and Assumptions: a Study in Electronic (Mis)Understandings". In Proceedings of the Thirteenth Australasian Conference on Information Systems ACIS 2002, Melbourne, Australia, Vol. 2, 509-521

Louis, M. (1980), "Surprise and Sensemaking: What Newcomers Experience in Entering Unfamiliar Organizational Settings". Administrative Science Quarterly, 25, 226-251

Nonaka, I. (1994), "A Dynamic Theory of Organizational Knowledge Creation". Organization Science, 5, 1, pp 14-37

Nonaka, I. and H. Takeuchi (1995), The Knowledge-Creating Company. New York: Oxford University Press

Penrose, E. (1959), The Theory of the Growth of the Firm. New York: Wiley

Polanyi, M. (1962), Personal Knowledge. Chicago, IL: University of Chicago Press

Polanyi, M. (1966), The Tacit Dimension. London: Routledge & Kegan Paul

Ryle, G. (1949), The Concept of Mind. Chicago IL: University of Chicago Press

Schon, D.A. (1983), The Reflective Practitioner. New York: Basic Books

Spender, J.-C. (1996), "Organizational Knowledge, Learning and Memory: Three Concepts in Search of a Theory". Journal of Organizational Change Management, 9, 63-78

Thomas, J.B., Clark, S.M. and D.A. Gioia (1993), "Strategic Sensemaking and Organizational Performance: Linkages among Scanning, Interpretation, Action and Outcomes", Academy of Management Journal, 36, 239-270

Tsoukas, H. (1996), "The Firm as a Distributed Knowledge System". Strategic Management Journal, 17 (Winter special issue), 11-25

Tsoukas, H. and E. Vladimirou (2001), "What is Organizational Knowledge?". Journal of Management Studies, 38, 7, 973-993

Wiley, N. (1988), "The Micro-Macro Problem in Social Theory". Sociological Theory, 6, 254-261

Wiley, N. (1994), The Semiotic Self. Cambridge: Polity Press

Weick, K.E. (1995), Sensemaking in Organizations. Sage

Weick, K.E. and K.H. Roberts (1993), "Collective Mind in Organizations: Heedful Interrelating on Flight Docks". Administrative Science Quarterly, 38, 357-381

Acknowledgement

This research has been conducted as part of the ARC SPIRT grant No C00002546 (2000-2002).

Part 2
Knowledge Management: Empirical Perspectives

Knowledge Creation in Organizations: A Multiple Study Overview[1]

Timothy M. Devinney[1], David F. Midgley[2] and Christine W. Soo[3]

[1] Australian Graduate School of Management, University of New South Wales, Sydney NSW 2052, Australia
[2] INSEAD, Boulevard de Constance, 77305 Fontainebleau Cedex, France
[3] Faculty of Business, University of Western Australia, 35 Stirling Highway, Crawley WA 6009, Australia

Introduction

The notion that knowledge is a source of competitive advantage has been advocated extensively in the management literature over the past decade (i.e., Winter, 1987; Quinn, 1992; Nonaka and Takeuchi, 1995). The value of intangible assets increases as goods and services become more sophisticated in content and production and the foundation of competition becomes intensively knowledge-based. As hypothesized by Teece (1998: 76), "the key sources of wealth creation at the dawn of the new millennium will lie with new enterprise formation; the renewal of incumbents; the exploitation of technological know-how, intellectual property, and brands; and the successful development and commercialization of new products and services".

One cannot dispute such statements as we witness the thriving of knowledge-based industries – the latest Fortune's Most Admired Companies listed General Electric, Intel, Cisco Systems, Microsoft, Charles Schwab and Dell Computer to be among the top ten companies – companies admired for their ability to innovate. We know that one of the keys to commercial success and longevity in today's economy lies in the ability to constantly create new knowledge and innovations, to develop and capitalize on the firm's knowledge base, and to "transform intellectual output into a service or a group of services embodied in a product" (Quinn, 1992).

1 The authors are listed alphabetically. This research has been supported by grants from the Centre for Corporate Change, Australian Graduate School of Management, the Australian Research Council, AT Kearney and INSEAD. All errors and omissions are those of the authors.

However, the more interesting question is "what are the factors that matter most to the development of new knowledge in organizations?"

There is an abundance of theoretical and empirical work (in the strategy, organizational behavior and industrial organization fields) on the factors that contribute to innovation (e.g., von Hippel, 1986; Powell et al, 1996; Henderson and Cockburn, 1994; Frost, 2001) and Soo, Midgley and Devinney (2003) show a strong and consistent relationship between new knowledge, innovation and performance. Where this paper differs is that we are interested in providing a more integrated view on how organizations create new knowledge (which can then lead to innovation) and whether differences in a firm's capability on this front are due to the firm's structure (i.e., whether it is firm specific) or the types of problems they are dealing with (i.e., whether it is problem specific). These are important questions because according to their answer we can draw on different streams of thinking to provide normative advice to firms. We attempt to answer these questions by integrating between-firm and within-firm analysis. This paper builds heavily on prior work (Soo, Midgley and Devinney, 2003; Soo, Devinney and Midgley, 2003a,b; Soo, Devinney, Midgley and Deering, 2002) and the reader is encouraged to examine this work in more detail for specifics on literature, frameworks, methodology and results. Our purpose here is to provide a more descriptive overview of this work.

Factors Influencing Organizational Knowledge Creation

There are several schools of thought that advocate for differential factors contributing to knowledge development within organizations. For example, social network theorists (e.g., Liebeskind et al., 1996; Nahapiet and Ghoshal, 1998; Steensma and Lyles, 2000) argue the importance of knowledge sourcing through network ties. Studies on dynamic capabilities and organizational learning (e.g., Teece et al., 1997; Miller and Shamsie, 2001) advocate the importance of adaptation and experimentation, while other studies (e.g., Leonard and Sensiper, 1998) examined more micro-level capabilities such as knowledge transfer in group problem solving.

Much of this literature is integrated with more basic work on knowledge-based strategy, which focuses on concepts such as firm resources (Wernerfelt, 1984; Barney, 1991), core competencies (Hamel and Prahalad, 1990), organizational capabilities (Stalk et al., 1992) and dynamic capabilities (Teece et al., 1990). The essence of this stream of work is that certain firm resources possess characteristics that are potentially rent-producing; i.e., if they are valuable, rare, durable, not easily traded and difficult to imitate (Barney, 1991) and hence for managers, the challenge is to "identify, develop, protect, and deploy resources and capabilities in a way that provides the firm with a sustainable competitive advantage and, thereby, a superior return on capital" (Amit and Schoemaker, 1993: 33).

One of the major criticisms of the resource based view of the firm, and indeed knowledge-based strategy concepts in general, is that it does not provide insights into 'how', 'when' and 'why' do certain firm resources generate superior returns for the firm. The literature on firm capabilities (e.g., Teece, et al., 1997; Levinthal and Myatt, 1994; Eisenhardt and Martin, 2000) is also predominantly silent on the specific sources of improved firm performance. In fact, Collis (1994: 151) argued that "the source of sustainable competitive advantage is likely to be found in different places at different points in time in different industries....this very unpredictability only reinforces the fact that prescriptions for building organizational capabilities are likely to be elusive".

Building on Collis' (1994) statement above and Nonaka and Takeuchi's (1995: 49) assertion that we understand very little about knowledge creation, we aim to develop a better understanding of the drivers of new knowledge. In doing so, we integrate various concepts in the literature such as social network theory (Liebeskind et al., 1996), absorptive capacity (Cohen and Levinthal, 1990), and socio-cognitive capabilities (Ginsberg, 1994) in developing a framework for understanding organizational knowledge creation, an area that has received little attention in the empirical research realm. We are interested in discovering the extent to which: (1) there is a generic way in which we can view the knowledge creation process that is subject to general empirical modeling, (2) we can distinguish effectively between the antecedents and outputs of this process, (3) new knowledge creation is a firm-specific or problem-specific phenomenon, and (4) the factors that affect new knowledge creation are moderated by the context in which they are embedded. From a managerial perspective these goals are important because they give guidance as to which factors matter most allowing managers to avoid needless investment in areas that may be out of their real control. Because knowledge is, by definition, intangible and difficult to measure, having a structure where the outputs are observable and their characteristics reasonably well defined would be a valuable addition to research and managerial thinking and practice.

The General Process of Knowledge Creation

A simple way of thinking about the knowledge creation process is with a sources-uses-outcomes approach as exhibited in figure 1. We have found this approach useful because it looks at knowledge creation in three ways, each building on streams in the prior literature. First, there must be ***sources of information and know-how*** on which an individual's knowledge base is built. These sources arise from the internal and external network opportunities open to the individual attempting to generate and utilize a knowledge base. Second, the organization and individual must have ***absorptive capacities*** for internalizing and integrating the information and know-how being extracted from the 'network' of contacts and sources (Cohen and Levinthal 1990). Third, because knowledge is 'actionable', it must be created through application. Hence, the catalyst of the knowledge creation process is the organizational problem solving context in which we investigate whether the acquired information and know-how influences the ***quality of the decision making process***. Specifically, we look at whether information and knowledge is utilized to generate higher levels of comprehensiveness (more thorough analysis of options), creativity (application of novel solutions), consensus (shared commitment to implement chosen options) and new knowledge (new ideas, insights, better problem solving processes and new ways of thinking) in decision making.

From this process, the organization puts itself in the position to generate knowledge-based outcomes; i.e., **innovation**. In our parlance, innovation is defined as a mixture of process and product outputs that include new or modified products and services, patents, new marketing techniques, new managerial tools and administrative processes, licenses and wider thought leadership represented by things like presentations at conferences and publication.

It is these outputs – and not the simple fact that know-how is created – that generate better financial and sales **performance**. Here "performance" is conceptualized broadly to include multi-year market share, profits, profit growth and sales growth, all relative to competitors.

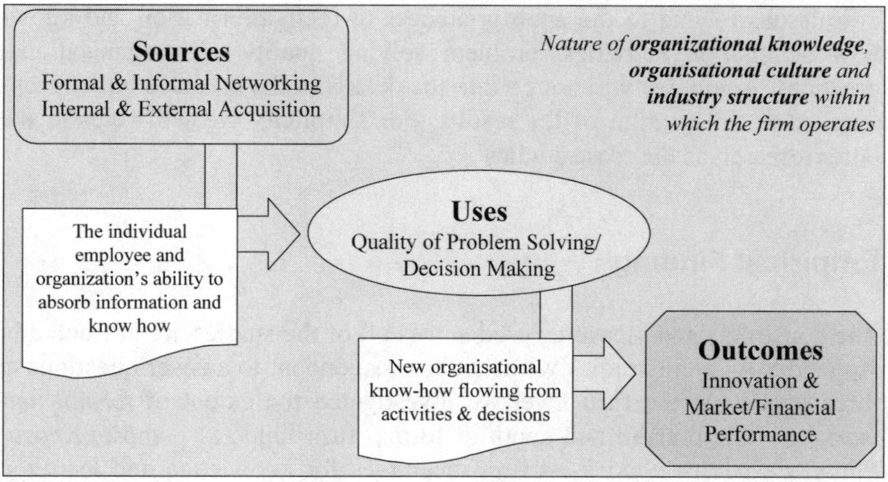

Fig. 1. The Process of Knowledge Creation and Innovation. *Source:* Soo, Devinney, Midgley and Deering (2002)

Another characteristic of this approach is recognition of the environmental milieu in which knowledge creation is taking place. There are two contexts that are important. The first is the simple **market/industry context**. This is most critical in determining basic structural factors that might affect the pool of available knowledge and innovation and the networking limitations as well as providing benchmarks for actual and potential innovative and market/financial performance. The second context is the **information and know-how context**. Certain business environments will have different information and knowledge structures in terms of the codifiability, teachability, observability, complexity, and cross-functionality of know-how and information (Zander and Kogut, 1995). For example, a legal firm tends to operate in a world with observable, teachable and function specific precedents that are driven by the nature of the legal system. This might be usefully contrasted with the different world in which, say, an advertising agency operates.

Soo, Midgley and Devinney (2003) and Soo, Devinney and Midgley (2003a) provide a comprehensive examination of the linkages operating in the knowledge creating process from a cross-sectional perspective by examining 317 firms across a host of industries. For simplicity we refer to this work as the 'cross-sectional studies'. Soo, Devinney, Midgley and Deering (2002) and Soo, Devinney and Midgley (2003b) expand this by investigating the general applicability of this model within the firm by examining projects in five different firms. This work compensates for the limitation of the cross-sectional studies by applying the model *within* firms facing specific issues related to the appropriateness of their information and know-how acquisition activities, problem solving quality and organizational practices. Again, we will not go into the details of the methods but concentrate on an integration of the results. For simplicity we will refer to the latter research as the 'case studies'.

Empirical Findings

The constructs and measures used across all of the studies are presented in Appendix A. In all studies we asked the respondent to answer questions at three levels. At the firm level we investigated the extent of *formal networking* – the breadth and depth of formal firm linkages – and *organizational absorptive capacity* – firm incentives for knowledge and learning. At the individual level we examined *informal networking* – the breadth and depth to which the individual interacted informally with other organizations and persons – *individual absorptive capacity* – the degree to which the individual engaged in knowledge acquisition and learning – *information sourcing* and *knowledge sourcing* – the breadth and depth of the individual's acquisition of information and knowledge from different sources. At the problem solving level we measured Ginsberg's (1994) socio-cognitive capabilities which were *comprehensiveness* – the exhaustiveness with which options where created – *creativity* – the creativity that was brought to bear on the problem – and *consensuss* – the extent of team work and consensus building utilized. Measures for new knowledge creation were developed by incorporating concepts from the organizational learning literature (i.e., Garvin, 1993; Fiol and Lyles, 1985), which included *new ideas, new insights and new ways of doing things that were generated from a problem solving situation.*

The major operational difference between the cross-sectional studies and the case studies is that the case studies utilized a manipulation where respondents were randomly selected to choose a *problem-solving context* for which the outcome was either 'more' or 'less' efficiently solved. The logic behind this is simple. In the cross-sectional studies the source of variation is firm differences. Hence, if the respondent is informed and the problem solved is representative we are reasonably confident that we are picking up the average differences between organizations. In the case studies, we have repeated measures of firm level variables and what we need to discover is whether there are project and problem solving contexts that matter. Hence the source of variance is across the firm, the individual and the problem being solved.

Samples

For the cross-sectional studies, the survey was mailed to 2,137 organizations (all with more than 20 employees) selected randomly from 17 manufacturing and service industries. After eliminating 26 surveys due to incomplete data, 317 responses were used in the final analyses. These firms were distributed across manufacturing (44%) and service (56%) sectors fairly evenly (see Table 1). Firm size was also well distributed, with 40% small firms (100 or less employees), 30% medium-sized firms (100 to 400 employees) and 30% large firms (more than 800 employees). The average and median sizes of these firms were 2,024 and 175 employees respectively. All respondents occupied middle-senior management roles with the average tenure at the organization, industry and current position was 12, 17 and 5 years respectively.

The case study data was collected from five firms – two of the firms were industrial in orientation with large labor forces – one in engine design and manufacturing and the other in railway design engineering. The other three were professional business service organizations that were large in their respective markets and also respected for their financial and service quality performance – one each in legal services, management consulting, and executive search. All but the railway design engineering and legal services firms operated in multiple countries and would be classified as large multinationals within their industry grouping.

Both the case study questionnaire surveys and the interviews targeted all three basic levels of the organization. Level 1 managers comprised the most senior management level such as CEOs, vice presidents and directors. Level 2 covered middle management positions such as project managers and marketing managers. Level 3 managers consisted of non-managerial staff such as technical officers, paralegals, associate consultants and business analysts (excluding administration/secretarial level staff). In the case of the larger organizations stratified sampling was used. In the case of the smaller organizations, all employees were surveyed although not all employees were interviewed. In the case of multinational firms, e.g., the consulting firm, we limited ourselves to a specific set of offices rather than surveying the company worldwide. Table 2 lists the number of returned surveys from each firm. Because we were able to gain senior management support from all five firms to conduct the studies, the response rates were relatively high, ranging from 70 to 85 percent.

Table 1. Distribution of Cross-Sectional Survey Respondents across Industries

Industries Included in the Study	Per cent of total responses	Per cent response within industry
Natural resources	23	11
Machinery and equipment	21	8
Banking and finance	12	9
Business and legal services	25	12
Health and other services	17	11

Source: Soo, Midgley and Devinney (2003)

Table 2. Description of Case Study Data

	Interviews				Surveys				
	Managerial Level				Managerial Level			Not Indicated	
	1	2	3	Total	1	2	3		Total
Executive search	7	7	4	18	9	19	17	0	45
Management consulting	4	7	6	17	18	15	17	1	51
Legal	4	6	8	18	22	50	22	0	94
Engine design	3	2	3	8	16	24	20	4	64
Railway engineering	5	6	7	18	20	53	32	10	115

Source: Soo, Devinney and Midgley (2003b)

Lessons from the Cross-Sectional Studies

The cross sectional studies examined two basic models. Soo, Midgley and Devinney (2003) examined the entire knowledge creation process outlined in Figure 1 with the proviso that the intermediate constructs of information/knowledge acquisition and problem solving quality were not disaggregated. The model tested is shown in Figure 2 along with the predicted effects associated with the paths in the model. Soo, Devinney and Midgley (2003a) disaggregate the networking component of the model and addresses the role of formal versus informal networking more closely as well as concentrating on the quality of knowledge and information. Figure 3 presents the results of both studies side by side.

There are several lessons that come from Soo, Midgley and Devinney (2003). First, the process as outlined appears to have some empirical legitimacy. All of the proposed linkages are significant. Indeed, tests versus alternative models show that the model presented dominates. Second, the main output of the knowledge creation process is innovation, defined broadly, and there is no residual effect of knowledge on performance, absent innovation. This is important because, should there be a residual effect of knowledge on performance sans innovation, then we must address how this gets capitalized into performance if not through administrative, process and product innovation. Third, and more critically, the strong fit of the model shows that we can indeed take a generalizable and quantitative approach to the study of knowledge creation that is based on survey research.

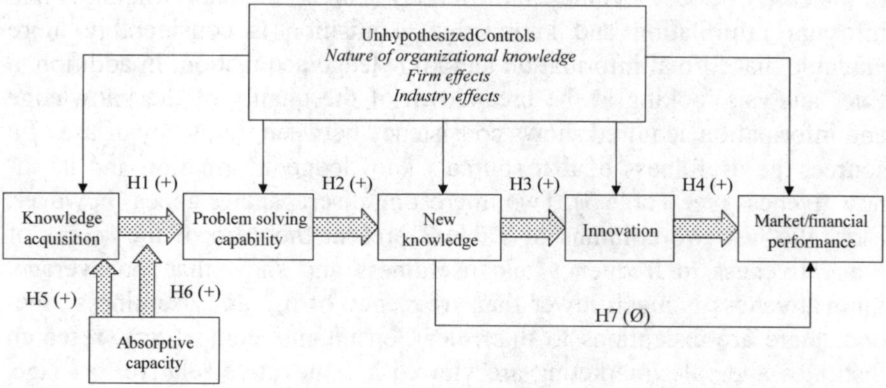

Fig. 2. Cross-Sectional Structural Equation Results

Note: Significant links only are presented and 'control' variables are not included in the above; **** $p < 0.001$, *** $p < 0.01$, ** $p < 0.05$. *Source:* Soo, Midgley and Devinney (2003); Soo, Devinney and Midgley (2003a)

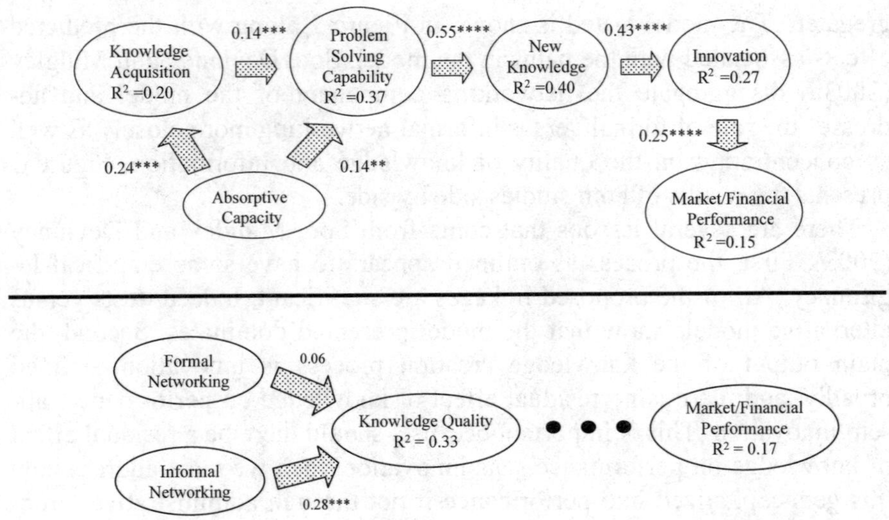

Fig. 3. A Model for Organizational Model Creation. *Source:* Soo, Midgley and Devinney (2003)

In the case of Soo, Devinney and Midgley (2003a) the main finding is that informal information and knowledge acquisition is considerably more valuable that formal information and knowledge acquisition. In addition, a finer analysis looking at the breakdown of the quality of the knowledge and information acquired shows consistency between frequency of use of a source, the usefulness of that source's knowledge/information and its innovativeness (see Table 3). Two interesting discrepancies appear however. First, the last two columns of Table 3 present the ratio of the scores of innovativeness to frequency and usefulness and show that, on average, innovativeness is much lower than frequency of use and usefulness. Second, there are exceptions to this rule. Consultants, competitors, research institutes and sales/marketing are viewed as innovative relative to usage. Third, some frequently used groups are not valued, relatively, in terms of innovativeness. In particular, customers are deemed to be the least innovative group when considered in light of their usefulness.

Table 3. Breakdown of Knowledge Sources and Knowledge Rating (Means)

						Innovation divided by	
	Frequency		Usefulness		Innovativeness	Frequency	Usefulness
Fellow colleagues	5.36	Fellow colleagues	5.47	Fellow colleagues	4.83	0.90	0.88
Parent/ subsidiaries	4.38	Parent/ subsidiaries	4.83	Consultants	4.38	1.15	0.92
Suppliers	4.15	Customers	4.82	Parent/ subsidiaries	4.18	0.95	0.86
Published material	4.11	Suppliers	4.79	Published material	4.10	0.99	0.90
Customers	3.94	Consultants	4.75	Suppliers	4.09	0.99	0.85
Consultants	3.81	Published material	4.57	Competitors	3.96	1.29	0.89
Sales/ marketing	3.38	Competitors	4.43	Customers	3.69	0.94	0.77
Competitors	3.09	Sales/marketing	4.07	Research institutes	3.63	1.19	0.92
Research institutes	3.04	Research institutes	3.96	Sales/ marketing	3.63	1.07	0.89

Note: Mean scores are presented in decreasing order. Each source is rated only if it is viewed as relevant. *Source:* Soo, Devinney and Midgley (2003a)

Lessons from the Case Studies

When examining the case studies we used two approaches. The first was a quantitative approach to determine what mattered more – the firm or the problem-solving context. We utilized two analyses. A MANOVA was used to examine the effect of the manipulation and the impact of that different problem solving contexts play in altering the antecedents of new knowledge creation. Second, a general linear model with the effects of the independent variables nested within problem solving context and firm was conducted which allows us to examine the marginal effect of specific variables on new knowledge creation. The second approach was a qualitative examination of the interview data in light of the quantitative modeling.

In the MANOVA the independent variables were the firm, the problem-solving context (efficiently or inefficiently solved) and the problem-solving context nested within the firm. These results are presented in Table 4. The most important difference to note is that all the problem specific variables are affected significantly by the problem-solving context and all the remaining firm and individual variables by the firm. There are additional firm effects on consensus, comprehensiveness and criticality and problem-solving context effects on informal networking. The only significant nested effect is with respect to new knowledge creation. From this we can conclude that we are indeed measuring the factors of interest at the level of analysis we are targeting.

Table 4. MANOVA Comparing the Effect of Problem Type Nested within Company on New Knowledge, Problem-Solving Variables and Firm and Individual Characteristics (F-Statistics)

	Direct Effects				Nested Effect: Context by Company	
Dependent Variable	Company		Context			
New Knowledge	0.91		27.99	***	2.30	**
Criticality	4.89	***	9.17	***	0.63	
Typicality	0.91		6.93	***	1.00	
Creativity	0.25		35.09	***	1.59	
Consensus	2.50	**	59.78	***	1.53	
Comprehensiveness	6.71	***	14.07	***	0.85	
Individual AC	7.09	***	0.06		0.71	
Organization AC	12.52	***	0.52		1.40	
Know-how Sourcing	3.71	***	0.31		0.41	
Information Sourcing	14.53	***	1.95		0.81	
Informal Networking	9.15	***	3.09	*	1.84	
Formal Networking	3.28	**	0.17		0.51	

Note: * $p < 0.10$, ** $p < 0.05$, *** $p < 0.01$. Direct company and nested effect with 4 df; problem solving context type with 1 df. *Source:* Soo, Devinney and Midgley (2003b)

The general linear model examines the role of networking, information and knowledge sourcing, absorptive capacity and problem-solving quality and context on new knowledge creation. Because our MANOVA indicated a possible problem context by company effect we have to run a model that looks at both nested and direct effects. The results are presented in Table 5.

Table 5. F-Test of Relationship between Knowledge and Problem Characteristics, Decision-Making Variables and Firm and Individual Characteristics

			Nested Effects				
Independent Variable	Direct Effect		Company		Problem Context		Company by Problem Context
Criticality	3.69	**	0.74		7.58	***	1.36
Typicality	0.52		0.40		2.03		1.08
Creativity	25.24	***	0.36		0.02		1.35
Consensus	11.82	***	0.68		4.93	**	0.40
Comprehensive-ness	1.06		0.66		0.32		0.91
Individual AC	0.00		2.34	**	NA		NA
Organization AC	0.43		0.44		NA		NA
Know-how Sourcing	5.89	***	0.74		NA		NA
Information Sourcing	0.55		0.30		NA		NA
Informal Networking	0.62		2.12	*	NA		NA
Formal Networking	0.06		0.54		NA		NA

Note: * $p < 0.10$, ** $p < 0.05$, *** $p < 0.01$ *Source:* Soo, Devinney and Midgley (2003b)

Knowledge sourcing and creativity in problem solving have significant direct effects on new knowledge creation, while consensus in problem solving has both direct and nested effects. This implies that not only do firms need to constantly acquire knowledge from their external and internal networks, but also that the way in which that knowledge is utilized to solve problems is just as important (Ryle, 1945). The 'criticality' of the problem-solving situation is found to be significant (both direct and nested effects) in influencing new knowledge creation. This implies that in situations where the problem (being addressed) has a 'critical' impact on busi ness performance, there is a higher propensity for firms to generate new knowledge. In the company-specific cases, both informal networking and individual absorptive capacity have positive effects on new knowledge creation. This is interesting as it tells us that firm differences in the ability to network and absorb knowledge is crucial in explaining propensity for new knowledge creation.

In summary, the survey results have revealed specific factors that are important to the process of new knowledge creation – i.e., the criticality of the problem being solved, creativity and consensus in problem solving, and knowledge sourcing – and pointed out that these effects are independent of both the firm and the problem-solving context. However, some effects are reinforced in more efficient problem-solving contexts – in the case of consensus – while others represent firm specific factors – for some firms, the effects of informal networking and individual absorptive capacity are magnified.
Specifically, our interview data provided important insights into specific organizational phenomenon that can inhibit knowledge sourcing, effectiveness of informal networking, and the quality of problem solving processes. We found that the main factors impacting on problem solving processes were (1) an inability to leverage individual employees' tacit knowledge, (2) an inability to transfer knowledge or best practices across business units, (3) a lack of incentive for knowledge sharing and, (4) a lack of effective database systems to capture and share information and structured learning forums to encourage the exchange of tacit knowledge. These four factors also explain why some firms fail to extract knowledge resources from their informal networks lessening their ability to absorb and assimilate external knowledge. Overall, these results present important managerial implications such as the need for explicit organizational policies to institute incentives for knowledge sharing and structured learning forums.

Conclusions

This quick overview of a complex mixture of projects was aimed at providing a picture of the validity of an approach to knowledge creation in organizations that is simple yet powerful. The lessons that we can take from this work operate on both intellectual and managerial dimensions.

From the more intellectual perspective we see that broad lessons can be drawn from our approach. Traditional examinations of organizational knowledge either confuse information with knowledge – demonstrating the need to be clearer about our definitions of the construct of interest – or rely on surrogates such as patent citations. What we have shown is that one can get an understanding of organizational knowledge by examining a mixture of: (1) access to sources of knowledge, (2) individual activities represented by individual absorptive capacity, (3) organizational incentives and practices represented by organizational absorptive capacity, (4) organizational problem solving capabilities and (5) innovative outputs. All of this, of course, must be conditioned on the environment in which the firm operates but that too appears to be less important than first believed. In addition, we are able to show that knowledge creation within the firm is driven by the problem solving context *much less* than by firm and individual differences. This also has important research implications since it seems to indicate that problem solving context can be compared across firms if the basic measures are broad and generic.

From the managerial perspective we have three clear implications. First, because our work shows that knowledge is capitalized through innovation, knowledge management becomes integrally bound to our understanding of the management of innovation and much less shackled by its links to information technology. Second, many knowledge management systems are driven by the formal structures that are both measurable and manageable. However, our findings indicate that it is the informal structures that generate the biggest effects on both problem solving quality and innovative output. This implies a need for a managerial reorientation to the intangible side of knowledge management, which is no doubt uncomfortable. Finally, we see that there is enormous variation within firms in the nature of the problems they are solving and the potentiality for knowledge creation. Failure to recognize this heterogeneity may needlessly restrict firms' abilities to learn and develop new knowledge.

References

Amit, R. and Schoemaker, P. (1993), "Strategic Assets and Organizational Rent." Strategic Management Journal 4: 33-46

Barney, J. (1991), "Firm Resources and Sustained Competitive Advantage." Journal of Management 17(1): 99-120

Cohen, W. M. and Levinthal, D. A. (1990), "Absorptive Capacity: A New Perspective on Learning and Innovation" Administrative Science Quarterly 35(1): 128-152

Collis, D. J. (1994), "How Valuable are Organizational Capabilities?" Strategic Management Journal 15: 143-153

Eisenhardt, K. M. and Martin, J. A. (2000), "Dynamic Capabilities: What Are They?" Strategic Management Journal 21: 1105-1121

Fiol, C. M. and Lyles, M. A. (1985), "Organizational Learning" Academy of Management Review 10(4): 803-813

Frost, T. S. (2001), "The Geographic Sources of Foreign Subsidiaries' Innovations" Strategic Management Journal 22(2): 101-124

Garvin, D. A. (1993), "Building a Learning Organization" Harvard Business Review July–August, 78-91

Ginsberg, A. (1994), "Minding the Competition: From Mapping to Mastery." Strategic Management Journal 15: 153-174

Hamel, G. and Prahalad, C. K. (1990), "The Core Competence of the Corporation." Harvard Business Review 68: 79-87

Henderson, R. and Cockburn, I. (1994), "Measuring Competence? Exploring Firm Effects in Pharmaceutical Research" Strategic Management Journal 15: 63-84

Liebeskind, J. P., Oliver, A. L., Zucker, L. and Brewer, M. (1996), "Social Networks, Learning, and Flexibility: Sourcing Scientific Knowledge in New Biotechnology Firms." Organization Science 7(4): 428-443

Leonard, D. and Sensiper, S. (1998), "The Role of Tacit Knowledge in Group Innovation" California Management Review 40(3): 112-132

Levinthal, D. and Myatt, J. (1994), "Co-Evolution of Capabilities and Industry: The Evolution of Mutual Fund Processing" Strategic Management Journal 15: 45-62

Miller, D. and Shamsie, J. (2001), "Learning Across the Life Cycle: Experimentation and Performance Among the Hollywood Studio Heads" Strategic Management Journal 22(8): 725-746

Nahapiet, J. and Ghoshal, S. (1998), "Social Capital, Intellectual Capital and the Organizational Advantages" Academy of Management Review 23(2): 242-266

Nonaka, I. and Takeuchi, H. (1995), The Knowledge-Creating Company New York: Oxford University Press

O'Dell, C. and Grayson, C. J. (1998), "If Only We Knew What We Know: Identification and Transfer of Internal Best Practices" California Management Review 40(3): 154-174

Powell, W., Koput, K. and Smith-Doerr, L. (1996), "Interorganizational Collaboration and the Locus of Innovation: Networks of Learning in Biotechnology." Administrative Science Quarterly 41: 116-145

Quinn, J. B. (1992), Intelligent Enterprise: A Knowledge and Service Based Paradigm for Industry New York: Free Press

Ryle, G. (1945), "Knowing How and Knowing That." Proceedings of the Aristotelian Society 46 (1945–46): 1–16

Stalk, G., Evans, P. and Shulman, L. (1992), "Competing on Capabilities." Harvard Business Review 70: 57-69

Steensma, H. K. and Lyles, M. A. (2000), "Explaining IJV Survival in a Transitional Economy through Social Exchange and Knowledge-Based Perspectives" Strategic Management Journal 21(8): 831-851

Soo, C. W., Devinney, T. M. and Midgley, D. F. (2003a), "The Role of Knowledge Quality in Firm Performance," in Tsoukas and Mylonopoulos (eds.) Organizations as Knowledge Systems. London: Palgrave, in press

Soo, C. W., Devinney, T. M. and Midgley, D. F. (2003b), "Knowledge Creation in Organizations: Exploring Firm and Context Specific Effects," Unpublished working paper, Australian Graduate School of Management

Soo, C. W., Devinney, T. M., Midgley, D. F. and Deering, A. (2002), "Knowledge Management: Philosophy, Pitfalls and Processes" California Management Review, 44 (4), 129-150

Soo, C. W., Midgley, D. F. and Devinney, T. M. (2003), "The Process of Knowledge Creation in Organizations." Unpublished working paper, Australian Graduate School of Management

Szulanski, G. (1996), "Exploring Internal Stickiness: Impediments to the Transfer of Best Practice Within the Firm." Strategic Management Journal 17: 27-43

Teece, D., Pisano, G. and Shuen, A. (1997), "Dynamic Capabilities and Strategic Management." Strategic Management Journal 18(7): 509-533

Teece, D. J. (1998), "Capturing Value from Knowledge Assets" California Management Review 40(3): 55-79

von Hippel, E. (1986), "Lead Users: A Source of Novel Product Concepts." Management Science 32(7): 791-805

Wernerfelt, B. (1984), "A Resource-Based View of the Firm." Strategic Management Journal 5: 171-180

Winter, S. (1987), "Knowledge and Competence as Strategic Assets" The Competitive Challenge: Strategies for Industrial Innovation and Renewal D. Teece (ed.), Cambridge, MA: Ballinger

Zander, U. and Kogut, B. (1995), "Knowledge and the Speed of the Transfer and Imitation of Organizational Capabilities: An Empirical Test." Organization Science 6(1): 76-92

Appendix A: Constructs and measures in the various model

Construct	Measure	Description
Absorptive Capacity		
	The extent to which individuals:	
Absorptive Capacity (Individual)	A	Seek information from external sources, other depts. and parent company
	B	Record and store acquired information for future reference
	C	Use the acquired information
	D	Distribute and share the acquired information
	E	Participate in academic/industry conferences
	F	Constantly update skills through training, workshops, or self-learning
	G	Constantly keep up to date with the latest technology and knowledge
	The extent to which org. policies/practices encourage employees to:	
Absorptive Capacity (Organization)	A	Seek information from external sources, other depts. and parent company
	B	Record and store acquired information for future reference
	C	Use the acquired information
	D	Distribute and share the acquired information
	E	Participate in academic/industry conferences
	F	Constantly update skills through training, workshops, or self-learning
	G	Constantly keep up to date with the latest technology and knowledge
Dimensions of Problem Solving		
	The extent to which:	
Criticality		The problem had an impact on organizational performance
Typicality		The problem occurs frequently in the organization
Comprehensiveness	A	The problem was solved through team effort
	B	The problem solving team was cross-functional
	C	More than one option was considered before the final decision was made
	D	Available options were formally tested before the final decision was made
	E	Orgn. structures/practices encouraged the generation of alternative solutions
Creativity	A	The final choice of solution was new, novel or creative
	B	Key decision makers were flexible in adopting new and innovative ideas
	C	People outside the orgn. provided new ideas or made suggestions

Construct	Measure	Description
	D	Orgn. structures/practices encouraged the generation of new/novel solutions
	E	There are pressures or incentives to be creative in solving problems
Consensus	A	The final solution was successful in solving the problem
	B	The problem was solved within the expected time frame
	C	There was a high level of consensus among key decision makers
	D	There was shared commitment towards the final goals and decisions
	E	Orgn. structures/practices encouraged the implementation of the final solution
New Knowledge	A	The new solution resulted in improved performance
	B	The new solution resulted in new ways of doing things
	C	The new solution resulted in new projects or product ideas
	D	The new solution resulted in wider organizational thinking
	E	The new solution resulted in increased ability to solve other problems
Know-How/Information Acquisition		
Information	Entropy index of frequency of acquisition from the following sources:	
	A	Customers, suppliers, competitors, other businesses, sales/distribution agents, universities, other research institutions, governments or government agencies, market research organizations, advertising agencies, consultants, parent company, overseas business units, other (in country) business units, fellow colleagues, libraries or other published materials, internet
Know-how	Entropy index of frequency of acquisition from the following sources:	
	B	Customers, suppliers, competitors, other businesses, sales/distribution agents, universities, other research institutions, governments or government agencies, market research organizations, advertising agencies, consultants, parent company, overseas business units, other (in country) business units, fellow colleagues, libraries or other published materials, internet

Construct	Measure	Description
Formal and Informal Networking		
Formal	Entropy index of frequency of collaboration with the following parties:	
(Organization level)	A	Customers, suppliers, competitors, other businesses, sales/distribution agents, universities, other research institutions, governments or government agencies, market research organizations, advertising agencies, consultants, parent company, overseas business units, other (in country) business units, fellow colleagues, libraries or other published materials, internet
Informal	Entropy index of frequency of interaction with the following parties:	
(Individual level)	B	Customers, suppliers, competitors, other businesses, sales/distribution agents, universities, other research institutions, governments or government agencies, market research organizations, advertising agencies, consultants, parent company, overseas business units, other (in country) business units, fellow colleagues, libraries or other published materials, internet
Innovation (14 Items)		
Entropy index of frequency of the following types of innovative output:		
		New product prototypes, products/services new to the market, product/services new to the firm but exist in the market, significant modifications to existing products/services, new/modified production techniques, new/modified administrative procedures, patents applied/pending/obtained, publications in scientific/technical/academic journals, formal presentations of discoveries, licenses/ technology rights sold/purchased
Market/Financial Performance (5 Items)		
Performance over the last three years relative to competitors on:		
	A	Return on investment (after tax)
	B	Market share in the primary market
	C	Annual increase in sales (sales growth)
	D	Annual increase in after-tax profits (profit growth)

Note: Controls are excluded

Knowledge Acquisition and Transfer in Strategic Alliances

Andrew Inkpen

Thunderbird, American Graduate School of International Management, 15249 N. 59th Avenue Glendale, Glendale, AZ, USA

There are various reasons why firms form strategic alliances, including the reduction of risk, economies of scale, access to new markets, and the search for legitimacy. Researchers have also suggested that an important explanatory factor for the alliance trend is that alliances provide a platform for access to new knowledge (Doz and Hamel 1991; Inkpen 1995; Ireland et al. 2002; Kogut 1988; Khanna et al. 1998). Through the shared execution of the alliance task, mutual interdependence and problem solving, firms can acquire knowledge from their partners. Unlike other learning contexts, the formation of an alliance reduces the risk that the knowledge will dissipate quickly (Powell 1987). Two or more organizations collaborate because of their different skills, knowledge, and strategic complementarity. The differences in partner skills and knowledge provide the potential trigger for knowledge acquisition by the alliance partners.

My objective in this chapter is to examine the factors associated with successful acquisition of alliance knowledge by an alliance partner. I will begin by reviewing the relevant theoretical background relating to knowledge acquisition through alliances. Building on this background, a framework of alliance learning is developed with an emphasis on key knowledge acquisition variables. I will then illustrate the framework using a case study of the NUMMI joint venture between General Motors and Toyota.

Definitional Background

Organizational knowledge can be defined as the capacity for action. In contrast to information, knowledge is often "sticky", difficult to codify, and of particular interest for this chapter, difficult to transfer. The firm is a repository for knowledge, with the knowledge embedded in business routines and processes. The firm's knowledge base includes its technological competences as well as knowledge about customer needs, supplier capabilities, competitors, and so on. Knowledge management is critical for firm success. Knowledge management involves various processes, such as the sharing of individual knowledge and its evolution to a collective state, the embedding of new knowledge in products and services, and the transfer of knowledge across organizational boundaries. The ultimate objective of knowledge management is the creation of new knowledge and innovations that can be deployed in the marketplace as the foundation for competitive advantage.

Knowledge transfer is defined as the process through which one network member is affected by the experience of another (Argote and Ingram 2000). The knowledge of interest in this chapter is knowledge directly associated with the skills of the alliance partner firm(s). For alliance knowledge to have value to the parent outside the alliance agreement, it must have the potential to be internalized and used by the parent. My interest is in how firms exploit the learning opportunity created by alliances and how knowledge is transferred.

A strategic alliance is a group of firms that enters into voluntary arrangements to exchange, share, or co-develop products, technologies, or services. In an alliance, knowledge access can be viewed from several perspectives. First, firms may acquire knowledge useful in the design and management of other alliances. Second, firms may acquire knowledge about an alliance partner that supports the firm's ability to manage the collaborative task. Third, firms may learn with an alliance partner when the partners jointly enter a new business area and develop new capabilities. Lastly, firms may acquire knowledge from an alliance partner by gaining access to the skills and competencies the partner brings to the alliance. For the purpose of our discussion, we focus on the last perspective, which concerns knowledge flows between alliance partners. This type of knowledge, called alliance knowledge in the remainder of the chapter, is directly associated with the skills of the partner firm(s) and may have value to the parent outside the alliance agreement. For the value to be captured, the knowledge must be acquired by the parent and applied to new geographic markets, products, and businesses. This potentially useful knowledge is knowledge the parent would not have had access to without forming the alliance.

Alliance Knowledge Acquisition and Transfer

The alliance knowledge acquisition and knowledge transfer process occurs in multiple stages. The first stage is the formation of the alliance and interactions between individuals from the two (or more) partners. The interactions and the individuals' exposure to partner knowledge may lead to the recognition of partner skill differences embodied in the alliance operation. This interactive and collaborative process creates the alliance knowledge, which in turn may lead to knowledge acquisition at the partner level.

Knowledge can be used strategically only to the extent that it is disseminated and integrated within the organization (Aguilar 1967; Jelinek 1979). A second stage, and the primary focus of the chapter, is the acquisition of alliance knowledge by the parent and the integration of the knowledge into the parent's knowledge base. For acquisition to occur, the parents must engage in efforts to transfer partner skill-related knowledge from the alliance to the parent. The third stage in alliance learning is the application of acquired knowledge within the parent firm to perform a discrete productive task. Over time, the knowledge may be incorporated into organizational routines. However, before this can occur, organizational members must reach some consensus on the framing of issues (Fiol 1994) associated with alliance knowledge.

Thus, learning through alliances should be viewed as a series of knowledge management stages, beginning with alliance formation and the creation of alliance knowledge. The focus of this chapter is on the second stage, knowledge acquisition. Of particular interest are the factors influencing both access to knowledge and effectiveness of knowledge acquisition efforts. The following section explores the knowledge acquisition process, beginning with the initial decision that provides the impetus for alliance knowledge acquisition.

The Valuation of Alliance Knowledge

A firm's initial valuation of alliance knowledge occurs prior to alliance formation, when the firm considers the value associated with gaining access to a potential partner's knowledge base (Inkpen and Beamish 1997). If gaining access to a partner's knowledge satisfies a firm's resource requirements an alliance may result. A firm may be intent on forming an alliance to substitute knowledge that it is lacking and cannot be created on its own (Hamel 1991). A firm also may see an alliance as a laboratory for learning about a broad range of new issues. Regardless of the intent, the formation of an alliance is a signal that the knowledge contribution of one partner has some strategic value to the other partner.

When an alliance is formed both partners have access to new knowledge, although the nature and ease of access will not necessarily be the same for all partners. At this point, alliance knowledge valuation takes on a different character and an alliance partner must consider the following question: is access sufficient or should additional efforts be made to acquire the knowledge at the partner level? Firms involved in alliances have a choice as to the resources and efforts that can be devoted to alliance knowledge acquisition. Acquiring alliance knowledge *enables* a partner to re-evaluate its commitment to collaboration. If a high strategic value is attached to knowledge access *and* acquisition, shifts in bargaining power become more likely because a partner firm placing a high value on acquisition will not be content with access alone. A high strategic value means that a firm may see a high potential in internalizing alliance knowledge and using the knowledge to enhance its strategy. On the other hand, a firm using an alliance as a substitute for knowledge it cannot create on its own may be content to remain dependent on a partner and may place a relatively low value on knowledge acquisition.

Alliance Knowledge Accessibility

Knowledge creation is initiated when organizations interact with their environments and are exposed to various sources of information. In the alliance context, a critical environment is the relationship between the partners and, in particular, the on-going nature of partner interactions. If one partner is to learn from another, the partners must interact and exchange knowledge. If there is no knowledge exchanged, obviously there can be no acquisition of knowledge by the partners. In some alliances, knowledge will be more accessible than in others. Two factors act as determinants of knowledge accessibility: partner openness and the complexity of alliance knowledge.

Partner Openness

The nature of partner interactions may range from operational information exchanges necessary to run the alliance to the sharing of more strategic information. Openness in the relationship should be a key element in determining the amount of information shared. With alliances, relationship openness can be defined as the willingness and ability of partners to share information and communicate openly. In a truly cooperative alliance, extensive communication between the partners is an essential feature of the relationship. The quality of inter-partner communications reflects the formal and informal sharing of meaningful and timely information (Anderson and Narus 1990). Hamel (1991) argued that openness between collaborative partners was an essential element in the learning process. This suggests that parent firms viewing their alliance relationships as open are more likely to invest resources in learning. Hamel also found that some organizations were more penetrable than others and systematic asymmetries in openness existed between Western and Japanese partners. These asymmetries had the potential to influence the learning process.

In considering openness, the degree to which partners are protective of their knowledge must be considered. Specifically, how tolerant are partners of the risk of knowledge leakage or spillover? Knowledge spillover occurs when valuable firm knowledge spills out to competitors and competitors can use the knowledge to gain competitive advantage (Cohen and Levinthal 1990). Knowledge spillover to an alliance partner has the potential to shift the balance of bargaining power that in turn, could lead to the initiation of changes in the partner relationship. When one partner acquires knowledge faster than the other, the learning partner no longer has the same partner need, which can lead to a situation of partner asymmetry (Inkpen and Bamish 1997). From a competitive viewpoint, a loss of knowledge by one partner may result in the creation of a new or stronger competitor.

The Complexity of Alliance Knowledge

The ease of knowledge acquisition is also influenced by the complexity of the underlying knowledge (Cohen and Levinthal 1990; Simonin 1999). Knowledge that is complex and difficult to transfer will likely include a sizable tacit component (Szulanski 1996). Spender (1996) suggested that tacit knowledge could best be understood as knowledge that has not yet been abstracted from practice. It is knowledge that has been transformed into habit and made traditional in the sense that it becomes "the way things are done around here" (Spender 1996). Tacit knowledge is highly context specific and has a personal quality, which makes it hard to formalize and communicate (Nonaka 1994). In contrast, explicit, codifiable or articulated knowledge is transmittable in formal, systematic language and may include explicit facts, axiomatic propositions, and symbols (Kogut and Zander 1992).

Skills, such as how to manufacture high precision products, will consist of a combination of both tacit and explicit knowledge. The explicit knowledge that can be expressed in schemata, diagrams, and charts is relatively easy to transfer and acquire. Because tacit and explicit knowledge are mutually complementary (Nonaka and Takeuchi 1995), there will be a strong tacit dimension associated with how to use and implement explicit knowledge. This tacit dimension is the "glue" that holds together the organizational routines associated with partner skills. Tacit knowledge is difficult to transfer and often sticky, which means a high incremental cost of transferring the knowledge to a specified location in a form usable by a given party (von Hippel 1994). A number of empirical studies have been carried out on the costs of transferring a product or process technology. For example, Teece (1977) examined 26 technology transfer projects in multinational firms and found that transfer costs varied widely for the projects in his study.

A further issue is that the greater the scope of knowledge being integrated within a capability, the greater the difficulty faced by competitors in replicating the capability. This suggests that in addition to tacitness, knowledge scope should also be considered. Scope refers to the degree to which knowledge incorporates multiple specialized tasks and functional capabilities. If knowledge is tacit, it will be broader in scope and, presumably, acquisition will be costly and time consuming for an alliance partner. Inkpen and Dinur (1998) found that the more tacit the alliance knowledge, the lower the organizational level through which successful transfers occurred and the less effective collective learning approaches were. In some cases, the effective transfer of tacit knowledge will require large amounts of knowledge to be transferred because the receiver does not know in advance which particular subset of knowledge will be most applicable to a specific problem (von Hippel 1994).

Knowledge Acquisition Effectiveness

Knowledge must be accessible before it can be acquired. However, accessibility does not guarantee acquisition. This section shifts the focus to the partner's ability to acquire alliance knowledge that challenges existing perspectives and paradigms akin to double-loop learning (Argyris and Schön 1978). Two factors are proposed as critical to effective knowledge acquisition: one, the knowledge connections between the parent and its alliance and two, the nature of alliance knowledge and its relatedness to the parent.

Knowledge Connections

Knowledge acquisition is an organizational process that can be managed by the partner firm (Hedlund and Nonaka 1993; Nonaka 1994) and improved upon (DiBella et al. 1996). Some organizations, like individuals, may lack the capacity to learn. Effectiveness at acquiring knowledge is closely related to Cohen & Levinthal's (1990) notion of absorptive capacity. Dyer and Singh (1998) referred to partner-specific absorptive capacity as the ability to recognize and assimilate valuable knowledge from a particular alliance partner. To develop an effective absorptive capacity, it is insufficient to merely expose individuals to new knowledge; the intensity of efforts is also critical. In the alliance context, parent learning efforts is a critical element because without active parent firm involvement, learning cannot occur. Firms must purposefully engage in actions and behaviors in order to capitalize on alliance learning opportunities.

Managers involved in an alliance will be exposed to various types of knowledge. In many cases, these managers will develop new ideas about their business. For knowledge in an alliance to be transferred to the parent organization level, there must be knowledge connections between the various organization levels. These connections create the potential for individuals to share their observations and experiences (Von Krogh et al. 1994). Knowledge connections occur through both formal and informal relationships between individuals and groups. These internal managerial relationships facilitate the sharing and communicating of new knowledge and provide a basis for transforming individual knowledge to organizational knowledge. The relationships also serve as the conduit for knowledge transfer to occur (Szulanski 1996). When one individual's or group's knowledge connects with other knowledge, it can be discussed, debated, and possibly discarded. The knowledge may also be further developed and move upwards in the organization. Individual knowledge is inherently "fragile" and, therefore, without knowledge connections new knowledge may be ignored or viewed as irrelevant (Von Krogh et al. 1994).

When an alliance partner has a strategic objective of acquisition and proprietary control over alliance knowledge, knowledge connections represent the mechanisms for knowledge transfer. Four generic management processes that create knowledge connections between alliances and parent firms were identified by Inkpen and Dinur (1998): personnel transfers between the alliance and parent; technology sharing; alliance-parent interactions, including visits and tours of alliance facilities; and linkages between parent and alliance strategies. Inkpen and Dinur (1998) found that the effectiveness of the various knowledge connection mechanisms depended on the tacitness of knowledge and the organizational levels involved in the process.

Knowledge Relatedness

Acquisition of knowledge is a cumulative process. Learning performance will be enhanced when the object of learning is related to what is already known and when there is a common language as the basis for interpreting experience (Grant 1996; Dyer and Singh 1998). Prior knowledge permits the effective utilization of new knowledge (Cohen and Levinthal 1990; Simonin 1999). As Powell et al. argued, "knowledge facilitates the use of other knowledge. What can be learned is crucially affected by what is already known" (1996: 120). In a study of internal knowledge transfers, Szulanski (1996) found that the ability of the recipient unit to value and apply new knowledge was critical for successful transfers. Lane and Lubatkin (1998) studied pharmaceutical-biotechnology R&D alliances and found that the similarity of the partners' basic knowledge bases supported interorganizational learning.

A paradox must be acknowledged here. The previous argument suggests that unrelated knowledge will be difficult to acquire and may, in fact, have limited value because of a lack of common language for understanding the knowledge. An alternative argument is that when there are significant differences between the partners, the learning opportunity is enhanced because of the potential new knowledge that is outside the firm's knowledge base. Continuing this line of thinking, the greater the differences between the partner firms, the more difficult it is to create a learning relationship, and the greater the probable value of learning. The counter to this view is that an enhanced learning opportunity that cannot be exploited ultimately has little value. If knowledge associated with firm differences is not recognized as valuable, it is unlikely that firms will initiate knowledge acquisition efforts. Lane and Lubatkin (1998) dealt with this problem by distinguishing between basic and specialized technological knowledge. Basic knowledge referred to general understanding of traditions and techniques. Lane and Lubatkin proposed that relatedness in basic knowledge supported the acquisition of different specialized knowledge.

As firms gain alliance management experience, they should become more efficient at utilizing alliances as learning opportunities because of a learning curve associated with the diffusion of learning within the firm (Westney 1988). This means that learning may be more difficult in new situations. If firms have a diverse background of alliance experience, there will be a more robust basis for learning because of the increased probability that incoming knowledge is in a form familiar to the parent. Firms that have a base of collaborative experience should have greater knowledge of how to manage, monitor, and appropriate value from their alliances (Simonin 1997). Once a firm begins collaborating, it develops experience in cooperation and a reputation as a partner (Powell et al. 1996). Alliance-experienced firms should be more likely to appreciate the learning opportunities created by their alliances.

Nummi Joint Venture

The NUMMI alliance between General Motors and Toyota is used to examine the framework introduced above. Data on the NUMMI alliance were collected through extensive interviews with current and former GM managers and via visits to the NUMMI plant and various other GM facilities. Data collection was completed in early 2003. In the early 1980s, GM and Toyota began negotiating a 50:50 equity joint venture (JV) to assemble small cars in the United States. After a year of negotiations, the two companies announced a partnership based at GM's plant in Fremont, California, which GM had closed in 1982. Toyota put up $100 million and GM provided the plant (valued at $89 million) and $11 million cash. The companies also raised $350 million to build a stamping plant. For Toyota, the main alliance objective was countering Honda and Nissan with minimal financial risk and learning to work with an American workforce (Weiss, 1997). The primary goals for GM were getting a small car replacement and utilizing an idle plant.

Learning was also a GM goal but there was not a consensus within GM about the value of the learning opportunity (Weiss, 1997). It was well known in the automobile industry that Toyota was much more productive than GM, Ford, and Chrysler. Keller (1989) said that Roger Smith was very interested in learning about Toyota's cost structure and how Toyota managed its plants. Smith spoke about the JV as a "learning experience - why not take the opportunity to get an insider's view of how the Japanese do what they do?" (Keller, 1989: 88). Weiss (1997: 292) reported that although GM's finance group favored the deal, GM manufacturing people were "dead set against a deal with Toyota" and were "confident in their own capabilities." Keller (1989) also argued that although a few GM executives recognized the opportunity for learning, there was deep resentment within GM about collaborating with a Japanese company.

Toyota was given overall operating responsibility for the plant. The first CEO was Tatsuro Toyoda, son of the founder of Toyota. The chief operating officer also came from Toyota and the general manager from GM. The JV agreement allowed GM to assign up to 16 managers to the JV (the actual number has sometimes been higher). A number of managers were also hired from outside GM and Toyota. One of the most important early decisions was to seek a different union agreement with the United Auto Workers. The union agreed to the adoption of the Toyota production system with its flexible work rules and broad job classifications.

Initial Years of the JV

Prior to its closure in March 1982, the GM plant in Fremont had about 800 pending union grievances and absenteeism regularly exceeded 20%. When the plant reopened as NUMMI, about 50% of the former workforce was rehired, which made up about 85% of the total production workforce. After about a year of operation, pending grievances were about 15 (Bussey & Tharp, 1986). More importantly, within a short period of time productivity and quality were the highest in the GM organization. Total hourly and salaried workers per vehicle averaged 20.8 at NUMMI in 1986, as opposed to 18.0 in Takaoka Japan, 40.7 in the comparable GM-Framingham plant, and 43.1 at the old GM-Fremont plant in 1978. Absenteeism was about 3% percent during the period 1984-1992, participation in the suggestion program increased to over 90% by 1991, and internal surveys of worker attitudes showed steadily increasing satisfaction from 1987 to 1991 (Adler & Cole, 1993). These results all became important triggers for learning and knowledge acquisition.

Later Years

In 1993 GM and Toyota agreed to extend the life of the JV beyond the original agreed termination date of December 1996. The Federal Trade Commission approved an indefinite extension of the original 12-year GM-Toyota agreement. In 2002 NUMMI built almost 370,000 vehicles, the most in its history. Employment in the plant in 2002 was at its highest level ever (about 5500) and four vehicles were being manufactured: Toyota Corolla, Pontiac Vibe, Toyota Voltz – a version of the Vibe for export to Japan, and Tacomas. The 2003 Pontiac Vibe and the 2003 Toyota Corolla, introduced in 2002, were more complicated than the vehicles that preceded them, requiring more parts and more people to build them.

NUMMI spent about $200 million preparing for the Vibe and Corolla launch in 2002.

Knowledge Transfer

In 2002 NUMMI entered its 18th year. Over that time period, GM significantly improved its manufacturing productivity and product quality. Based on public reports and data collected for this study, NUMMI has played a key role in GM's organizational improvements and knowledge has been successfully transferred. In this section I explore how GM managed the knowledge transfer process and exploited its alliance learning opportunity.

Alliance Knowledge Accessibility

When NUMMI was formed, GM found itself in an interesting position. As 50% owner of NUMMI, GM now had access to a Japanese-managed plant. Interestingly, Toyota was quite open in providing access to GM, even though GM and Toyota were major competitors on a global basis. Toyota's willingness to share its knowledge was the result of various factors. One, Toyota management recognized the importance of being viewed as a good corporate citizen from a U.S. political perspective. Partnering with GM could help make that happen. Two, Toyota has always been proud of its manufacturing leadership position and has openly shared the Toyota Production System (TPS) with other firms. Three, the Toyota and GM relationship was a strong relationship and in typical Japanese corporate fashion, close partners usually share information. In that sense, knowledge accessibility for GM was assured, although learning and knowledge transfer were not.

Although GM had excellent access to new knowledge via the NUMMI venture, acquiring the knowledge proved to be a significant challenge. In the early 1980s the U.S. automakers had limited knowledge of Japanese manufacturing processes and lean manufacturing as a concept had not yet been developed. When GM was first exposed to NUMMI, there was moderate understanding of the potential value of the Toyota knowledge but limited understanding of the complexity associated with the TPS. As a result, GM's initial efforts at knowledge transfer were not very successful because the underlying reasons for the knowledge differences were not well understood. Previous research (Inkpen 1996; Inkpen and Crossan 1995) found a similar situation in their analysis of Japanese-American joint ventures. Inkpen (1996) documented a case of an American firm that began its alliance with a low assessment of the value of alliance knowledge. The following is a quote from a senior manager in the American partner:

"Initially, we thought there was nothing to learn from our partner. When we first went to Japan we thought our partners wanted a JV so they could learn from us. We were shocked at what we saw on that first visit. We were amazed that they were even close to us, let alone much better. We realized that our production capabilities were nothing [compared with the Japanese firm]. Our partner was doing many things that we couldn't do" (Inkpen 1996: 132).

Thus, although partner openness created accessible knowledge for GM, the complexity of the knowledge significantly increased the difficulties of acquiring the knowledge. Grant (1996: 382) described General Motors' process of upgrading its manufacturing capability as "a slow and painful process" because the Toyota knowledge was deeply embedded with Toyota's history and culture. In particular, General Motors needed to learn about the Toyota production system and its emphasis on cost efficiency, quality, flexibility and innovation. In the next section, I consider factors that increased the effectiveness of knowledge acquisition and helped GM overcome their initial challenges.

Knowledge Acquisition Effectiveness

Knowledge in organizations gets created through social relationships and interactions between people in smaller groups or communities (Edmonston 2002). GM's challenge was to transfer the "sticky" knowledge of the NUMMI community to the GM manufacturing community. During the 1980s, various GM managers were exposed to NUMMI through assignments and visits to NUMMI. These mangers were creating a community of shared understanding and practice and were expected to be the "brokers" that carried the message (Brown and Duguid 1998). However, as seen above, the knowledge did not move easily. What was initially missing was knowledge connections, or organizational mechanisms, that create the social interactions necessary for knowledge to be transferred. Over time, GM put a variety in mechanisms in place and a systematic approach to knowledge acquisition and transfer emerged. These mechanisms include: a more systematic approach to selection and management of GM managers assigned to NUMMI; extensive visits to NUMMI by GM personnel; and the establishment of the NUMMI technical liaison office to manage knowledge acquisition. As well, GM leadership increased their commitment to knowledge acquisition from NUMMI.

Earlier I argued that knowledge acquisition will be enhanced when the knowledge is related to what is already known and when there is a common language as the basis for interpreting experience. Unrelated knowledge will be difficult to acquire and may have limited value because of a lack of common language for understanding the knowledge. Within communities, there is a shared understanding based on practice and experience that allows knowledge to move easily. Between communities, as in the case of two alliance partners or an alliance and its parent, knowledge movement must overcome different standards, different priorities and different evaluating criteria. As the number of managers exposed to NUMMI increased, a learning network of NUMMI-experienced managers emerged in GM. This network readily accepted the NUMMI knowledge and accelerated its distribution within GM. As NUMMI-experienced managers became more senior in the company, the distribution of the knowledge became easier. In addition, GM's increased experience in managing NUMMI (in part supported by GM's experience with other Japanese automakers such as Suzuki and Isuzu), can be viewed as a broadening experience that added to the firm's capacity to assimilate new experiences and increases its absorptive capacity.

Knowledge Movement Over Time

When GM first formed NUMMI, expectations of learning were unclear. Although initially some senior managers in GM had the mistaken belief that the learning could be finite, by the late 1990s, there was an understanding that the learning opportunity was continuous. The alliance learning challenge that GM faced was in the nature of the knowledge sought. It was not a set of explicit guidelines or tools; it was tacit and deeply embedded in the TPS. Embedded knowledge is difficult to transfer, as the following quote suggests:

"When knowledge is embedded, particular problems arise. The knowledge is not available in simple, unitized packages that can be bought for cash. For one organization to secure embedded knowledge from another, its personnel must have direct, intimate, and extensive exposure to the social relationships of the other organization" (Badaracco 1991: 98).

For knowledge originating in NUMMI to become internalized in GM, a socialization process had to occur and that would take time, as explained above. With exposure to NUMMI and experience in managing the alliance, GM was able to leverage the knowledge. The first application of NUMMI knowledge in a greenfield site came in 1992 in Eisenach Germany. NUMMI was the model for Eisenach. NUMMI also was the basis for a major turnaround effort in GM do Brasil. Eisenach was followed by greenfield plants in Argentina, Poland, Thailand, and China. As the international greenfield plants were built, lean production knowledge levels increased and the network of knowledge expanded. With each greenfield plant, the objective was greater manufacturing efficiency than the previous one. Within North America in the late 1990s, lean production began to impact all aspects of manufacturing. The most visible outcome of the knowledge transfer in the United States was the new Lansing Grand River plant opened in early 2002. However, the impact was not just in the greenfield sites. Old established plants were also being improved and the Global Manufacturing System (GMS) was developed as GM's standardized approach to lean manufacturing. By 2002, GMS was seen within GM as a core competence that, although its roots were the TPS, had evolved to become a unique GM approach to manufacturing.

Conclusion

Although there is clearly widespread interest in the knowledge management area, researchers continue to wrestle with questions such as "How do firms acquire knowledge?" and "What factors contribute to effective knowledge transfer?" To provide some insights to these complex questions, I have focused on one aspect of the broad knowledge management area – learning and knowledge acquisition through alliances. Within the alliance area, knowledge management and alliances has established itself as an area of scholarly interest. However, previous research in this area has been primarily concerned with the outcome of knowledge management. This chapter brings a degree of integration to the area and incorporates an emphasis on specific aspects of the knowledge acquisition process.

The management of knowledge is emerging as an important role of top management. To be successful, organizations must not only process information but also acquire and create new information and knowledge. A theme throughout this chapter is that there can be a significant payoff in collaborating, namely knowledge acquisition. As collaboration increasingly becomes a fact of life in the business environment, exploiting the knowledge potential of alliances will become more important. As a research area, knowledge management and alliances is fertile ground for future study. Research directed at exploring the underlying processes of alliance learning and more generally, the processes associated with transferring knowledge across organizational boundaries will enhance our understanding of organizational learning and knowledge acquisition. As von Krogh (1998:148) noted, the key challenge for knowledge researchers is "to find further enabling conditions for the fragile processes of knowledge creation." Using alliances as a specific context, this chapter has presented a framework of conditions that enable firms to acquire new knowledge.

References

Adler PS, Cole RE (1993), Designed for learning: A tale of two auto plants. Sloan Management Review, 34 (Spring): 85-94

Aguilar FJ (1967), Scanning the business environment. MacMillan, New York

Anderson JC, Narus JA (1990), A model of distributor firm and manufacturer firm working partnerships. Journal of Marketing 54 (1): 42-58

Argote L, Ingram P (2000), Knowledge transfer: A basis for competitive advantage in firms. Organizational Behavior and Human Decision Processes 82: 150-169

Badaracco JL (1991), The knowledge link. Harvard Business School Press, Boston

Argyris, C, Schön DA (1978), Organizational learning. Addison-Wesley, Reading, MA

Bussey J, Tharp J (1986), NUMMI auto venture is termed success: GM, Toyota, UAW are nearing their goals. Wall Street Journal May 20, A1

Cohen WM, Levinthal DA (1990), Absorptive capacity: A new perspective on learning and innovation. Administrative Science Quarterly 35: 128-152

DiBella AJ, Nevis EC, Gould JM (1996), Understanding organizational learning capability. Journal of Management Studies 33: 361-379

Doz Y, Hamel G (1998), Alliance advantage: The art of creating value through partnering. Harvard Business School Press, Boston

Dyer JH, & Singh H (1998), The relational view: Cooperative strategy and sources of interorganizational competitive advantage. Academy of Management Review 23: 660-679

Edmonston A (2002), The local and variegated nature of learning in organizations: A group-level perspective. Organization Science, 13: 128-146

Fiol CM (1994), Consensus diversity and learning in organizations. Organization Science 5: 403-420

Grant RM (1996), Prospering in dynamically-competitive environments: Organizational capability as knowledge integration. Organization Science 7: 375-388

Hamel G (1991), Competition for competence and inter-partner learning within international strategic alliances. Strategic Management Journal 12: 83-104

Hedlund G, Nonaka I (1993), Models of knowledge management in the West and Japan. In Lorange P, Chakravarthy B, Roos J, Van de Ven A (eds) Implementing strategic processes: Change learning and cooperation: Blackwell, Oxford, pp 117-144
Inkpen AC (1996), Creating knowledge through collaboration. California Management Review, 39 (1): 123-140
Inkpen AC (1995), The management of international joint ventures: An organizational learning perspective. Routledge, London
Inkpen AC, Beamish PW (1997), Knowledge bargaining power and international joint venture stability. Academy of Management Review 22: 177-202
Inkpen AC, Crossan MM (1995), Believing is seeing: Joint ventures and organization learning. Journal of Management Studies 32: 595-618
Inkpen AC, Dinur A (1998), Knowledge management processes and international joint ventures. Organization Science 9: 454-468
Ireland RD, Hitt MA, Vaidyanath D (2002), Alliance management as a source of competitive advantage. Journal of Management 28: 413-446
Jelinek M (1979), Institutionalizing innovations: A study of organizational learning systems. Praeger, New York
Keller M (1989), Rude awakening: The rise fall and struggle for recovery at General Motors. William Morrow, New York
Khanna T, Gulati R, Nohria N (1998), The dynamics of learning alliances: Competition cooperation and relative scope. Strategic Management Journal 19: 193-210
Kogut B (1988), Joint ventures: Theoretical and empirical perspectives. Strategic Management Journal 9: 319-322
Kogut B, Zander U (1992), Knowledge of the firm combinative capabilities and the replication of technology. Organization Science 3: 383-397
Lane PJ, Lubatkin M (1998), Relative absorptive capacity and interorganizatioal learning. Strategic Management Journal 19: 461-477
Nonaka I (1994), A dynamic theory of organizational knowledge. Organization Science 5: 14-37
Nonaka I, Takeuchi H. (1995), The knowledge-creating company: How Japanese companies create the dynamics of innovation. Oxford, New York
Powell WW (1987) Hybrid organizational forms. California Management Review 30 no. 1: 67-87
Powell WW, Koput KW, Smith-Doerr L (1996), Interorganizational collaboration and the locus of innovation: Networks of learning in biotechnology. Administrative Science Quarterly 41: 116-145
Simonin BL (1999), Ambiguity and the process of knowledge transfer in strategic alliances. Strategic Management Journal 20: 595-624
Simonin BL (1997), The importance of collaborative know-how: An empirical test of the learning organization. Academy of Management Journal 40: 1150-1174
Spender JC (1996), Making knowledge the basis of a dynamic theory of the firm. Strategic Management Journal 17 (Winter Special Issue): 45-62

Szulanski G (1996), Exploring internal stickiness: Impediments to the transfer of best practice within the firm. Strategic Management Journal 17 (Winter Special Issue): 27-43

Teece D (1977), Technology transfer by multinational firms: The resource cost of transferring technological know-how. Economic Journal 87: 242-261

von Hippel E (1994), Sticky information and the locus of problem solving: Implications for innovation. Management Science 40: 429-439

Von Krogh G, Roos J, Slocum K (1994), An essay on corporate epistemology. Strategic Management Journal 15: 53-71

Weiss SE (1997), Explaining outcomes of negotiation: Toward a grounded model for negotiations between organizations. In Lewicki RJ, Bies RJ, Sheppard, BH (eds) Research on Negotiations in Organizations, Vol. 6. JAI Press, Greenwich, CN, pp 247-233

Westney DE (1988), Domestic and foreign learning curves in managing international cooperative strategies. In Contractor F, Lorange P (eds) Cooperative strategies in international business. Lexington Books, Lexington MA, pp 339-346

Knowledge Management and Indian Industrialization

V.S. Arunachalam[1] and Robin King[2]

[1] Carnegie Mellon University, Pittsburgh, PA 15213, USA
[2] Georgetown University, Washington, DC 20057, USA

Introduction

India's industrialization since Independence in 1947 presents a unique opportunity to study how its institutions acquired knowledge and how successful they have been in assimilating it. Unlike other countries that became independent during the same period, India inherited a rich reservoir of traditional knowledge built over centuries, and this got added to the knowledge pool acquired later. It also inherited a first-class higher educational system, educated and trained human resources and a catalogue of achievements in science and technology, commerce and international trade. In 17th and 18th centuries, India was one of the largest manufacturers of iron and steel in the world, an enviable exporter of high quality textiles and a shipbuilder for the British Royal Navy[1]. Western craftsmen traveled to India to learn the secrets for printing fast colors in cotton textiles and constructing men-of-war[2]. The Industrial Revolution that replaced muscle power by machines changed all that and radically reduced the country's leadership in trade and manufacturing. Large-scale manufacture of factory-centric goods of quality and reliability from Britain made handcrafted Indian products non-competitive. Within a century, from being an exporter of commodities and manufactured goods, India became a net importer of

---

1 See *The Cambridge Economic History of India, Volume* 2, Dharma Kumar and Tapan Raychaudhuri, New York: Cambridge University Press, 1983, especially Chapter VII by Morris D. Morris on "The Growth of Large-Scale Industry to 1947" and Chapter X by K.N. Chaudhuri on "Foreign Trade and Balance of Payments (1757-1947). On ships, the Indian Navy's web site proudly recounts India's illustrious ship-building past, found at "indiannavy.nic.in/maritime_history.htm".

2 Jawaharal Nehru, *The Discovery of India*, Garden City, NY: Anchor Books, 1960 (reprint of original published by the John Day Company, Inc., in 1946).

manufactured and engineering goods[3]. Missing the Industrial Revolution had cost the country dearly.

Irrespective of the loss in trade and commerce, India improved its educational system during this period patterning it after the British universities, and adopted English as the medium of instruction in its colleges and universities. For the first time, the entire country had a common language for higher education. It also incorporated the many products of the Industrial Revolution such as railways, electricity, and telegraphs into its infrastructure. Private entrepreneurs adopted the factory system for manufacturing textiles, metals and chemicals. But these trysts with industrialization were modest and dwarfed by large-scale imports from Britain, its colonial ruler. It was only after it became independent that India seriously embarked on projects to modernize and enlarge its infrastructure and set up new industries. In this paper we shall discuss the role of knowledge, both imported and indigenous, in India's industrialization, adding our thoughts on the role of traditional knowledge during this process. We shall also discuss the social environment that is peculiar to India in determining the localization, spread and transfer of knowledge.

Traditional Knowledge in the Classification of Knowledge

Polanyi's definition of tacit knowledge invokes knowledge acquisition through experience or practice – learning by doing – and through discussions and is not formally structured or codified[4]. It is this kind of knowledge, in the hands of an expert chef, that transforms a run-of-the-mill dish into a culinary marvel. It is also this knowledge – an addition of an element there or control of a pouring temperature there – that makes a metallic casting defect-free. The size and richness of this type of knowledge is determined more by the number and variety of innovations in practice than by formal education. The acquisition and dissemination is dependent on the availability of opportunities for learning, and the absence of barriers, social or economic, for its transfer and assimilation. For instance, information on intricacies involved in steel plate rolling would have no relevance

[3] See Chaudhuri in Kumar and Raychaudhuri, above. Perhaps the scholar whose work on this topic has reached the most readers worldwide is Eric Hobsbawm. For example, see *Industry and Empire: from 1750 to the Present Day*, London: Penguin, 1999, especially Chapter two on "the Origin of the Industrial Revolution" and a later chapter on "Britain in the World Economy."

[4] Michael Polanyi, *Personal Knowledge; Towards a Post-Critical Philosophy.* Chicago: University of Chicago Press, 1958.

to a country with no steel rolling mills, or to a receiver of information who has no access to steel industries. Knowledge without a context is redundant information that is quickly forgotten.

Codified or formal knowledge comes in the form of instructions, manuals, blue prints and through lectures and textbooks. A bridge design handbook, for instance, provides the necessary information on construction materials, design criteria and details of design calculations. The interchange between tacit and codified knowledge is dynamic with elements of tacit knowledge that could be clearly articulated and structured entering into the realms of codified knowledge. Parts of codified knowledge, in turn, may become obsolete and may get discarded. Manuals and instructions for repairing a mechanical typewriter or assembling a vacuum tube radio are not now in circulation. With recurrent use, some elements of codified knowledge may turn out to be so commonplace that they may no longer require formal description. In this sense, the codified becomes tacit. One does not write, for instance, that clockwise rotation of a screwdriver tightens the screw while an anti-clockwise loosens it.

How does one classify traditional knowledge in these two categories? It can be classified as tacit, as more often than not, it gets transferred through oral exchanges. One could equally well argue that it should be classified as codified as the person conveying the information might not have acquired it through practice or by learning by doing, but through inheritance or deliberate learning. The absence of appropriate documents and blueprints could be attributed to India's cultural tradition of oral transmission. Manuscripts, when available, are on palm-leaves in languages and scripts that are not now in vogue. A few projects are now under way in India to transfer knowledge from ancient palm scripts to digital memory. The Council of Scientific and Industrial Research in India (CSIR), at one of its institutions, the National Institute of Science Communication and Information Resources (NISCAIR), is pursuing a program to formally catalogue all such information available on Indian medicinal plants and traditional Indian medicine in a structured way. This initiative is expected to help India defend its knowledge heritage from intellectual property challenges from the West[5].

---

[5] For further information on this Traditional Knowledge Digital Library (TKDL) see: www.niscair.res.in/ActivitiesandServices/MajorProjects/majproj.htm.

Constraints in Knowledge Dissemination in India

Sharing of knowledge is a social issue and, in India, it was governed strictly by caste or *varna* considerations. Each caste was traditionally assigned a specific profession that was hereditary: a weaver's son was to be a weaver and a blacksmith's son, a blacksmith. Women were generally excluded from such inheritances even though it wasn't uncommon to see women in some professions, working mainly as laborers or artisans. *Sudras* were assigned all tasks considered menial by the upper castes. A strict adherence to the caste system ensured the smooth transfer of resident knowledge, but curtailed the growth of any profession or injection of new knowledge or innovation from other communities. By restricting formal learning only to upper castes and professional practices to the so-called lower castes, the rigid caste system curtailed any two-way exchange of knowledge and practice. Innovations were therefore rare. Traditional production practices were followed for generations without any changes. Physical labor and experimentations by educated higher castes were frowned upon except in the practice of medicine. Indian traditions with its debilitating caste system could not have produced a James Hargreaves or a Richard Arkwright. One could argue that the caste system was not dissimilar to the membership of guilds that were in vogue in Europe in the 14th century[6]. But the guilds were created to regulate the number of practitioners for preserving the monopoly of craft, and one could buy one's way into the guild membership through money and apprenticeship. The guilds also took upon themselves to regulate the quality of products manufactured by their members. The caste system provided no such opportunities for entering into a profession nor did it ensure the quality of goods produced by different castes. Karl Marx argued that with the introduction of railways, India would free itself from the stagnating poverty and inertia to growth. He felt that the caste system would also be eliminated by the easy mobility that the railways offered[7]. Contrary to his expectations, the caste system proved to be more impervious. Unlike in the US, the railways couldn't enable the indigenous industrialization.

Social changes that have made caste less relevant for pursuing a profession or practicing a trade came only gradually, through social reform

---

6 There is a vast and controversial literature on the caste system. The most scholarly piece in the West is generally considered to be Susan Bayly, *Caste, Society and Politics in India: From the 18th Century to the Modern Age*, New York: Cambridge University Press, 1999.

7 Karl Marx, letter to *New York Daily Tribune*, dated July 22, 1853, published August 8, 1853.

movements in the country and by laws enacted by the parliament after India's independence. This began with Article 15 (4) of the Constitution which allows the state to make "special provision for the advancement of any socially and educationally backward classes of citizens or for the Scheduled Castes and the Scheduled Tribes" and Article 16 (4) providing for job reservation for "any backward class citizens … not adequately represented in the services under the state." Reservations for jobs in the government, and in admissions to professional colleges and universities to members of the so-called lower castes are now practiced to attempt to ensure that there are no caste based barriers to acquiring knowledge or practicing professions. It is not now uncommon to find ace software engineers from communities that were once relegated to menial labor. Many Indian political leaders and social reformers believe that such reservations should continue for many more years before knowledge acquisition and practice becomes truly egalitarian, determined solely by individual competence and not by the caste to which one is born. Chief Minister of Karnataka S.M. Krishna in March 2001 suggested that the reservation system in place in the public and education sectors be extended to the private sector as well[8].

Knowledge Management in Independent India

To study knowledge transfer and management in modern India, we must examine the trajectories of different products and sectors in Indian economic development. Soon after Independence, the Indian Government implemented its policy of public ownership of industries in a number of sectors of the economy arguing that only through the "commanding heights" of the public sector would it be possible for India to industrialize rapidly[9]. Steel plants, fertilizer factories, electric power companies all became publicly owned. The infrastructural industries such as railways, telecommunications and broadcasting also came under the public ownership.

---

[8] See "CM for quota for SCs in pvt. Sector," in *The Hindu*, Monday 19, 2001, available at www.hinduonnet.com/thehindu/2001/03/19/stories/0419402u.htm. More recently, in April 2003, he stated that this extension may be inevitable stemming from the need to combat discrimination in the newly privatized and globalized environment. See "Infosys Chief favours selective reservation," April 15, 2003 at www.indiainfo.com/2003/04/15/15infy.html.

[9] See T.N. Srinavasan, *Eight Lectures on India's Economic Reforms*, New Delhi: Oxford University Press, 2000, for a discussion of the early plans including Sir M. Visveswaraya's 1934 *Planned Economy for India* and the Industrial Policy Resolution of 1948.

In addition, the central government took over various strategic and science-intensive sectors such as atomic energy, space and electronics forming autonomous commissions, emulating the USAEC and NASA. Even before Independence, manufacturing in the defense sector was under the government. For example, the Defense Research and Development Organization (DRDO), formed in 1948, also came under the tutelage of the central government. The Defense Research and Development Organization (DRDO) was set up on the recommendations of Prof. P.M.S. Blackett, a British Nobel Laureate, and a socialist like Nehru, who in a brief report commissioned by the Indian Government argued for India developing its indigenous capability in defense research, development and manufacture of equipment. He did not recommend India pursuing the development of advanced systems like radars and aircraft, which he called as "competitive". Instead, he favored the development of more conventional ("non-competitive" in his jargon) systems like guns and ammunition. This initial hesitation to pursue state-of-the-art projects likely stunted the growth of knowledge in many advanced areas of engineering.

Private industries were permitted only in some sectors with stringent licensing conditions that fixed the quota for production[10]. Improvements in manufacturing that would have increased production, and development of new products were not encouraged as these would have made the allotted licenses, permits and quotas irrelevant.

Research laboratories in various areas of science and technology were set up; the existing ones in areas such as agriculture were strengthened. New higher educational institutions including Indian institutes of technology were founded to produce the large number of professionals that India needed. It was said that Pandit Jawaharlal Nehru's love for science and anything scientific began even as a student in Cambridge. He had many friends among scientists both in England and in India. When he became independent India's first Prime Minister he sought the help of a number of distinguished Indian scientists to establish research laboratories, which he called the temples of modern India. The Planning Commission also has had as members from the Indian scientific community. Nehru was concerned about the acute scarcity of scientist and engineers for building India's infrastructure and industries. The Indian institutes of technology were set up because of this concern. By bestowing autonomy for these institutions, and freeing them from the bureaucratic controls of state governments

---

10 The "licensing raj" is addressed widely by economists, such as Srinavasan above, and politicians, such as former President Clinton, in his address to the Indian Joint Session of Parliament on March 22, 2000 (at clinton4.nara.gov/WH/New/SouthAsia/Speeches/20000322.html).

and the endemic poverty of the Indian University Grants Commission, he sowed the seeds for the growth of engineering education of quality. This major contribution of Nehru has not been adequately recognized. It is of interest to point out that when a former British Prime Minister Harold Wilson was asked to identify a major contribution of his government to the country, he chose the setting up of Open University that provides access to university education of quality for a large number of people who couldn't afford to join the more formal British university system.

Constraints in Knowledge Dissemination

One could argue that with such a consortium of laboratories, industries and institutions of higher learning, India should have become a major industrial power rivaling China or South Korea, and contributed more to International trade and scientific and technological innovations. A major part for this deficiency could be attributed to the public ownership of manufacturing in several key sectors[11]. As India did not have its own technology in many areas, it had to depend on imported know-how and manufacturing equipment. The imported know-how was targeted for the manufacture of a specific product with the chosen hardware and operational procedures. The transferred knowledge was not sufficiently up-stream or versatile to encourage innovation or spill-over, where knowledge acquired in a particular area becomes relevant in other areas. Rather, the technology transfer represented technology frozen in time, and generally already mature (read: old) by the time it reached India[12]. For many years, India had to depend on foreign aid for establishing large industries, and this aid came in the form of equipment and know-how that was not easily transferable to another plant that was being set up with support from yet another country. In these cases, the "know how" was blindly transferred, while the "know-why, " critical to generating spillover effects, did not make the journey. A number of cases provide examples of this phenomenon. For instance, the Soviet steel making technologies (using large open-hearth furnaces) wasn't very useful

[11] See Deepak Lal, *Unfinished Business: India in the World Economy*, New Delhi: Oxford University Press, 1999.

[12] Here Raymond Vernon's Product Cycle Theory captures India's predicament, well within the less developed country category, receiving technology and producing new goods only once the product is very mature, that is, at the very end of the cycle. See Raymond Vernon, International Investment and International Trade in the Product Cycle," *Quarterly Journal of Economics*, Volume 80, pages 190-207, 1966.

for manufacturing steel using the LD process. Another classic example was of a foundry in South India built by the Soviets that had snow cleaning equipment included as part of the package. The average annual temperature is about 30 degrees Celsius, and snow is unknown, yet that equipment was, in the Soviet donor's mind, required. Many of these transfers of industrial technology occurred in vertically integrated packages, further dissuading innovation. For example, investment in the aircraft engine field was turbine specific, limiting the potential for innovative linkages, as specialization locked in – and limited – markets. In the U.S., on the other hand, investment casing for many types of turbines was more the norm, and the need to service multiple markets led to improvements spilling over across markets.

Even innovations within a plant were not encouraged by the know-how givers. Maintenance of the *status quo*, without any disruption in production or in product quality, was seen as their main interest. The know-how givers were also reluctant to guarantee the performance of new innovations generated independently by Indians. For instance, when an Indian laboratory was ready to substitute aircraft brake pads, as they were not easily available from the Soviet Union, the Soviet collaborating industries objected as they feared that the indigenous product could adversely affect the braking performance of the aircraft. It was only with strong political pressure that the Soviet objections were overruled so that indigenous brake pads could be introduced in Indian fighter aircraft. Once such nationally developed knowledge was recognized, many innovations in friction materials technology quickly followed, making India a recognized manufacturer and exporter of friction materials. For example, one Chennai-based firm, Sundaram Brake, received the Deming Application award in 2001 from the Japanese Union of Scientists and Engineers in recognition of its excellence in total quality management.[13]

Indigenous Knowledge Generation and Dissemination

Indigenous knowledge generation blossomed in areas where there was no flow of know-how from other countries. Their absence could have been due to many reasons, including India's inability to pay for such purchases from abroad, or its needs being specific to India alone. There were also instances, especially in defense, space and nuclear energy sectors, where export controls prevented India from acquiring such technologies. It there-

[13] "Sundaram Brake gets Deming award," in *The Hindu* online edition, October 13, 2001.

fore became essential for India to generate the needed knowledge and skills indigenously. This, the country, seems to have accomplished well though it took longer as the Indian organizations first learned to collaborate. The recent successful testing of cryogenic engines for space rockets, and fly-by-wire systems for a fighter aircrafts suggest that generation and diffusion of knowledge is dependent on the availability of customers and their confidence in Indian products, and their willingness to invest in their development. A detailed tale on the acquisition of knowledge for an advanced system like a cryogenic rocket engine is given in a report commissioned by the Eisenhower Institute.[14]

Unfortunately, even when it was possible, private industries were not successful either in knowledge generation or on its diffusion or spillovers. Because of the license-quota-regime and assured supply of customers, it became easy to ignore innovations. These could become such a farce that a particular model of an Indian automobile was known more for the year of its manufacture than for the incorporation of any new feature!

Three Success Stories

Three major Indian successes in knowledge generation and its successful diffusion are in agriculture, computer software and in pharmaceuticals. These have emerged because of particular combinations of characteristics, including endowments, policies, and traditions. We will very briefly address each, emphasizing the role of knowledge in each case.

1. Agriculture

Innovations in cereal production, known popularly as the Green Revolution, came out of a close collaboration between the US and Mexican laboratories, and Indian agricultural research institutes[15]. The speed with which

---

[14] See http://www.eisenhowerinstitute.org/programs/globalpartnerships/fos/new-frontier/ arunarticle.htm.

[15] There is a large, diverse literature about the Green Revolution. Illustrative, but non-exhaustive examples are cited below. For purposes of this paper, however, suffice it to say that the literature is in general agreement that dramatic increases in cereal production occurred. See M.S. Swaminathan, editor, *Wheat Revolution: A* Dialogue, Madras: Macmillan India, 1993; International Food Policy Research Institute Issue Brief Number 11, "Green Revolution: Curse or Blessing," Washington: IFPRI, October 2002; Lester R. Brown, *Seeds of Change: The Green Revolution and Development in the 1970s*, New

new high yielding and hardy mutants were developed and the diffusion of the know-how for their cultivation and harvesting shows the results of the evangelic initiatives of agricultural extension workers in an environment where the stakeholders were interested, and many of the necessary complementary policies and inputs were available. The users of the technology – the farmers – had a large stake in its success and their livelihood depended on the success of the Green Revolution.

2. Computer Software

After Independence, India set up a number of engineering universities in different parts the country[16]. Admission to these was based more on academic merit than on other considerations. The graduates from these institutions working both in India and abroad have made significant contributions to the growth of Information Technology (IT) industry. There have been many reports speculating on reasons for India's success in this area of high technology[17]. Various explanations from familiarity with the English language (that appears to be essential to any development in computer software), to Indian students' ease with arithmetic, to the availability of good engineering education have been offered. To this list we must also add that as IT is a totally new technology, it does not depend either on the pre-existence of any specific infrastructure, tacit know-how, nor has it been subject to the license raj. Because of the nature of its product, knowledge, the market is global and not dependent on the existence of a national market with all its distortions. Even after a decade, Indian export earnings in this sector are more than its national sales. In 2002-3, for examples, exports totaled US $9.5 billion while the domestic market absorbed only $2.5 billion[18]. Fortunately, because of the decentralized nature of this sector's

York: Praeger Publishers, 1970; and Andrew C. Pearse, *Seeds of Change, Seeds of Want: Social and Economic Implications of the Green Revolution*, New York: Oxford University Press, 1980.

[16] The history of individual universities can be found in their promotional literature. For example, see "IIT History" at www.iit.org/about_iit_history.htm, accessed August 19, 2003.

[17] For example, see Ashish Arora, V.S. Arunachalam, Jai Asundi, and Ronald J. Ferandes, "The Globalization of Software: The Case of the Indian Software Industry: Final Report to the Sloan Foundation," February 2000. Available at www.heinz.cmu.edu/project/india/pubs/Sloan_Report_final.pdf.

[18] National Association of Software and Service Companies, "Indian IT Industry – A Success Story," NASSCOM Fact Sheet, June 2003, available at www.nasscom.org/download/it_industry.pdf.

infrastructural needs – a few computers with some connectivity will do – the pressure for the government to invest was not strong. The government thus allowed all entrepreneurs to enter into the fray providing incentives for this nascent industry. The center of this industry is located in Bangalore in the Highlands of the Karnataka State. Because of its climate, past experiences with many areas of high technology and laissez-faire attitude of its citizens, it was easy to set up a large number of IT industries. The location and the availability of appropriately trained and motivated human resources are providing opportunities for easy diffusion of knowledge and its spillovers[19]. Already, Indians are moving up-scale in the type of problems they address in software. The quality of its products are now recognized by customers in the US and elsewhere.

3. Pharmaceuticals

The Indian pharmaceutical industry has also come of age. Initially, this industry was mostly foreign-owned, but provided opportunities for the workers to learn the relevant technologies[20]. With demands for more drugs, there were many incentives for entrepreneurs to start new industries in this sector. As Indian drug patents are only process-specific, as opposed to product-specific like in the U.S. and other Western countries, opportunities to innovate in both proven and new compositions have existed, allowing competition – with its benefits of lower costs and more variety – to flourish. Lower overheads also contribute to cheaper Indian manufactured pharmaceuticals. This environment has led to an international dispute as a result of offers in early 2001 from Indian pharmaceutical company CIPLA to sell AIDS drugs to South Africa far more cheaply (at $1/day) than the western pharmaceuticals' previous offers[21]. A counter-offer of cheaper

---

[19] For example, see "Calling Bangalore," in *Business Week International* of November 11, 2002, available at www.smallco.com/education-articles.asp and V.S. Arunachalam, "Home Improvement: An Indian Tale," in *Foreign Policy*, July/August 2003, p.79.

[20] For more on the history of the this industry in India, see Felker, *et. al.*, *The Pharmaceutical Industry in India and Hungary: Policies, Institutions, and Technological Development*, World Bank Tech Paper #392, December 1997, especially Chapter 2 (pp. 6-26) by Shekhar Chauduri.

[21] Sitaraman Shankar, "Cipla says Cheap AIDS Drug Exports Taking Off," Reuters News Media, September 4, 2001, available at www.aegis.com/news/re/2001/RE010902.html.

drugs from the western firms followed after much debate[22]. Here it is easy to see the consumer costs, i.e., higher costs, of the monopoly protection that patents confer in Western countries such as the United States. In India, on the other hand, the consumer – and society through the public good of public health -- is benefiting from widespread knowledge! As in the case of computer software this area has also been profited by the availability of a large number of well-trained chemical engineers. Chemical engineering is one of the oldest engineering disciplines taught in Indian universities, and the graduates are always in demand because of the opportunities in many private sector chemical industries. India also has a long tradition in synthesizing chemicals for textile industries and over many decades, has built a rich repertoire of tacit knowledge in these areas. This strength in applied chemical knowledge is strongly aided by the smooth transitional from lab to manufacturing plant than in other areas.

Conclusion

We suggest that "ownership" is a critical parameter for studying knowledge growth. This can arise either from personal profit (not necessarily financial; it could even be a solution to a mathematical problem!) motives or patriotic fervor. Public ownership of civilian industries and strict governmental controls of private industries offer neither of these options. On the other hand, the Green Revolution that made the farmer richer or a fighter design that freed the country from a vulnerable foreign dependence provided the appropriate incentives. The rapid growth of IT in India is due to the ownership provided to individual entrepreneurs by the hands-off policy of the government, opportunities for profit from exports, unsullied

[22] This is one example of heated debate on the right balance of intellectual property rights to provide incentives to spur innovation while maximizing public welfare, and the role of the international trading regime as a way to enforce intellectual property rights worldwide. In the academic world, see especially Keith Maskus, *Intellectual Property Rights in the Global Economy* (Washington, DC: Institute of International Economics, 2000). For more general resources, see "IPRsonline" at www.ictsd.org/iprsonline/resources/iprs.htm". This specific case has also helped to spur movement within the World Trade Organization (WTO) to allow some leeway in the implementation of TRIPs (Trade Related Aspects of Intellectual Property Rights) obligations for developing countries addressing public health challenges such as fighting AIDS. See "WTO News Press Release: Intellectual Property: Decision removes final patent obstacle to cheap drug imports," August 30, 2003, at www.wto.org/english/news_e/pres03_3/pr350_e.htm.

by local corruption, and a well-educated human resource base. However, the state cannot just sit back and watch. It needs to pursue policies which aid in the development and dissemination of knowledge throughout society.

It is possible that many years of Indian investments in higher education, its social restructuring that is attempting to make caste irrelevant, and industrial deregulation and privatization that freed many industries from public ownership are all contributing to India's overall economic growth. Only with such growing opportunities and a non-stifling and more egalitarian environment will it be possible for the society to take full advantage of its potential in knowledge generation and its dissemination.

Social Capital: The Driver for Corporate Success in the Knowledge Era

Laurence Lock Lee

Innovation Services, Computer Sciences Corporation, Macquarie Park, Sydney, NSW 2113, Australia

Introduction

Social Capital as a concept has its roots in the field of sociology, being largely applied to describe organisational effects developed through socially derived connections in the broader communities, societies and cultures (Baker, 2001; Nahapiet and Ghoshal, 1998). Traditionally, the context of social capital for private sector firms is seen as their contributions (usually financial) to the communities within which they operate. While often seen as corporate philanthropy, claims have been made that such good corporate citizenship can contribute to improved business performance (Allee, 2000; Roman, Hayibor and Agle, 1999).

The traditional view of Social Capital, as described above, is "industrial era" thinking. Many commentators have argued that we are currently transitioning from the industrial era to a knowledge era (Drucker, 1993; Savage, 1996), where the traditional factors of production of land, labour and capital are being replaced by the creation of value through knowledge. In the knowledge era the boundaries between firms, governments and society at large will become increasingly blurred. In the knowledge era, firms will become embedded within a complex web of interconnections that span markets, governments and communities, rather than simply managing an interface between a private and public sector. In this world the concept of Social Capital can take on a whole new dimension for the "firm".

This paper explores the concepts of Social Capital, as it applies to the corporate sector. The notion of how world markets are migrating from being industrially based to knowledge based is discussed. A relationship is drawn between the concept of Social Capital and the concepts of "Intangibles" and their impact on company valuations. An argument is then put forward for the use of Social Capital as a unifying theme for developing a suite of management heuristics for intangibles. Finally some case study examples of how Social Capital could be measured at the individual, group and marketplace levels, are provided. These examples further illustrate how markets and firms are moving from an industrial modus operandi to a networked model, further supporting the argument for the use of Social Capital as a unifying concept for managing in the Knowledge Era.

What Is Social Capital?

Definitions for Social Capital are many and varied as the concept broadens from its traditional sociological base to more fully embrace corporate sector activities. There are however a set of common themes that can be drawn from definitions offered by noted authors in the field (Baker, 2001; Nahapiet and Ghoshal, 1998, Putman, 1995; Cohen and Prusak, 2001; World Bank, 2003):

- Strong levels of network/contacts;
- High levels of trust and shared understanding;
- High levels of co-operative action; and
- Operates at individual, group and marketplace level.

Continuing the theme of "corporatising" Social Capital one could look at the traditional societal context for Social Capital through a Corporate lens. The following table provides a corporate interpretation of a traditional context provided by the Australian Bureau of Statistics (ABS, 2000).

Table 1. Traditional versus Corporate Context for Social Capital

Traditional Societal Context	Potential Corporate Context
Social Networks and Support Structures	Communities of Practice, Industry bodies
Empowerment and Community Participation	Membership of Communities of Practice or Industry bodies
Civic and Political Involvement	"Bottom up" initiatives; Industrial body initiatives.
Trust in People and Social Institutions	Trust in Management. Trust in Community leadership
Tolerance of Diversity	Cross functional teams, cross industry initiatives
Altruism and Philanthropy	Investment in local communities, environment etc.

One can see that a corporate context can be easily aligned with the tradition context for Social Capital. One could add that the corporate context for Social Capital when presented this way looks like a list of modern management "best practices", strengthening the argument for Social Capital as a leading focus for corporate success.

Social Capital, Intangibles and the Knowledge Era

Charles Savage in his book on Fifth Generation Management (Savage, 1996) describes the transition to the knowledge era as a continuum of our evolution from initially the Agricultural Era through to the Industrial Era and now the Knowledge Era (see Figure 1). Other writers on the knowledge era have chosen to use a human analogy to emphasise the organic and adaptive nature of firms and markets operating in the knowledge era (de Geus , 1997; Dawson, 2003).

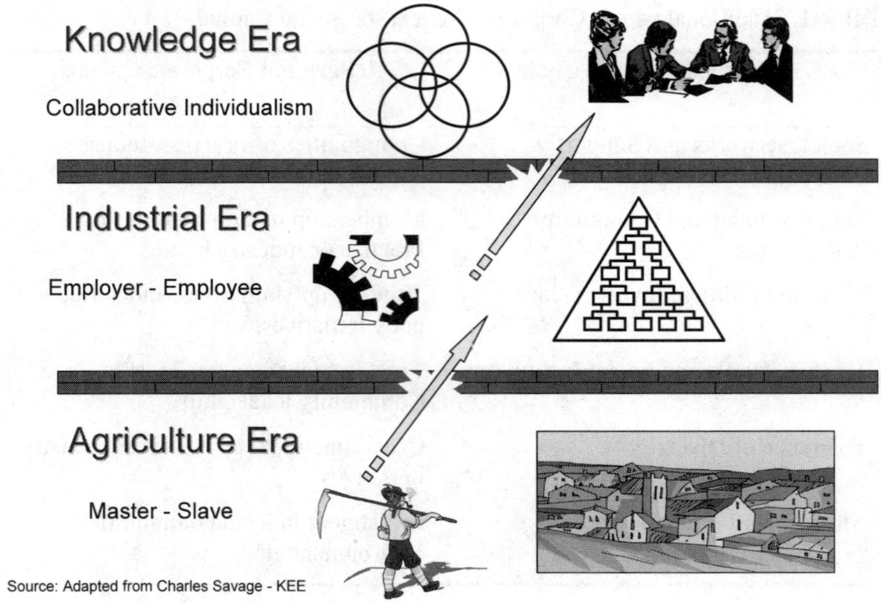

Fig. 1. Knowledge Era Transition

While there is much support for the view that we are now in the knowledge era, this view is far from universal. The artefacts of the industrial age still surround us and traditional industrial age management methods are still proving effective. So what evidence is there that we are actually in transition to a different era? Perhaps the most tangible evidence can be seen by looking at the world's stock markets and Fortune 500 lists. Over the past 10 to 15 years, industrial companies are overwhelming being replaced by knowledge based service companies on these lists. Intangible, rather than physical assets now largely determine shareholder returns.

Looking at the top 10 stocks by market valuation on the Australian Stock Market as an illustrative example (Table 2), one can see clear evidence of the demise of the industrially based firms. In fact the two survivors on the list, BHP Billiton and Rio Tinto are both diversified mining companies which have had to grow to being in the top 3 of diversified resources companies world wide, to retain their places in the Australian top 10.

Table 2. Top 10 Stocks on the Australian Stock Exchange by Market Valuation

1989	2003
BHP	News Corporation
BTR Nylex	NAB
NAB	*BHP Biliton*
CRA	Commonwealth Bank
Westpac	Telstra
Western Mining Corporation	Westpac
Elders IXL	ANZ
ANZ	AMP
News Corporation Inc.	*Rio Tinto Limited*
Coles Myer Limited	Woolworths

It is also clearly evident from the market valuation of the global stock markets that there has been a notable change over the past 10 to 15 years. Figure 2 tracks the movement in the S&P500 and NASDAQ indices over the past 30+ years. While earnings and book valuations have grown modestly over the past 30 years, market values have both exploded and retracted in the past 5 years alone. The impact of intangibles and the market's inability to value them are clearly providing a roller coaster ride for shareholders, to an extent that has not been seen before. Is this evidence of a growing transition from an industrial era to a knowledge era?

One can see from Figure 2 that the high technology stocks as represented in the NASDAQ had experienced the largest swings, but it also apparent that industrial stocks are also being impacted to a greater degree by intangibles than ever before. Figure 3 provides an illustration of the differing fortunes of industrial sectors of Resources, Steel and Petroleum.

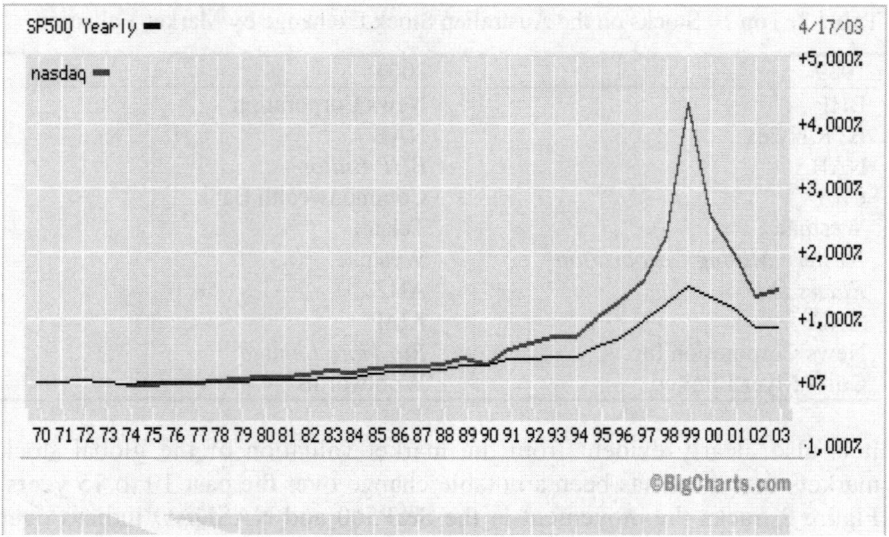

Fig. 2. S&P500 and Nasdaq Indices since 1970.

One can see from Figure 3 that intangible values as measured by the ratio of market to book values have grown modestly in the Resources sector, grown strongly in the Petroleum sector and actually reduced in the Steel sector.

Looking more closely at how the nature of firms has been changing, we are now seeing firms involved in many more joint ventures, alliances and partnerships. Outsourcing and co-opetition is making it increasingly difficult to identify the firm boundaries. Figure 4 illustrates this transition for a traditional industrial firm, Du Pont.

The increasing importance of intangibles was initially identified by Swedish researcher Karl-Erik Sveiby in his co-authored work on "Company Knowhow" (Sveiby and Risling, 1986). Since this time a plethora of literature has been published in support of new methods for measuring and managing intangibles (Sveiby, 1997; Edvinson and Malone, 1997; Lev, 2001; Johanson et al, 1999). From Sveiby's Intangible Asset Monitor (Sveiby, 1997) and Kaplan and Norton's Balanced Scorecard (Kaplan and Norton, 1996), increasingly sophisticated scorecards have been built (Wall and Doerflinger, 1999; Liebowitz and Suen, 2000; Mouitson et al, 2000). Intangible Capital has been decomposed into intellectual capital, structural capital, human capital, customer capital, innovation capital, external capital, stakeholder capital, knowledge capital….and the list goes on. Clearly many of these concepts are interdependent and difficult to measure and operationalise. As an adjunct to the traditional balance sheet or profit and loss statement, they may eventually become useful analytical tools. How ever, in order to operationalise these concepts, a suite of simplifying intangible asset management heuristics need to be developed.

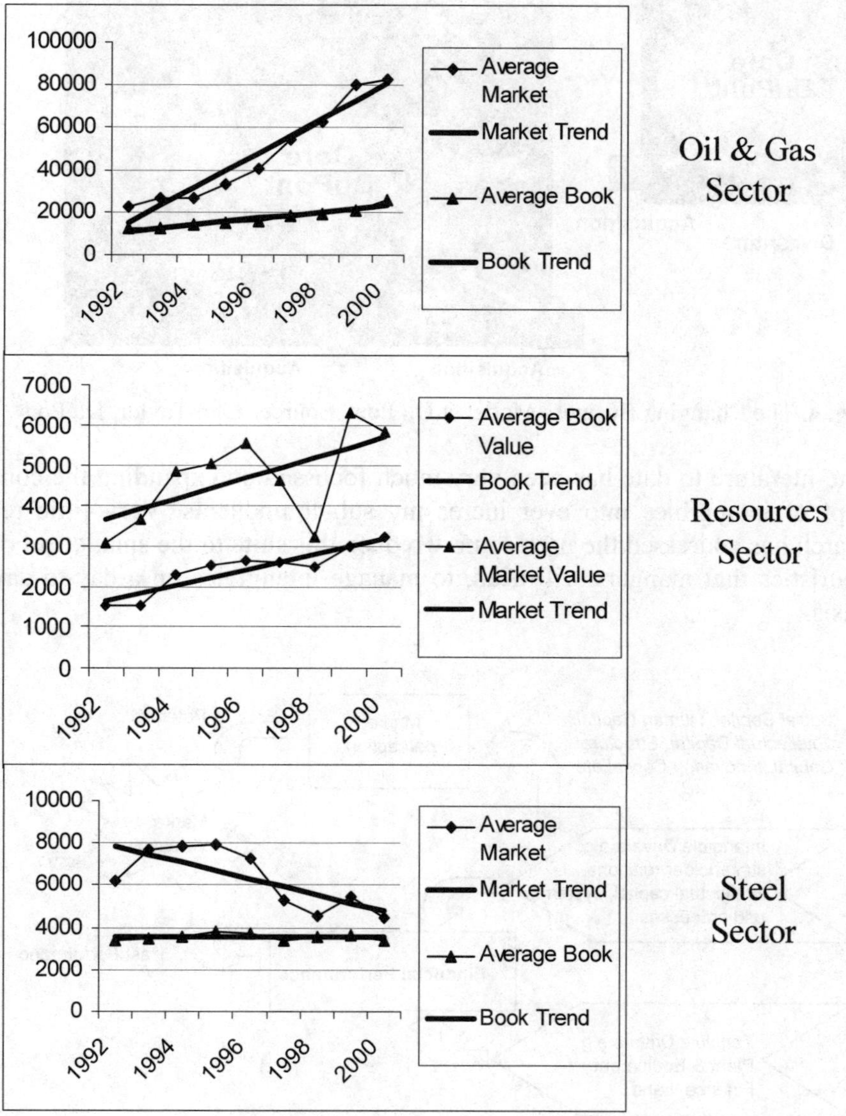

Fig. 3. Intangible Value Trends for Selected Industrial Sectors

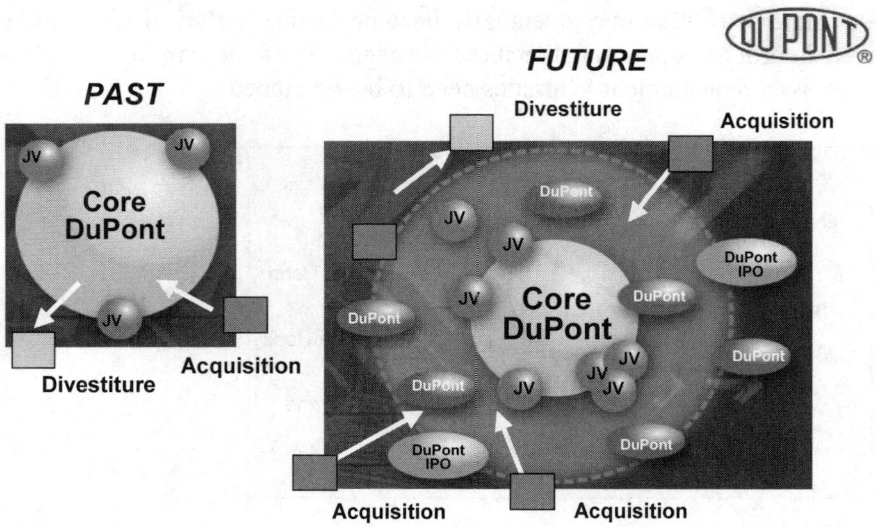

Fig. 4. The Changing Business Model at Du Pont. Source: John Taylor, Du Pont

The literature to date has been very much focussed on expanding the concept of intangibles into ever increasing sub-components. Very little research has addressed the need to now reduce this suite to the smaller set of heuristics that mangers will need, to manage intangibles on a day-to-day basis.

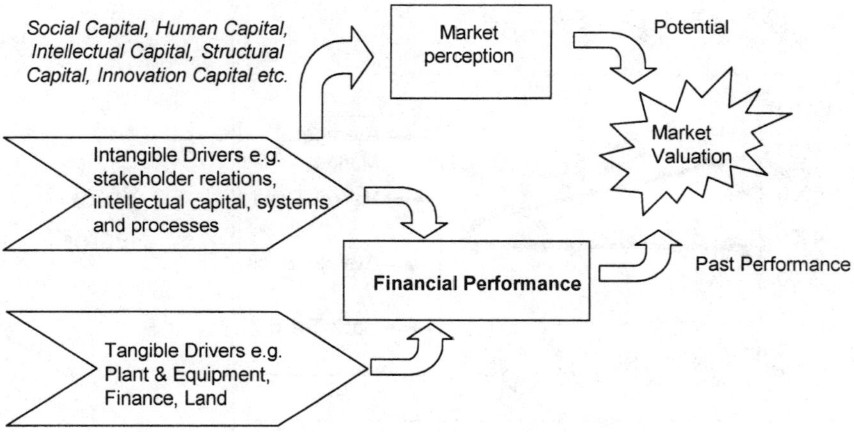

Fig. 5. Conceptual Framework

Why Lead with Social Capital?

The following conceptual framework is offered to provide a basis for thinking about the impact of intangibles on market valuations.

Performance drivers can largely be divided into the traditional physical assets a firm has available to it and the intangible assets it can apply or leverage. Both asset forms contribute to the eventual financial performance of the firm. The historical financial performance of the firm will make a contribution to the firm's market valuation. The second input to a firm's market valuation is the market's perception of what might happen in the future i.e. the firm's potential performance. This perception is driven by intangibles, which have been variously described as Social Capital, Human Capital, Structural Capital, Innovation Capital etc.. There is anecdotal evidence that intangibles are becoming the dominant factor in market valuations. Being able to clearly describe and articulate which intangible factors have most impact on market valuations is a key aspect of intangibles research to date.

In assisting managers to manage the non-financial aspects of their businesses, various intangible asset scorecards have been developed. Perhaps the best known are the Balanced Scorecard (Kaplan and Norton, 1996), and the Intangible Asset Monitor (Sveiby, 1997). Both scorecard methods attempt to decompose non-financial factors into component parts and then provide a suite of measures for on-going monitoring. For retrospective analysis of performance these tools provide a valuable analytical aid. However, to make the management of intangibles a pragmatic reality, a simpler conceptual theme, or set of heuristics is required to guide today's executives. In the financial world, heuristics like "cash is king", "sweating your (physical) assets", "look after your pennies and the pounds will look after themselves", need some equivalents in the intangible world. The following table provides a list of key intangible elements and the perceptions that they invoke.

Table 3. Intangible Elements and the Perceptions They Invoke

Intangible Element	Perception
Human Capital	Competency
Intellectual Capital	Patents
Internal Capital	Systems and Processes
External Capital	Brand
Social Capital	*Trustful Relationships*

Looking at each factor individually, an argument could be made to select any of them as the leading indicator for intangibles performance. For example, one could argue that if a firm has high human capital i.e. highly skilled and experienced staff, then they will build intellectual capital, design and operate great internal processes and work effectively with suppliers, partners and customers. A counter argument might be that just because you have highly skilled people, it doesn't necessarily follow that they are great collaborators or that they have the natural ability to put their knowledge to work to create new intellectual capital. Each factor will have its pros and cons as a leading indicator. The argument for selecting Social Capital as the leading indicator is based on the author's perception that it has more pros and less cons than the other major themes. In supporting this argument one could argue that to be recognized as having excellent social capital one would need to:

- Be successful in searching for competent people to co-operate with, both internally and externally (human capital);
- Select collaborators on the basis of the intellectual capital that can be exchanged;
- Have built a reputation for excellent internal processes (internal capital) and seek out those with similarly strong internal process to collaborate with; and
- Achieved a good brand and market reputation to attract the right sort of collaborations (external capital).

There are detracting views on promoting Social Capital as a leading theme. Typically these criticisms relate to highly cohesive groups becoming blind to diverse opinions, and therefore limiting the potential for new innovations i.e. innovation capital (Florida et al, 2002; Cohen and Prusak, 2001; Locke, 1999). These are fair comments when related to groups within firms or even communities in the general public. However, if we look back at the common definition for Social Capital it also defines that it must operate at the *individual and group levels*. One could argue that for innovation to succeed, the "innovators" would need excellent Social Capital skills at both the individual, then group levels to be able to shepherd a new invention through to a successful innovation. As such, a highly cohesive group that appears to be not open to engaging in diverse conversations and promoting innovation could be seen, by definition, as having a lower level of social capital. Of course the degree of cohesiveness of a particular network can be entirely contextual. A study of structural and relational embeddedness in the Steel and Semiconductor industries (Rowly, Behrens and Krackhardt, 2000) illustrates that for highly dynamic industries, where continuous and radical innovations are the norm, the structure of the networks will be more exploratory, reaching out to more diverse groups and having far less redundant links than say a Steel industry network. In the Steel industry the networks are more closed with many redundant links as companies concentrate on perfecting common practices i.e. exploiting rather than exploring innovations. The networks for the Semi-conductor and Steel industries will structurally be quite different, but one could argue that excellent companies in either industry are exhibiting high levels of Social Capital.

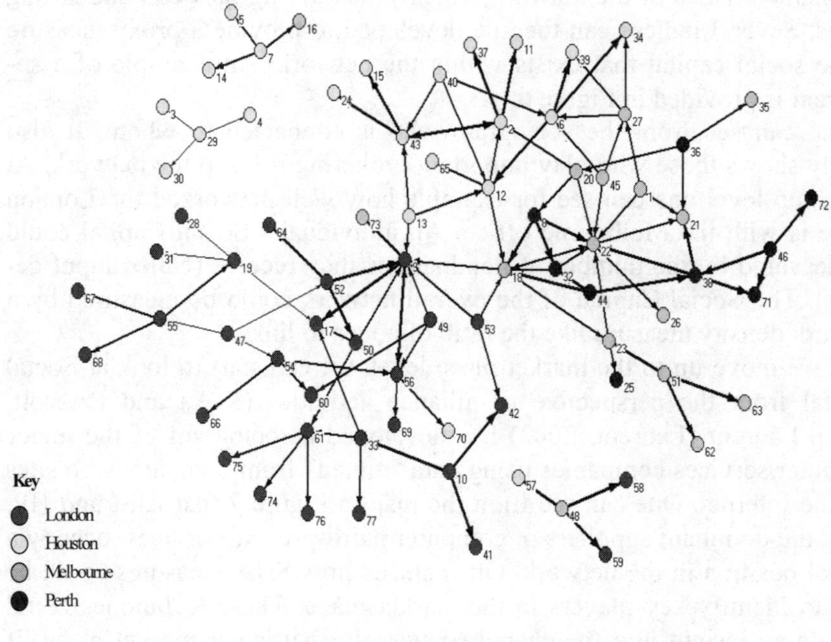

Fig. 6. Example Sociogram (Pajek mapping software used)

An additional counter argument could be made relating to the observations that in today's market place, successful firms need to be more collaborative than their industrially focused predecessors. It is rare that one would see a firm recognized for its innovation, not also recognized for its Social Capital in the market place e.g. Xerox, HP, 3M, etc.. While the above arguments could be seen as purely manipulating definitions, it is perhaps the trends to a more networked and collaborative market place and the fluidity of knowledge flows compared to physical flows which provide the strongest arguments for leading with Social Capital.

New Methods for Measuring Social Capital

While there has been many attempts at measuring Social Capital in a social science context, i.e. Social capital within communities, developing countries etc..(ABS, 2000; Spellerberg, 2001; World Bank, 2003), very few attempts have been related to the corporate world. One technique that has had its genesis in social science but is rapidly finding use in the corporate world is Social Network Analysis (SNA). Typically SNA involves surveying individuals on who they collaborate and share information and knowledge with. This data can then be used to generate a sociogram showing who is connected to whom. SNA statistical methods can be used to analyse the characteristics of the network, quickly identifying its weak and strong points. Several indices can then be developed to provide a proxy measure of the social capital that exists within the network. An example of a sociogram is provided in Figure 6.

One can see from the sociogram who is connected to whom. It also clearly shows those who play important brokering roles in the network. At the group level one can see for example how well networked the London office is with the Melbourne office. An individual's Social Capital could be measured by the number of nominations they receive (called input degrees). The Social Capital of the overall network could be measured by a network density measure like the ratio of nodes to links.

If we move up to the market place level, we can start to look at Social Capital from the perspective of alliance activities (Koka and Prescott, 2002). Laurent (Laurent, 2002) has developed a sociogram of the major computer services companies using data "mined" from company web sites and the Internet. One can see from the map in Figure 7 that IBM and HP, being the dominant suppliers of computer hardware and services, occupy a central position in the network. One can see how SNA measures could be used to identify key players in the market place. These techniques could provide an insight into the characteristics of a particular market place. If the network representation of a market place is seen to be highly connected, with many redundant links, one could assume that it might be difficult for a new player to break into the market. Conversely, if network representation of the marketplace appears more open and exploratory in nature, there will be opportunities for new entrants to become part of, and perhaps influence the network / market.

Electronic usage based proxy measures for Social Capital are now being developed to overcome the need to conduct time consuming and expensive SNA surveys. In many instances these proxies, like discussion group activity, on-line communities and even e-mail traffic are proving to be reasonably good approximations to the true human networks (Lock Lee, 2003; Guimera et al, 2002; Boudourides, Mavrikakis and Vasileiadou, 2002). While these examples are preliminary in nature, it is clear that Social Capital metrics will start to emerge to support corporate executives in making decisions relating to intangibles and improving shareholder value.

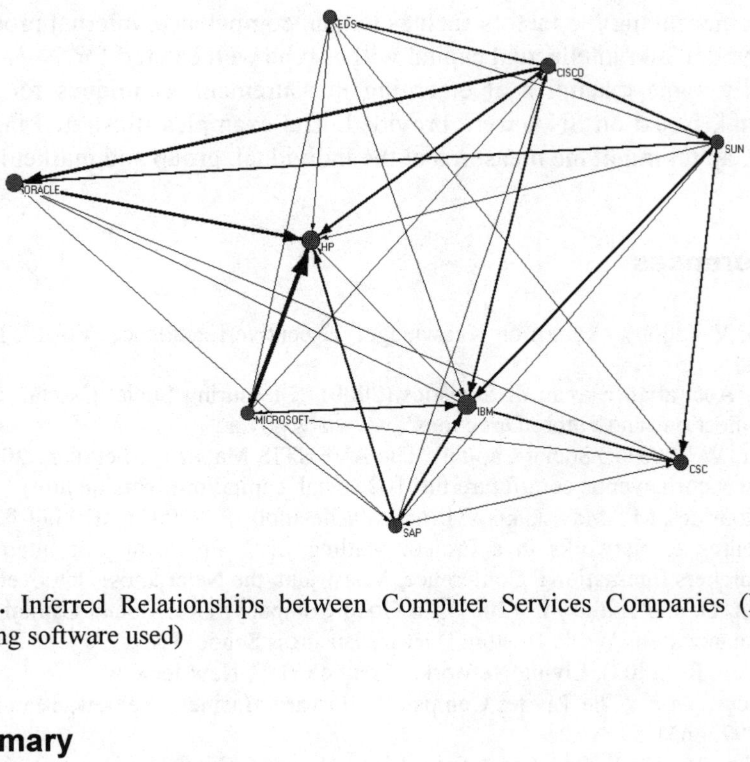

Fig. 7. Inferred Relationships between Computer Services Companies (Pajek mapping software used)

Summary

This paper has introduced the concept of Social Capital as it might apply to the corporate sector, in support of increasing shareholder value through the prudent management of intangibles. It has been argued that as world markets evolve from an industrial era into a knowledge era, the management of intangibles will become increasingly important in assuring market valuations, and hence maximizing shareholder value. The large and dynamic movement of share prices on world markets over the past 10 to 15 years is being attributed to a poor understanding of the effect of intangibles like human competence, intellectual capital, brands and Social Capital. While it is acknowledged that developments in balanced scorecards and intangible asset monitors will provide powerful analytical aides for reviewing non-financial performance, what is missing is the simple heuristics that managers rely on for day-to-day activities. These heuristics exist in financial management, they don't in intangible management.

To assist managers develop such heuristics, an argument has been made for the use of Social Capital as the basis for developing management heuristics. It is argued that a leading focus on developing trustworthy networks at the individual, group and market levels will create an assurance that other intangible factors such as human competence, internal processes, innovation and intellectual capital will also be well catered for.

Finally some examples of emerging measurement techniques for Social Capital, based on SNA were provided. The examples illustrated how Social Capital might me measured at the individual, group and market levels.

References

Allee, V. (2000), 'Return on Knowledge', Executive Excellence, Vol.17, Issue 9, pg8

ABS: Australian Bureau of Statistics (2000), 'Measuring Social Capital: Current Collections and Future Directions', www.abs.gov.au

Baker, W. (2001), 'Social Capital', The AVENTIS Magazine, February 2001 (see www.corp.aventis.com/future/fut0102/social_capital/printversion.htm)

Boudourides M., Mavrikakis, M. and Vasileiadou, E. (2002), 'E-Mail Threads, Genres & Networks in a Project Mailing List', Proceeding of Internet Researchers International Conference, Maastricht, the Neterlands, Octobver 13-16

Cohen, D. and Prusak, L. (2001), In Good Company: How Social Capital Makes Organizations Work, Boston: Harvard Business School Press

Dawson, R. (2003), Living Networks, Prentice-Hall, New Jersey

de Geus, Arie, 'The Living Company', Harvard Business Review, March-April 1997, pp51-59

Drucker, P. (1993), Post Capitalist Society, Harper Collins, New York, NY

Ednvinsson, L. and Malone, M. (1997), Intellectual Capital: Realizing Your Company's True Value by Finding its Hidden Brainpower, Harper Business, New York

Florida, R., Cushing, R. and Gates, G. (2002), 'When social capital stifles innovation', Harvard Business Review, August

Guimera, R., Danon, L., Diaz-Guilera, A., Giralt, F. and Arenas, A., 'The real communication network behind the formal chart: community structure in organisations' http://galadriel.ffn.ub.es/articles/email_networks.pdf

Johanson, U., Martensson, M. and Skoog, M. (1999), 'Measuring and Managing Intangibles: Eleven Swedish Qualitative Exploratory Case Studies', International Symposium on Measuring and Reporting Intellectual Capital: Experience, Issues and Prospects, Amsterdam, 9-10th June, 1999

Kaplan, R. and Norton, D. (1996), The Balanced Scorecard: Translating Strategy into Action, Harvard Business School Press, Boston

Koka, B.R and Prescott, J.E. (2003), 'Strategic Alliances as Social Capital: A Multidimensional view', Strategic Management Journal, 23:795-816

Laurent, D. (2002), "Understanding External Relationships in the Knowledge Era: An Exploratory Study that Applies Social Network Analysis to the World Wide Web", unpublished Honours Thesis, School of Information Technologies, Sydney University

Lev, B. (2001), Intangibles: Management, Measurement and Reporting, Brooking Institution Press, Washington DC

Liebowitz, J. and Suen, C. (2000), 'Developing knowledge management metrics for measuring intellectual capital', Journal of Intellectual Capital, Vol , No.1, 2000, pp54-67

Locke, E. (1999), 'Some Reservations about Social Capital', Academy of Management Review, 24(1), January:8-9

Lock Lee, L. (2003), 'Does your Community Leave a Digital Footprint?', KM Challenge 2003, Melbourne, April 2003. (Proceedings published by Standards Australia)

Mouritsen, J. et al. (2000), A Guideline for Intellectual Capital Statements, Danish Agency for Trade and Industry, (see www.efs.dk)

Nahapiet, J. and Ghoshal, S. (1998), 'Social Capital, intellectual capital, and the organizational advantage, Academy of Management Review, 23(2):242-266

Putman R. (1995), 'Bowling Alone: America's Declining Social Capital', Journal of Democracy 6: 65-78

Roman, R., Hayibor, S. and Agle, B. (1999), 'The relationship between social and financial performance', Business and Society 38(1), 109-125

Rowley, T., Behrens, D. and Krackhardt, D. (2000), 'Redundant Governance Structures: An Analysis of Structural and Relational Embeddedness in the Steel and Semiconductor Industries' Strategic Management Journal 21:369-386

Savage, C. (1996), Fifth Generation Management, (www.kee-inc.com)

Spellerberg, A. (2001), 'Framework for the Measurement of Social Capital in New Zealand', (see www.stats.govt.nz)

Sveiby, K. and Risling, A. (1986), Kunskapsforetaget (the Know-How Company), Liber, Malmo

Sveiby, K. (1997), The New Organizational Wealth: Managing and measuring Knowledge-Based Assets, Berret-Koehler, San Francisco, CA

Wall, B. and Doerflinger, M. (1999), 'Making Intangible Assets Tangible', Knowledge Management Review, Sept/Oct 1999

World Bank on Social Capital (2003), www.worldbank.org/ poverty/scapital/ methods/

Part 3
Knowledge Management: Practitioner Perspectives

The Intellectual Division of Labor

Charles Lucier[1] and Jan Dyer[2]

[1] Ex-Booz Allen Hamilton, McLean, Virginia, USA
[2] Ex-Booz Allen Hamilton, McLean, Virginia, USA

We live in what has been referred to as the knowledge age. We buy knowledge-based products and services, do knowledge work and search the internet in hopes of finding ever improved knowledge. Knowledge is increasingly the source of competitive advantage. Yet, despite some enormous successes – like Booz Allen Hamilton's knowledge program – few systematic programs to "manage knowledge" have produced significant results.

The evidence for the limited success of knowledge management is widespread. In a Bain & Company survey, managers ranked knowledge management as the second *least* satisfactory tool among the most widely used management tools[1] in North America. Both the dollars spent on knowledge management and the numbers of "Chief Knowledge Officers" at major corporations have declined for several years.

The principal reason for knowledge management's limited success has been a mismatch between the solution and the problem. Knowledge management can dramatically improve innovation, but it does not improve productivity – the objective of many failed efforts. Successful knowledge management programs have typically occurred in consulting firms and applications engineering businesses like the oft-cited case of Chapperel Steel. Chapperel employees, working furiously to develop new solutions for customers, gladly built on new ideas and techniques developed by their colleagues, once a knowledge management program made it easy. But this kind of voluntary sharing and use of knowledge can't drive improved productivity and efficiency, especially in slow growing companies where increased productivity means fewer jobs. Why would employees share or use ideas that could put them out of work? To stimulate sharing and use, some industrial companies (e.g., Ford) promised workers that no jobs would be lost because of knowledge sharing – a promise that virtually guaranteed that improved productivity wouldn't result. Tim Devinney's extensive em-

---

1 Bain & Co., *Management Tools 2001: The Good, the Bad, the Ugly of Management Tools*. Available on the internet.

pirical work[2] confirms that knowledge management, as it has been practiced, contributes primarily to innovation but not to improved productivity.

With the increasing quantity and importance of knowledge, it is reasonable to expect that managing knowledge should be the key to unlocking improved productivity and profitability for companies. But to unlock improved productivity, we need to think about how to manage knowledge differently. Instead of emphasizing how to enable people to share knowledge, we need to focus on how to effectively *use* knowledge. Following Charles Babbage,[3] we call this approach an intellectual division of labor.

An Example

Our experience with Booz Allen's knowledge program illustrates the challenge and, we think, part of the solution. The heart of Booz Allen's knowledge efforts is the sharing of ideas, tools, and techniques that have proven successful in working with clients, continuously updated in a repository which is available globally, 24x7. Each consulting team, guided by partners with appropriate expertise, creates an entirely new and unique strategy for a client, building on the accumulated knowledge in the repository. Booz Allen's pioneering program exemplifies what has become classic, innovation-oriented knowledge management.

In implementing our knowledge program, however, we quickly discovered that we didn't want people to try to improve *all* of the knowledge in the repository; we wanted some knowledge used without modification. Graphics templates – a seemingly innocuous tool – provide a wonderful example. In the late 1980's, Booz Allen hired graphics communications experts to develop templates for exhibits used in client reports. In 1995, we found that more than 40% of our client reports contained at least one exhibit with a modified graphics template. When a panel of four outside graphics experts reviewed a sample of 200 exhibits that didn't conform to the templates, they found that 11% *might have* resulted in better communication; 42% communicated about as well as the template, and 47% resulted in *significantly poorer* communication to clients.

Those statistics had major implications for the firm. Forty-seven percent of the non-standard exhibits were a lose-lose-lose proposition: the quality of communication was worse, staff worked harder and longer because they had to create the different format, and our report production costs were

---

2 Cite chapter from this book.

3 Babbage,Charles, On the Economy of Machinery and Manufactures. New Jersey: Augustus M. Kelley, Publishers, 1986, (1832).

higher because our graphic artists were working with unfamiliar exhibits requiring additional discussions with the client team. Taken together with the forty-two percent that delivered comparable communications with the templates, this means that eighty-nine percent of the time, staff worked harder and our costs were higher without any benefit to clients. Clearly, we would have been better off if our staff just used the templates without modifying them.

When told of the findings, our staff's push back was "don't you want us to be creative?" The answer, of course, was, yes, we wanted them to be creative. We wanted them to be creative in developing unique answers for clients; in how they worked with their clients to develop and implement these unique answers; and in how they adapted and applied the concepts and tools learned in their MBA programs. We didn't, however, want them to be creative about a lot of the tools we gave them – not only graphics templates, but also methods for performing standard analyses like estimation of scale curves, and the computer hardware and software they used.

Our task as managers was to help our staff understand where we wanted them be creative and where we wanted them to use the tried-and-tested tools that Booz Allen provided. It wasn't a complex change management challenge, it was largely a communication issue. We didn't need a new incentive program or better tools. Our measurement and reward system already rewarded staff for focusing their efforts where we wanted them to be creative. Staff were evaluated and promoted based on the powerful answers they developed for clients and their ability to establish client relationships – not for new graphics. And our staff had world class tools. We had long before embraced the management responsibility of equipping our staff with the best tools available.

Explicit communications about where we wanted people to focus and be creative and where we wanted them to use tools triggered a virtuous cycle:

- The quality of our analysis and our communication to clients improved.
- Clients received better work because our consultants were focusing their efforts on what really mattered to clients, not on low value tasks like reinventing graphics or rediscovering ways to do analysis.
- Because the proportion of time staff spent on their highest value tasks increased, value added/person increased, fueling improved compensation.

- Staff satisfaction increased because they worked fewer hours to produce high quality work.
- Confident that our staff would use the tools provided, Booz Allen invested in additional tools – allowing additional improvements in work quality and value added/person.

The Intellectual Division of Labor

Charles Babbage in his aforementioned book 'On the Economy of Machinery and Manufactures', first published in 1832, developed the concept of intellectual division of labor to explain how in the late eighteenth century, the French developed the most complete and most accurate tables of logarithmic and trigonometric functions (seventeen large folio volumes of tables). The French divided the task in three parts:

- Developing Algorithms: Five or six of the most eminent mathematicians in France worked together to identify algorithms that could be "readily adapted to simple numerical calculation". These mathematicians had little to do with the actual numerical work.
- Simplifying and Verifying: Seven or eight people with "considerable acquaintance with mathematics," translated the algorithms into templates to enable both simple calculations and later verification procedures that did not require them to examine all of the detailed work.
- Calculating: Sixty to eighty people, with only rudimentary mathematical ability, performed the calculations using nothing more than simple algebraic operations.

Dividing the overall activity into three parts, each requiring different levels and types of knowledge, produced improved quality and productivity, much like the physical, task-based division of labor Adam Smith described in his famous pin factory.

After two hundred years of automating physical tasks and more than fifty years of automating the flow of transactions, most of the benefits of Adam Smith's task-based division of labor have been realized. However, few companies are effectively managing the intellectual division of labor. How and where can the intellectual division of labor be applied?

To apply the intellectual division of labor, begin by asking how much knowledge should reside in the individual's mind and how much in the organization (see Figure 1). The vertical axis represents the amount of knowledge about a given activity possessed by an individual: novice, journeyman, or expert. The horizontal axis represents organizational expertise: ranging from processes to link the toughest problems with the appropriate expert to methodologies to powerful algorithms that define exactly what should be done. The three *natural knowledge models* identified on Figure 1 define an efficient frontier of choices.

- In the WHO model, most expertise resides in individuals. Organizations need "yellow pages" and business processes to ensure that experts handle the toughest problems – both to achieve the best solution and to provide experts with the continual diet of the most difficult problems necessary to deepen and renew their expertise.
- A formal, structured methodology is the heart of the HOW model. Using the methodology, people with only moderate levels of expertise can solve difficult problems.
- The WHAT model requires algorithms powerful enough to tell people exactly what they should do in a variety of situations. With algorithms functioning as "black boxes," individuals need only minimal expertise.

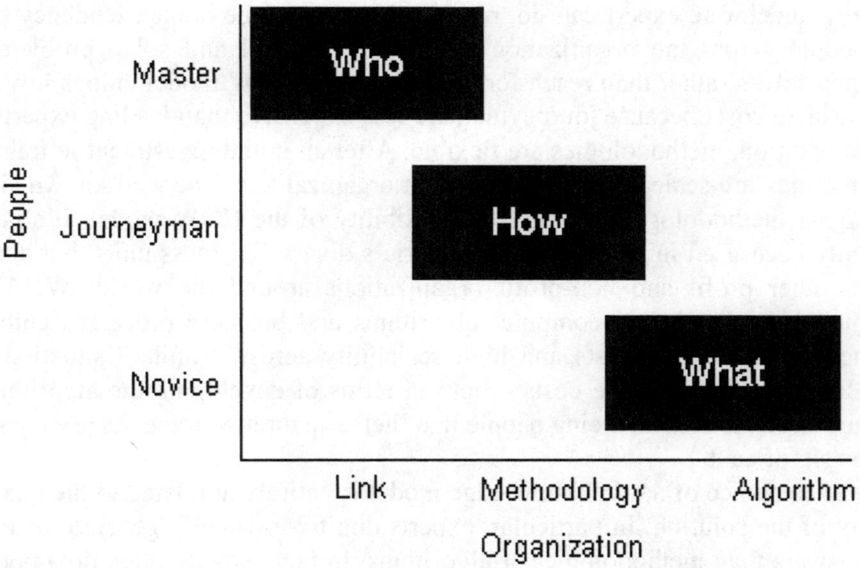

Fig. 1. Natural Knowledge Models

The approach used by the French to calculate logarithmic and trigonometric tables divided tasks among the natural knowledge models. In the WHO model, experts identified the analytical expression most suited to the task.

Using a HOW model, supervisors with a journeyman understanding of mathematics defined specific tasks for WHAT model execution.

One way to improve effectiveness and productivity is to apply the intellectual division of labor explicitly, moving from today's almost random assortment of individual and organizational expertise to structuring work around the natural knowledge models. The Booz Allen graphics template is a simple example of moving to an effective WHAT model. Our knowledge repository includes WHATs and HOWs as well as a variety of material to help teams develop unique solutions – under the guidance of an expert WHO. For us, a more important initiative was to implement a WHO model for our principal content expertise, explicitly identifying our leading experts and creating processes and internal incentives to bring those experts in to help with our clients' most difficult problems.

A second way to improve productivity is to shift from one natural knowledge model to another, usually a shift away from WHO to one of the other models. The three models differ significantly in their costs and scalability. Although the WHO model enjoys low fixed costs, it has the highest variable costs: experts command a higher level of compensation. The WHO model is also the least scalable, not only because of the limits on how much one expert can do, but also because of the human tendency of people across the organization to maintain control and solve problems themselves rather than reach for an expert. The HOW model enjoys lower variable costs because journeymen are less expensive than leading experts. In addition, methodologies are flexible. After an initial investment in training, they are scaleable across divergent organizations. The well-known six sigma methodology illustrates the flexibility of the HOW model: it's not only been used in all of General Electric's diverse business units, but also in other profit and non-profit organizations around the world. WHAT models embedded in computer algorithms and business processes enjoy near zero variable costs and high scalability across "similar" situations. However, the one-time costs – both in terms of developing the algorithm and in terms of convincing people that their situation warrants its use – can be significant.

The choice of natural knowledge model is entirely unrelated to the quality of the solution. In particular, experts don't consistently generate better answers than methodologies or algorithms. In fact, experts often do a poor job on routine tasks that don't hold their attention. The team that developed the tables in Charles Babbage's example found that people with limited mathematical skills generally produced the most accurate answers. In addition, because human experts have limited ability to quickly assimilate masses of data and instantaneously explore all alternatives, algorithms based on systematic analysis of history, rigorous analysis of alternative actions, and integration of rapidly changing information, often yield better results. The quality of a solution depends on using the best expertise for each situation. Quality is knowledge and situation-specific.

Examples

The intellectual division of labor can enhance productivity at three levels within an organization: equipping people at the activity level; as part of a broad change program at the functional or business unit levels; or as the centerpiece of a company's strategy. At the activity level, credit decisions provide a good example of improving productivity through the intellectual division of labor. Most companies use credit scoring algorithms combined with the most up-to-date information available about a customer to make 80% or more of their credit decisions, focusing a few credit experts on the small number of most difficult cases. As another example, consider the success of leading consumer package goods companies in equipping salespeople with sophisticated, analytically-based algorithms that enable them to eliminate costly promotions that fail to result in sustained volume or increased profit. Using algorithms – a form of the WHAT model – is not the only way to improve productivity at the activity level. Powerful new approaches, HOWs, can significantly enhance productivity. Call center methodologies for handling customer inquiries are an obvious example. Often, the most significant productivity improvements at the activity level come from the using a mix of the models. For example, the best approach to equipment maintenance has evolved from preventative or predictive to "reliability-centered." Shifting to the reliability-centered approach includes using a new methodology as well as a variety of analytical tools.

When applied broadly, across entire functions or business units, HOWs or WHATs have constituted powerful productivity-enhancing change programs. For example, Jack Welch launched a series of methodologies (HOWs) across all of General Electric's businesses, including demand flow manufacturing, digitization, and most famously, six sigma. According to Welch: "we went from 3,000 Six Sigma projects in 1996 to 6,000 in 1997, when we achieved $320 million in productivity gains and profits, more than double our original goal of $150 million....By 1998, we had generated $750 million in Six Sigma savings over and above our investment and would get $1.5 billion in savings the next year." [Welch, p 335][4] AT&T's "concept of one" offers an example of a WHAT-driven produc-

[4] Welch, Jack, Jack: Straight From the Gut, New York: Warner Business Books, 2001.

tivity program. The "concept of one" means: do it once, do it right, and do it everywhere. That is, develop the best way to do a task and replicate that approach across the company. According to *Fortune* [2003, 134], AT&T saved $2 billion over four years in network and customer-care operations through its "concept of one" initiative.

At the strategic level, successful service businesses (and service activities within manufacturing businesses) are often structured around one of the knowledge models. Management consulting is a powerful example. Traditional management consulting uses the WHO model. Firms like Booz Allen Hamilton and McKinsey are structured around partner-experts, each supervising about seven experts-in-training. In the late 1970s, Andersen Consulting (now Accenture) pioneered HOW model consulting, based on the "Method 1" methodology to develop and implement software. Andersen's business model enjoyed much better economy-of-scale than the WHO strategy firms in part because it was based on less expensive journeymen and journeymen-in-training, and in part because the methodology allowed each partner to supervise 30 staff. Even after the higher costs of recruiting and training so many staff, the HOW business model generated about twice the profitability per partner – part of which was reinvested in lower prices and rapid growth. Recently, the segment of the consulting industry growing most rapidly has been WHAT-based outsourcing of information technology and business processes. Success in the outsourcing business requires disciplined use of standard ways to do business and develop algorithms which together enable each "partner" to supervise at least 500 staff. This kind of WHAT business model generates about four times the profitability of a WHO business model. Admittedly, that's before sharing many of the savings with customers to motivate them to outsource, but even after passing along savings, the economics of WHAT far exceed those of WHO.

Table 1. Strategic Use of the Natural Knowledge Models. Economics of Management Consulting

	Partner/Staff	Profit contribution per partner
WHO	1/7	$1 million
HOW	1/30	$2 million
WHAT	1/1000	$5 million

Different models are best suited for different types of challenges. WHO model consulting is best suited to developing unique, often new-to-the-world strategies or to partner with clients in large-scale global change programs. HOW model consulting works best for tailoring a proven solution to a client's unique needs, whether the solution involves information technology or a new manufacturing or marketing discipline. The WHAT consulting model executes a standard, low cost way to provide a service within a customer's unique environment. On strategy problems, where no one has yet developed an effective methodology, CEOs demand a WHO approach. Most operational issues, like supply chain management, lend themselves to HOWs and WHATs. As a result, the consulting business continually shifts down and to the right on the efficient frontier of the natural knowledge models.

Of course, to say a business operates in the WHO model doesn't mean that every activity requires an expert. For example, Booz Allen's commercial consulting is a WHO business because more than 80% of our value added activities use the WHO knowledge model. This explains our staff's confusion about our insistence that they stick to prescribed graphics templates. Because they were used to WHO, they didn't know how to think about HOW and WHAT. The key, for us, was to identify the activities that were the exception to WHO.

Beyond Taylor: The New Definition of Jobs

Frederick W. Taylor's scientific management has been denounced in recent years for its dehumanizing impact. But, AT&T's "concept of one" and our celebration of WHATs and HOWs seem to smack of Taylorism's "one best way." Does the intellectual division of labor, especially the WHAT model, imply a next stage of dehumanizing work – turning people into mindless, stationary automatons? No, we don't think so.

Rather than forcing people into narrowly defined specialties, the intellectual division of labor – when properly applied – actually results in new, more integrated, more interesting jobs. It can enrich peoples' working lives and enable them to increase their compensation. The Booz Allen graphics story is a simple illustration of the principle: using the templates allowed consultants to focus on the activities where their creativity most benefited clients, enabled them to manage their time better, and, by increasing their value added, resulted in increased compensation.

At the heart of the win-win-win for customers, employees, and owners is a definition of a job that includes some activities where the individual can use her talents and knowledge, as well as other activities where HOWs and WHATs are used. The message to the individual worker is not the dehumanizing message of Taylorism: "do your job exactly the way we say, faster than you did it last year. Rather, the message of the intellectual division of labor is: "focus on using your talents and creativity on these outcomes and activities, using these methodologies and algorithms in the mundane parts of your job." Like in the case of the Booz Allen graphics format, effective use of knowledge is about being freed to focus on performing the most important, and usually most interesting, part of a job.

The redefinition of the salesperson's job over the past twenty years illustrates the opportunity (see figure 2). Initially, the salesperson focused only on selling, and had to contact others in the company about non-standard pricing, credit, actual product lead time, order status, and to get direction about which new accounts to target. Most companies now equip salespeople with algorithms to assess credit, respond to most non-standard pricing requests, plan promotions, offer immediate delivery dates and order status. In addition, salespeople apply methodologies to target potential new accounts, know who to call within the company to help address difficult customer problems, and enjoy access to up-to-date information about purchases and profitability of each of their accounts. Effective use of the division of labor across each of these activities not only increases productivity by eliminating many jobs in support functions, but also improves the quality and timeliness of the expertise delivered to customers. It also fundamentally changes the nature of the salesperson's job. No longer a simple order taker, sounding-board or "gofer" for customers, today's salesperson can truly manage each account, including its profitability and the value realized by the customer. While restructuring work around the intellectual division of labor usually required a significant change effort, salespeople have welcomed the opportunity to use the algorithms and methodologies because it has expanded and enriched their job and enabled them to add more value.

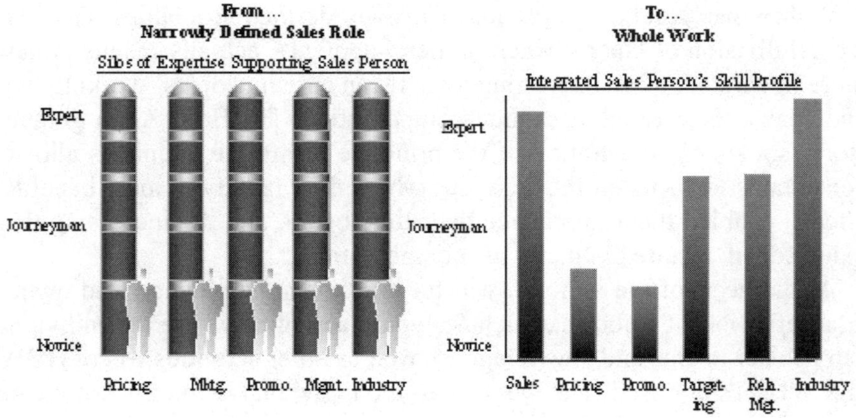

Fig. 2. "WHOLE WORK" Sales Force Example

Effectively implementing the intellectual division of labor requires what we call "whole work thinking:" Instead of focusing on activities to improve productivity, focus on how an important job can be restructured to be more effective and efficient while remaining challenging and becoming even more rewarding for the individual. Start by asking what a better, more efficient, more attractive job for a sales person might look like. Then, using the intellectual division of labor, apply methodologies and algorithms to implement the new vision. Sometimes, task-by-task application of the intellectual division of labor achieves the same result as it generally has for salespeople. But as often, the task-by-task approach results in dehumanized, mindless jobs and prompts enormous push-back from employees.

While "whole work" thinking helps eliminate self-defeating applications of the intellectual division of labor, it doesn't eliminate employee resistance – or the need for change agents and managers. People resist change, especially change that causes them to lose control and depend on others and others' ideas. In addition, increased productivity, by definition, means more output per worker and fewer jobs. Finally, while the intellectual division of labor is theoretically about producing more output by working smarter not harder, many workers would prefer to work smarter and produce the same amount of output by taking it a bit easier. Of course, in the knowledge age, few workers would trade fulfillment in their work for ease – at least in the advanced market economies. Just ask any career counselor or human resources manager.

We conclude by posing a question: where can you improve the productivity of your organization by effectively using the model of intellectual division of labor proposed in this paper.

The Significance of Knowledge Management for a Large Company

Jürgen Biesner and Gerhard Brüggen

Robert Bosch GmbH[1], Department BFV2, P.O. Box 10 60 50,
D-70049 Stuttgart, Germany

Introduction

In a study of any market, you are likely to find successful companies side by side less successful companies within the same market sector. What is the reason for this difference? What is the reason behind a good performance? The good performers may have had a little bit more luck in the past, but usually they tend to also have better management and better processes.

But why should less successful companies find it so difficult to have good management? The methods and tools for management seem to be well known, taught in business schools and universities, and they are more or less the same in each company. The organizational structure of companies may differ, but, within each structure, companies can post a typically good or poor performance. So it seems to be rather difficult to manage a company while the "proven" concepts taught in business schools and implemented by advisors might not be as reliable as those actually needed.

In the following pages the fundamentals behind the state-of-the-art approach to the management of a company will be described. It will be shown that these fundamentals may be insufficient and may even be wrong. Then an alternative basis for a company will be described focusing on knowledge and knowledge management and yet without being able at the present time to suggest suitable methods and tools for the management of a company from that point of view.

---

1 Bosch is a company operating world-wide with 220,000 employees and sales worth 34 billion Euros in 2002. The core business is automotive technology while other business sectors are industrial technology and consumer goods. Bosch runs its business on the basis of technological innovations and has an R&D annual expenditure of about 2 billion Euros.

Definition

Many different definitions of knowledge exist. In this article "knowledge" means: information, skills (know what), capabilities and abilities (know how) and rules, relevant to the company.

Managing a Company – A Big Task

In principle, management of a typical company works as follows:

1. Determine the company's current market situation and evaluate how things have developed up to now.
2. Think about what form the future might take and how the company should be positioned.
3. Draw up a plan describing what operational steps should be taken in order to turn this future possibility into reality for the company.
4. Make sure that efficiency is maintained and the company is permanently in line with the goal. Monitor the implementation of this plan and, additionally, the activities within the company in general.

This is a very short description of management. But what is being managed here? A company and its processes consist of:

- many different elements: projects, products, internal and external services, customers, competitors, departments, units,…
- a wide range of functions: purchasing, sales, development, production,…
- various influences: markets, economic developments, interest rates, competition,…
- many measurable quantities: market share, number of employees, profit/loss, sales, customer satisfaction, growth,…
- a high degree of interaction between the various items: market share affects profits and revenues; customer satisfaction influences market share etc.

A company builds up simultaneously both a complicated and a complex system: this system consists of very many different items and the interaction between the items is very often non-linear and often depends on the actual status of other items. A company is far from being fully transparent in all its items and cannot be controlled by dealing with each factor and quantity in isolation.

The primary question that we pose in this paper is how do we effectively manage a complicated and complex system at all? In other words, how is it possible to monitor a more or less non-transparent system and then steer this system in the right direction when there are hundreds of possible directions to pursue

How Do We Manage a Company?

To simplify the complexity of the system a *model of the company* is used, very much smaller than the company so that the complicated and complex system can then be handled. This company model is based on the assumption that there are a few *key factors* that have to be precisely monitored, measured and controlled since they represent the impact made by the company. All other factors are of secondary importance: they are either directly linked to the key factors, thus allowing them to be portrayed in conjunction with the latter, or, they are of minor importance so that they do not have to be taken into account when managing the company. This model of a company is the basis of all the operational and strategic controlling and steering measures. The key factors form the basis for defining optimization strategies and for implementing them in the company.

The company's "really relevant factors", commonly known as "factors of production" are:

- labor
- capital
- facilities and raw materials

At first sight it might appear rather surprising that the very complicated system "company" can be reduced to only these three items and that the non-linear interactions are not explicitly mentioned in this model, but, as we will now show, this is the world we now live in when we talk about, and work in, the management of a company. This way of looking at things in a company has its origins in the 19th century.

Today this company model offers a wide range of methods and tools for handling these "factors of production" in the operational and strategic management of a company, in order to monitor, plan and implement optimization measures:

- monitoring labor-time, planning resources, head count, etc. focuses on *labor*
- controlling, cost centers, balance sheets, budget planning, etc. focuses on *capital*
- capital expenditure account, (fixed) cost accounting, write-offs, etc. focuses on *facilities and raw materials*.

These methods and tools are constantly being adapted and refined by business experts.

Also at the operational level these three factors of production are the main focal points.

Managing a development project, for example, demands tight control of the labor and capital factors in the starting phase by reducing budgets as much as possible and by planning the optimal use of human resources; in the working phase rigid control has to be exercised over money and the labor investment (people, working hours). Even in the strategic area these three factors of production build the basis for new optimization strategies: lean management (labor factor), shareholder value (capital factor), lean production, just-in-time production and outsourcing (investment and raw materials) are examples from the last decade. If something very important has to be done in a company, these three factors of production have to be kept in focus.

Additionally, these factors of production represent values and so there is a kind of business philosophy behind this model: earnings and profits are more or less proportional to the use of these factors. The possession of these factors of production and their investment in a real product brings its own rich rewards.

The situation is described here in such detail as to make it clear that this really is the common model of the company. Managing a company means thinking and acting according to this model. Of course, it is not a bad thing to use a model when dealing with complicated and complex systems. In fact, it is the only way to act sensibly and not just leave it to chance.

Nevertheless, one big problem still exists: is the model the right one or the best one possible? If not, wrong decisions might be taken in the company and wrong optimization strategies might be set up. If a better model for companies existed, its implementation would bring more clarity and better opportunities for control and, consequently, it would cause fewer problems and generate higher profits.

How can this model be tested?

Firstly, a good model should explain the current situation: what is happening within the company? How can we explain certain events, processes or results?

Secondly, it should provide hints for optimization strategies.

Testing the Model

The model should be able to describe effects, events, processes and measurable quantities within the company. What can this model tell us?

Here are just a few questions (Q) and answers (A):

Q: *What is sold?*

A: Products and services.

Q: *What is knowledge?*

A: Knowledge (know-how or experience) is intangible and comes into existence when work is being done on new (material) products. It can also appear spontaneously or be generated intentionally at creativity workshops (ideas, visions etc.). Knowledge is an attribute of our products and processes. It is generated while work is being carried out on the product.

Q: *How should knowledge be handled?*

A: It should be stored, shared, distributed, etc. (for example, according to the elements of Probst's circle of knowledge).

Q: *What can be done to ensure success for the company in the future?*

A: Invest work and money in development projects. This pays off when certain success factors are taken into account such as the monitoring and control of the amount of money, labor and investment spent on the projects.

Up to now, the model has given us reasonable answers to the questions. However, there are simple questions to which the model either cannot give any answer or merely gives answers that are unsatisfactory or irritating:

Q: *From dishwasher to millionaire – how is that possible?*

A: Not at all! The labor has already been sold and there is neither capital nor facilities. There cannot be any gain from, or any combination of, the three factors of production.

Q: *How does the software industry make its money?*
A: ?

Q: *How can a estate agent earn so much money by injecting so little investment, so little money and – as the clients often say – so little work?*
A: ?

Q: *How is growth achieved? Where does it come from?*
A: ?

The answer to the first question is somewhat curious: the great American Dream cannot be explained by conventional methods of looking at companies. Actually, the history of most companies is not explainable using this model because they all started off as very small enterprises.

The software and estate agent questions ask why there are such large differences in the gains achieved from labor. Do other companies also have such huge gains from their use of labor? Moreover, if a company is part of the "Old Economy" with production facilities (investments), its profits should be significantly higher than if it were part of the "New Economy" because it also uses the two other factors of production. And this should result in additional gains.

These questions may be simple but they are of a fundamental nature. It is really annoying that these questions cannot be answered.

It should also be noted that even after using the company model for 150 years, it could be said that we still end up facing similar, even identical, problems in managing the company, in spite of all the extensive controlling and steering measures intensified in the last years by all the IT-based ones.

Therefore, one might come to the conclusion that the company model is inadequate.

It doesn't fit.

This might also be the reason for the permanent search for better management methods and for the searchers' lack of success. It may be that we cannot develop suitable management methods and tools within the framework characterized by the three traditional factors of production.

The Knowledge-based Model of the Company

We suggest that *knowledge* is the important factor when it comes to ensuring the success of a company. This model has the following fundamentals:

- only by having knowledge about product functions, production processes, markets and internal organizations can a company successfully manufacture and sell products or services
- knowledge is not part of a product but rather its precondition
- a company's competitiveness is achieved by its advantage over its rivals in the field of knowledge. An important consequence of this is that the company requires exclusive, proprietary knowledge. It is not enough to use the knowledge that is publicly available
- the employees work in processes either to create new knowledge or to apply existing knowledge.

Testing the Knowledge-based Model

The most fundamental question is: *How is business done?* The answer reveals a rather different picture of the nature of the company.

Five processes define the business of a company:

1. Knowledge is bought by the company in the form of employees, licensing rights, components, machines and assembly plants, etc.
2. Knowledge is used for the (existing) products and for optimizing the efficiency of the processes. This keeps the company state-of-the-art in those areas which do not belong to its core competencies. Additionally, this knowledge is the basis for the next process:
3. Knowledge is newly created. When all the available state-of-the-art knowledge is applied, it will add that little bit extra and so achieve an advantage over competitors.
4. Knowledge is converted by the production process into a marketable form, i.e. into a service or product.
5. Knowledge is sold in its converted state.

To sum up, the company's business is to buy, use, create, convert and sell knowledge. The other factors of production (labor, capital, investments and materials…) are needed to run the processes to use this knowledge. They largely depend on the amount and complexity of the knowledge involved: the amount of knowledge needed lies in conjunction with the company's efficiency in the application and creation of knowledge and the effort needed for the conversion of such knowledge.

On the basis of this model, the tricky questions mentioned previously can easily be answered in a consistent manner:

- the dishwasher possesses knowledge about the market and the needs of its customers. He also possesses knowledge about product functions or services and the ways to offer these to the customers. This knowledge he can sell.
- the software industry offers IT-based knowledge which the company needs in order to increase the efficiency of its processes. The company buys this knowledge, which is also available to the public, in order to keep pace with its competitors. The profit of a software company does not come from invested labor, but from the market value of the knowledge generated.
- the estate agent sells his or her knowledge of the market, not his/her labor.
- growth is based on the company's ability to generate efficiently the right knowledge for the market.

Preliminary Conclusions from the Knowledge-based Company Model

Taking a closer look at the knowledge and knowledge management (KM), some preliminary conclusions can be drawn:

- KM has two tasks: of course, it has to ensure that the existing knowledge is efficiently applied in the processes and converted into the products. This is the typical task of KM in today's organizations. In addition, it has to manage the effective and efficient creation of new knowledge for the future business of the company.
- KM is not an additional process which runs parallel to the existing product development and production processes, but it should be the core of the management process itself.
- Projects are seen to be different by their amount of knowledge creation and knowledge conversion. Only the latter type can be managed (monitored and steered) in the conventional way by focusing on work. The other project type must be managed by focusing on the knowledge needed and knowledge creation.

- The role of the employees is then also defined differently: we need creative employees who can create new knowledge as well as employees who can transform this knowledge efficiently and with determination into products. These are different roles with different requirements.

Implementation of the Knowledge-based Company Model

Today it is easy to think in terms of the concept of a knowledge-based company model, but it is hard to act according to it. Up to now no common units exist to represent knowledge or the knowledge needed as we have for labor (hours, number of employees) or capital (money). When we have solved this problem, the difficult task remains to develop the methods and tools for monitoring and steering the company's processes with regard to knowledge. Many of today's common methods and tools of knowledge management may be useful and might be applied, but this will only be recognized after close analysis of the knowledge requirements of the company's processes. Some initial ideas already exist but they have not yet been fully developed and there is a lack of extensive testing and optimization.

Perfection can be realized only in the long run, but it should be kept in mind that today's methods of management also have a history of development over more than 100 years – and are still not working completely satisfactorily.

Conclusion

We have shown that present day company management is based on a model of the company, which might be insufficient and thus constrain the development of efficient and effective management methods and tools. We have presented here an alternative company model based on knowledge that might have the potential to open up the way towards a new and better understanding of the company and could lead to a new and better operative and strategic management. The result is that knowledge management is no longer an additional task for the company – but the core of the company management itself.

Knowledge Sharing Through Storytelling

Steve Denning

Formerly: World Bank, Washington DC, USA

4515 Klingle Street NW, Washington DC 20016
email: steve@stevedenning.com

Introduction

This paper addresses some questions that we've been discussing here, particularly the last question, "How do you enlighten a CEO?" And "How do you spark culture-change in an organization?" The answer that I am going to suggest to these questions might surprise you: organizational storytelling.

The Response of Academia to Organizational Storytelling

Organizational storytelling? In academia, a resort to story might seem implausible, even outrageous. Meddling with narrative risks being seen as infringing a taboo, which stems from the 17th Century when René Descartes, the philosopher and scientist, cut a turf deal with the Pope in order to get the freedom to do scientific research. Descartes' deal was that science wouldn't mess with the soul, the mind, the imagination or the emotions: they would remain the exclusive jurisdiction of the Church, so long as science could claim the physical realm for its own. This deal set the tone and direction of the Western intellectual activity for the next couple of centuries, dividing human experience into two artificially distinct and separate spheres that could never overlap.[1] The use of story in organizations with its direct appeals to subjective understanding and emotions breaches this deal, and hence is automatically looked at with suspicion in academia. Nevertheless the practical benefits of re-examining the deal are so large for organizations today that some reconsideration of the deal is inevitable.

---

1 Candace Pert, *Molecules of Emotion* (1997, Simon & Schuster).

My Initiation into Organizational Storytelling

I got into the issue of organizational storytelling in a rather unexpected way.

It began for me in February 1996. Prior to that, I grew up in Australia. I was born in Sydney. I studied psychology and law here at Sydney University. Then I studied in England at Oxford University. And then I joined the World Bank.

I was a very analytic abstract kind of thinker – sharp, clear, crisp, the very things that big organizations love. And so I climbed up the managerial ladder of the World Bank. By February 1996, I was the Director of the Africa Region. Now the Africa Region handles about a third of the operations in the World Bank. So I was beginning to think that this was a pretty important kind of position.

And then, as these things happen in large organizations, the scene unexpectedly changed in the management and things were not looking too bright for me in the World Bank. So I went to the senior management and asked them whether they had anything in mind for me. And they said, "Not really."

I pressed them a little as to whether they had really nothing at all for me. And they said finally: "Why don't you go and look into information."

In February 1996, unlike today, information in the World Bank had about the same status in the organization as the garage or the cafeteria. So this was not exactly a promotion that was being offered to me. Essentially, I was being sent to Siberia.

But I was kind of interested in information and computers, and so I went and looked into information. And I saw a scene that is familiar to anyone working in a large organization. We were drowning in information. We were spending a ton of money on it and getting very little in the way of benefits. We couldn't find anything when we needed it.

And we obviously had to fix this up and we were equally obviously going to save a lot of money when we did that. But something else started to become clear to me as I thought about the situation. Even if we fixed up the situation in information, we would still be a rather old-fashioned lending organization. And our future as a lending organization wasn't looking too bright.

Many years ago, we had had a virtual monopoly in lending to the less developed countries. Now the scene had changed. Now a whole set of private banks had emerged that were lending far more than the World Bank could ever lend. And they were doing it faster and cheaper and with less conditionality than the World Bank. There were even world-wide campaigns to close the World Bank down. There was a political slogan chanted by protesters, "Fifty years is enough!". So our future as a lending organization was not looking too bright. .

So some of us started to have a different idea. We thought: why not share our knowledge?

Over the previous fifty years, we had acquired immense expertise as to what worked and what didn't work in the field of development. We had all this know-how on how to make development happen in countries around the world. But it was very hard to get access to this expertise and know-how. It was very hard to find it. If you were inside the organization and you knew somebody who had the expertise, and could talk to them, you were o.k. But if you didn't know someone, you were in trouble. And if you were outside the organization, it was practically impossible to get access to the World Bank's expertise unless you were engaged in a lending operation.

So there were only very few people around the world who were actually benefiting from the World Bank's immense expertise. So we started to ask ourselves: why don't we share our knowledge more widely? Technology was changing and it was now becoming possible for us, if we so chose, to share our knowledge with the whole world. It was becoming possible for us to become a knowledge sharing organization, and in the process, we could be a pretty exciting organization with a bright future.

So I tried all the traditional methods of explaining the case for change. But no one seemed to be able understand the change idea. I tried charts. I tried reason. Nothing of the things that had been such a strength for me all my life seemed to work. No one seemed to able to grasp the significance of my idea. I was hitting a brick wall.

The Zambia Story

And then I stumbled on something else. I would be talking about the future, and the future of the World Bank. Well, the future is obviously going to be different. But how? What will the future look like? "Well," I said, "the future is going to look like today. Let me tell you about something that happened just a few months ago."

We are still in early 1996, and I would say something like the following.

"In June 1995, a health worker in a tiny village in Zambia logged on to the website for the Center for Disease Control in Atlanta, Georgia, and got the answer to a question on how to treat malaria".

Now remember: this was June 1995, not June 2015.

And this is not the capital of Zambia, but a tiny small village six hundred kilometers away.

And this was not a rich country: this is Zambia, one of the poorest countries in the world.

But you know the most important part of this picture for us in the World Bank? The World Bank isn't in this picture. We didn't have our know-how organized in such a way that we could share our knowledge with the millions of people in the world who make decisions about poverty. But just imagine if we did. Just imagine if we got organized to share our knowledge in that way, just think what an organization we could become!

And yes, that did start to resonate. That started to connect with managers. And in fact, it was only later that those managers were able to get to the president of the organization. And on October 1, 1996, at the Annual Meeting of the World Bank, in front of 170 finance ministers, the President of the World Bank, Jim Wolfensohn, announced that we were actually going to be doing this thing. We were going to be a knowledge sharing organization, from top to bottom. We are going to become "the knowledge bank".

Well, that was not the end of the war. That was just the beginning, because the people who had sent me to Siberia suddenly realized, "The man from Siberia is back!" And worse than that, he has this strange vision of turning us into a knowledge organization. And he's somehow co-opted staff and managers and now even the president to pursue this vision. This is bad news!" In effect, they were thinking that this was their worst-case scenario. And that's when they started using real bullets, instead of rubber bullets in the process. Now there was a chance that this thing might actually happen.

So in fact, over the next couple of years, we had major struggles, confrontations, and battles at the upper level of the organization as to what this thing called "knowledge management" was, and how we were going to go about implementing it. People like me – and Carlos Braga – were trying to persuade people to implement the vision that the President had already announced. My experience was that the only thing that carried us through those battles was telling a story, like the Zambia story and other stories, which are described in my book, *The Springboard*.[2]

What I discovered was that there was a certain pattern to a story that could spark people into action. I'll just say a few things about it in the short time we have.

---

2 Stephen Denning, *The Springboard: How Storytelling Ignites Action in Knowledge-Era Organizations*, (2000, Butterworth Heinemann).

Communication: Our Reaction to Abstractions

Let me start by explaining how does a story work. What is it that is being explained by the story? As we all know by now, knowledge management is a complex idea. I don't know whether it has ten dimensions, or twenty dimensions, but it's certainly got lots of dimensions that need to be mastered if it is going to implemented successfully. Let's say for the sake of argument that knowledge management has sixteen dimensions.

Now if I say to you, "Let me explain to you in detail and depth right now each and every one of the sixteen dimensions of knowledge management," you're already looking at your watch and thinking, "How do I get out of this meeting without causing an international incident?" You are not looking forward to a comprehensive explanation of knowledge management's sixteen dimensions.

Communication: Our Reaction to Narratives

But if I say, "Let me tell you something that happened in Zambia," that is to say, a story, you're immediate reaction is, "Yes, I'd like to hear about it." You're not sure what I'm going to pop out at you, but you've heard so many interesting stories, in your life, you have a positive attitude and expectation to the prospect of hearing a new story. And I may lose your interest by telling a boring story, or by telling an interesting story poorly, but your initial attitude and expectation towards the story is positive. Unlike the abstract explanation or the chart, I start out on a positive note.

Communications: The Download Theory of Communication

But you might ask, "How could this possibly work? How could a 29 word story like the Zambia story that I just told you, how could that 29 word story possibly convey to you a sixteen-dimensional concept like knowledge management? Surely that's not possible?"

And if you take the standard view of communications, the download theory of communications, it surely can't work. The standard view of communications runs something like this. I am talking to you. So my head must be full of stuff. So you are sitting there silent, listening, so your heads must be empty. And the object of my communication is to download the stuff which is in my brain into your empty heads. In other words, some kind of computer dump.

Communication: How Narrative Communicates

That's total nonsense of course, but that's the standard view of communications. There are many things wrong with the picture. I don't happen to have all the answers to the questions to give to you. And even if I did, I couldn't transmit them to you in the time that I have available. But the main thing that's wrong with this picture is: your heads are not empty. Your heads are full of all sorts of understanding about how the world works, what malaria is, and where Zambia is, All of those things you have in your mind. And all I need is a tiny fuse of a story that can link up with all of this tacit understanding that you have in your minds, and if it succeeds in igniting that understanding, then suddenly a new pattern of understanding can flash into your mind, and you can suddenly see how the world fits together in quite a different way from what you had been thinking. A new pattern of understanding emerges in your mind.

Communications: The Little Voice in the Head

In fact, there are two listeners in the room that we need to be thinking about When I look at someone, I see the physical person in front of me, but there is also, the little voice in the head. And we all know what the little voice in the head is. And if you're asking yourself, "What is he talking about? What on earth does he mean by 'the little voice in the head'?", well, that's exactly the little voice that I mean! And so there are two listeners. I am talking to you about Zambia. And the little voice in the head may well be saying, "I've got all these problems back in my office, my in-box is filling up, I've got email to answer. How can I get out of here without causing an international incident!" So the little voice may not be listening at all to what you are talking about.

And the conventional view of communications is: let's just ignore the little voice in the head. Let's just hope that it doesn't get in the way and let's hope that everything goes o.k. Unfortunately, that often doesn't happen. The little voice gets busy, and before you know it, the listener is getting a whole new and often unwelcome perspective on what the speaker is talking about.

What I am suggesting to you is something different. What I am saying is: exploit the little voice in the head. Take advantage of it. Make use of it. And the way that you do that is that you tell a story in a certain way that elicits a second story. The little voice in the head tells another story. In effect, what I am doing is: I am giving the little voice in the head something to do.

So when I say, "Let me tell you about something that happened in Zambia, I am hoping that the little voice in the head is saying, "We're working in highways. Why couldn't we do this?" Or if you are working in finance, "Why don't we do this in finance?" Or if you are working in Latin America, "Why don't we try this in Latin America?" In effect, the little voice starts to imagine a new story, a new set of actions for the listener, another kind of future. And if things are going well, the little voice in the head starts to flesh out the picture. It starts to say: "Of course, we would have to have a community. We would need to get organized. We would need budgets to make it happen. And we would have to get more people involved. But why don't we do it? Why don't we get on with making this happen?"

And when this happens, the little voice is already racing ahead to figure out how to implement knowledge sharing in the organization. And because the listener has created the idea, it regards the ideas as his or her own baby. And of course, you love your own baby. You created the idea. It's yours!

The Story Is Told in a Minimalist Fashion

So the story is told in a minimalist fashion. You'll recall that I told you about that health worker in Zambia. Was it a nurse or a doctor? Was it a man or a woman? Was it hot or cold? Was it wet or dry? I didn't tell you anything about that health worker in Zambia because I didn't want you thinking about Zambia. I wanted to leave a lot of room in your mind for the little voice in your head to be crafting a story about how you could launch knowledge sharing in your environment. If I tell you all about Zambia, you might get interested in Zambia, instead of crafting your own story.

The Necessity for a True Story

It's very important that it be a true story. It's not a fictional story. It's a true story, because when you tell one of these stories, one of the first things that happens is that people go and check it out to find out if it actually happened the way I said it happened. And if they find it was true, they race back and announce loudly, "It didn't happen. It's just a myth." Then everyone can relax and go back to the standard ways of doing things.

I've had no success at all with an imaginary story like, "Just think what the World Bank would be like if it adopted knowledge sharing." The answer to this kind of story is, "That will never happen around here. It might happen in some good organization, but not here in the World Bank." And if the story is imaginary, that is usually the end of that. But if the story is true, one can say, "This already has happened. It happened right here. Here's the guy it happened to. Go and check it out. It actually happened." Then it's the truth of the story that shakes the listener out of their complacency. They have grapple with the fact that the story actually happened. So maybe it *could* happen here, after all.

And it must be authentically true. It's not just a story that's factually accurate as far as it goes. An example of a story that is factually accurate but not authentically true is the following:

Seven hundred happy passengers reached New York after the Titanic's maiden voyage.

The story is factually accurate as far as it goes. It omits the detail that the ship sank and 1500 other people drowned. Once that fact becomes clear, then the backlash on the story and storyteller is massive. But the ironic thing is that many, if not most, corporate communications are exactly in this format. They paint a rosy picture of some scene, but just below the surface or just around the corner is some other unedifying fact that, once it becomes known, creates a massive negative impact on the story and the storyteller. If you want to understand why trust levels in big organizations are at their current abysmal levels, you might want to examine these "Titanic stories" which are proliferating in these organizations.

The Necessity for a Happy Ending

Most important, Hollywood is right. It's got to have a happy ending. I have had no success in telling a story: "Let me tell you about an organization that didn't implement knowledge management and it went bankrupt." No success at all with this kind of story.

If I tell you a story with an unhappy ending, that company that bankrupt because it didn't implement knowledge management, what seems to be happening is that these ancient parts of the brain, the limbic system kicks in and the message is: "Fight! Flight! Get out of here! Trouble! Something bad is happening!" and so on.

But by contrast, if I tell you a story with a happy ending, what seems to be happening is that the limbic system kicks in with something called an endogenous opiate reward for the human brain, the cortex. Basically, it puts the human brain on drugs. It pumps a substance called dopamime into the cortex and this in turn leads to "a warm and floaty feeling," the kind of feeling you have after you have just seen a wonderful wonderful movie. And this is the perfect frame of mind to be thinking about a new future, a new identity for yourself or your organization. You are ready for anything. "Let's do it." That's why the story has to have a positive tonality.

So I wrote a book about this kind of story, *The Springboard*, in 2000. In December 2000, I left the World Bank and since then, I've been going around coaching various organizations how to use the power of storytelling to get results in their organizations. A lot of big organizations have got pretty interested, even excited about it: GE, Shell, McDonald's, Bristol Myers Squibb. These companies face huge problems. The world economy is going through these wrenching changes and obviously the companies have to change if they are going to survive. Change is irresistible. But when they start explaining to their staffs that they are now going to have to do things very differently, no one wants to hear this message, when it's explained in conventional abstract terms. So change is irresistible but the organization is immovable. The financial impact of the storytelling can be massive.

And more and more organizations are realizing that a key part of their future depends on effective storytelling.

- It relates to *communicating the need for change*. This is what I was writing about in *The Springboard*.
- It relates to *communicating identity and branding*. Who is this firm? What sort of an organization is it? Why does it have a bright future? They need to be able to tell an effective story.
- *Knowledge sharing* also depends on storytelling. A lot of high value knowledge resides in stories that the staff and clients tell each other. Understanding this, and capturing those stories becomes a key part of knowledge sharing.
- Stories can *tame the grapevine.* A particular form of story can in certain circumstances stop rumors.

But each of these different purposes needs a different pattern of story. If you understand the pattern, you can find the right story much more easily. I'm currently writing a book on highest value forms of organizational storytelling.

Two Types of Cognitive Functioning

Jerome Bruner suggested that there are two distinct forms of cognitive functioning. On the one hand, there is what he called the logico-scientific or paradigmatic mode of thinking, or what is usually called abstract or analytic thinking. On the other hand there are narratives or stories. Bruner said that they are separate realms. Abstractions cannot be reduced to narratives and narratives cannot be reduced to abstractions. One reason for that is this phenomenon of the little voice in the head. Storytelling is always a dialectic between the storyteller and the listener. It's a conversation. The storyteller is saying one thing, and the listener is thinking that, but also something else, namely, whatever the little voice head is saying. There is a great deal going on between the storyteller and listener.

Mapping the Narrative Dialectic

You actually can map this dialectic along the two key dimensions of true/imaginary and negative/positive tonality.

Here's the springboard story. The storyteller's story is a true story with a positive tonality. This leads to the listener imagining a new story about their own story which is in the future, and hence fictional, but it's very powerful because it drives the listener to action.

By contrast, a knowledge sharing story would be over in the top left hand corner. We learn more from our mistakes than our successes. Hence knowledge sharing stories are about issues and difficulties and how they were resolved. It also leads to a new story for the listener, but because the story is negative, it generally doesn't spark the positive excitement that you can get from a successful springboard story. A knowledge-sharing story tends to be sobering. The listener is sadder but wiser. He or she realizes how difficult it is to make things happen in the real world. So a knowledge sharing story takes the listener some of the way, towards a positive future story, but not the whole way.

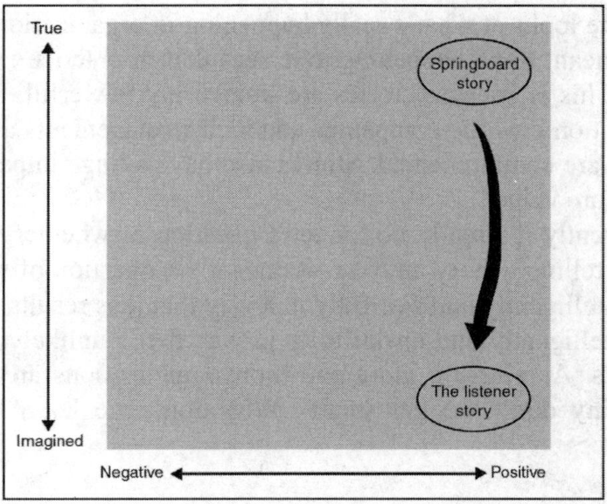

Fig. 1. The Springboard Story

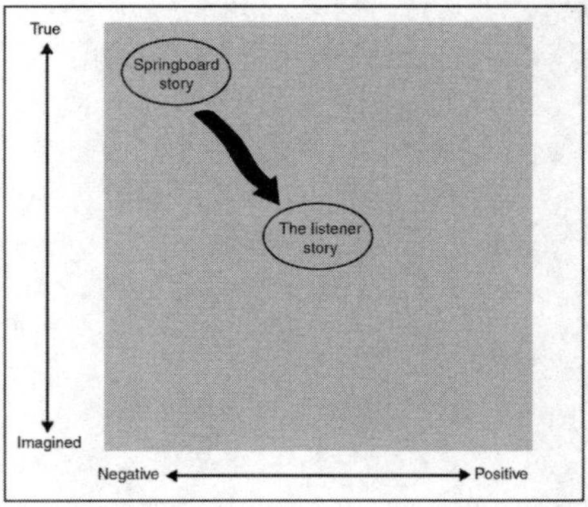

Fig. 2. The Listener Story

Conclusion

Narrative is a different way of understanding and interacting with the world, and is central to the key management challenges facing organizations today. Narrative modes of communication are proving to be a quicker and more effective tool for explaining complex concepts, and strange new ideas, in comparison with analytic abstract thinking.

When one looks at what's really happening in organizations, as opposed to what's meant to be happening, one sees that in practice everyone is using story. This is because stories are immensely powerful. Stories have a huge impact on how the companies and their managements are viewed and how issues are communicated. Stories also have a huge impact on how the companies are valued.

Consequently it's really no longer a question of whether to tell a story. People are telling a story anyway. Rather it's a question of whether to tell the story intelligently and skillfully in a way that gets results, or whether to tell it unintelligently and unskillfully in way that's unlikely to get the desired results. As a result, more and more organizations are asking themselves: "Why don't we get smart? Why don't we learn how to use a story?"

Knowledge Management Experiences: India's Light Combat Aircraft

Kota Harinarayana

Vice-Chancellor, University of Hyderabad, Central University P.O., Hyderabad – 500 046, India

Introduction

Aviation is a knowledge-intense activity. Its direct contribution to economic prosperity is a measure of its success in pioneering the "Knowledge Society". The people directly employed in the aviation enterprises are highly skilled "knowledge" workers, well practised in the use and exploitation of advanced technologies including the new digital information technologies. Others working in the laboratories push forward the technological frontiers developing the knowledge that is crucial for economic growth.

In aviation the largest investments are made on military aircraft development since they are linked to national security. Military aircraft also have the most demanding and the most diverse performance requirements. It is therefore not surprising that the best technologies and often the best science emerge from the development of military aircraft. These technologies then find their way into civil aviation sector and often to one's delight, also to non-aviation sector.

Taking into consideration, the military and financial aspects, the Indian Light Combat aircraft program was initiated in the mid-eighties. This fighter aircraft is world's smallest, lightweight supersonic fighter of its class. This necessitated development of new infrastructure, new enabling technologies and new core technologies. Collaborative effort between academic institutions, R&D laboratories and Industry was undertaken on a very large scale. Hundreds of new products, processes, facilities and technologies were developed as a part of this program. This paper outlines the strategy adopted to develop and manage the knowledge base.

Indian Light Combat Aircraft (LCA)

LCA is the world's smallest, lightweight, multi-role supersonic aircraft designed to meet the stringent requirements of Indian Air Force (IAF) as its frontline, multi-mission single-seater tactical aircraft for the 21st century (Fig. 1).

The Key requirements are:

- Higher agility and maneuverability
- Multi-mission capability
- All weather, day and night missions
- Cockpit compatible with night vision systems
- Capability to carry
  - Precision guided weapons
  - Conventional bombs and rockets
  - Close Combat and beyond visual range missiles
  - Sensor and Electronic counter measure pods
- High survivability in ECM/ECCM environment
- Adequate range for close support and interdiction

Fig. 1. LCA in Flight

The need was that performance must be superior to fighters such as F-16 of American origin, Mirage-2000 of French origin and Mig-29 of Russian origin. Another requirement was that the technology deployed should enable aircraft remain current for duration of its service without major upgrades. It was evident that goals of performance and life could be achieved only if the best of technologies available in the field of aviation were harnessed in the making of LCA (Fig. 2)

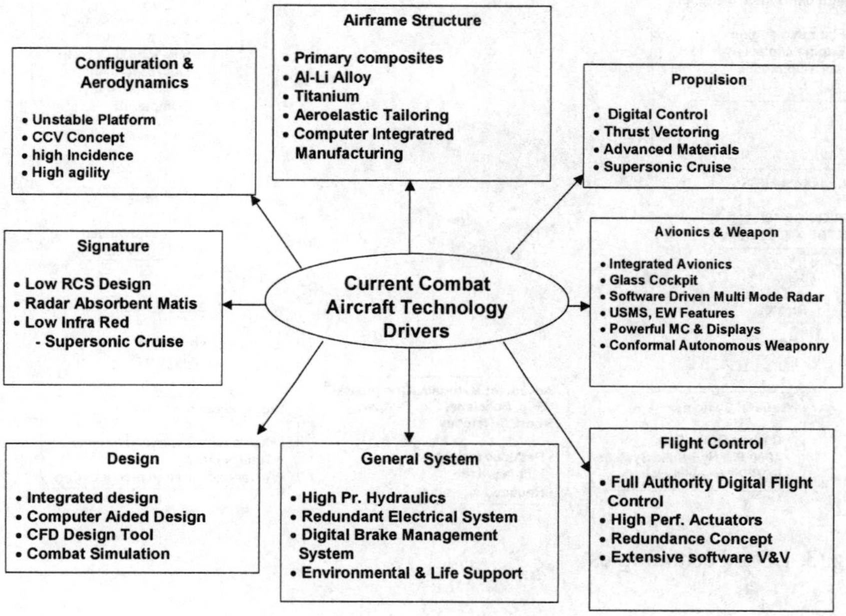

Fig. 2. Current Combat Aircraft Technology Drivers

Core Technologies and Design Concepts of LCA

LCA integrates modern design concepts and state-of-art technologies such as compound delta plan form with relaxed static stability, fly by wire flight control system, advanced digital cockpit, multimode radar, integrated avionics system, advanced composites for airframe and a state-of-art, high performance engine (Fig. 3).

LCA is a total weapon system capable of precision weapon launch. There are eight weapon stations with capability to carry and deliver a wide range of missiles (close combat, beyond usual range, air-to-air, air to surface and air to sea), bombs, rockets, etc.

In addition to the multimode radar, which is the prime sensor of LCA, it is designed to carry additional sensors such as FLIR (forward looking infrared sensor), IRST (Infrared search and track system), LDP (Laser designation Pod) and Reconnaissance Pods.

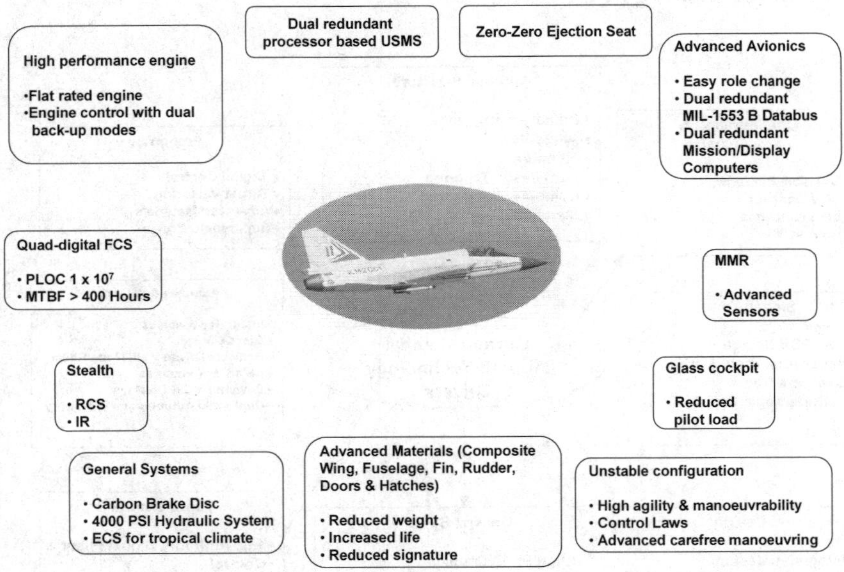

Fig. 3. LCA Technologies

Enabling Technologies for LCA Design, Development and Production

LCA is packed with latest technologies relevant to contemporary fighters. The performance, weight and cost targets specified by the customer demanded not only the best of core technologies but also best of design processes, manufacturing technologies, testing infrastructure/ testing facilities/ testing technologies, software development, testing and validation methodologies and a host of other enabling technologies and management tools. Some of the enabling technologies needed for development of LCA were:

- Computer Aided Design (CAD)
- Computer Aided Manufacturing (CAM)
- Computer Aided Engineering (CAE)
- Digital Prototype Assembly (DP)
- Virtual Prototyping (VP)
- Rapid Prototyping (Rapid Tooling (RP/RA)
- Reverse Engineering (RE)

- Product Data Management (PDM)
- Enterprise Resource Planning (ERP)

A few of the CAD tools such as CATIA were available in the commercial market. However, most of the CAD/CAE/CAM/DP/VP/RP/RA tools needed to be developed by the LCA teams as they were not available in the commercial market. The Aircraft Industries develop these tools in-house and would not like to part with them as they are their knowledge base and provide them competitive advantage. The Indian Industry had not developed any of these tools and technologies earlier as they did not have a development program which demanded such tools and facilities.

Challenges of Knowledge Generation and Knowledge Management

For a proper understanding of the significance of LCA for Indian Aeronautics, one needs to know a little bit about the historical background of fighter aircraft design and development in India. The last fighter prototype, the HF 24, Marut flew in 1961. This aircraft development was undertaken in India under the leadership of a German design team using mostly imported materials, equipment and processes. This aircraft was a contemporary fighter. However, no follow-on program was undertaken for next two and half decades. As a result the knowledge base, not only did not grow but even the existing knowledge base got dissipated. In a field such as aviation, one has to continue to develop new technologies and products to retain their position, whereas in India, no significant initiative was taken to develop new technologies. Thus the base was very weak.

Unlike the previous generation aircraft, LCA systems are totally software dependent. The flight control system is an all digital system incorporating safety critical onboard software. The Glass Cockpit does not incorporate any discrete instruments. The multifunction displays are driven by software and instruments on demand are created. The onboard avionics computer is driven by onboard mission critical software which not only manages vehicle management functions but also carries out multiple functions such as control of displays, weapons management, sensor management, systems health management, electronic counter measures and a host of other related tasks. The software is so critical that new development and testing technologies were required to be established and mastered.

The new generation fighters such as LCA are highly integrated systems, each element is dependent on many other elements and together they serve the multiple objectives of vehicle management, mission management, life management, vulnerability/survivability management. Development of such an integrated system, needed concurrent engineering approach and related tools; ground rigs for testing at component, subsystems and system level; simulators mimicking the major systems, the vehicle itself and also the complex environment in which the vehicle has to operate. Development of a complex system such as LCA needed a structured process of validation and verification leading to certification for safe flying leading to service induction. The testing involves not only on ground but also flight testing. It is a complex process needing lot of know-how and know-why along with excellent professional management skills. This is a complex knowledge and resource management which was developed from scratch.

A complex system such as LCA needed thousands of scientists/engineers/technicians with expertise in multiple disciplines. No single organization within India had the abilities to develop these complex knowledge bases and technologies. Hence along with knowledge innovation there was a need to bring in organizational innovation to achieve the objectives. Fig. 4 outlines major innovations that were achieved in the process of developing the LCA.

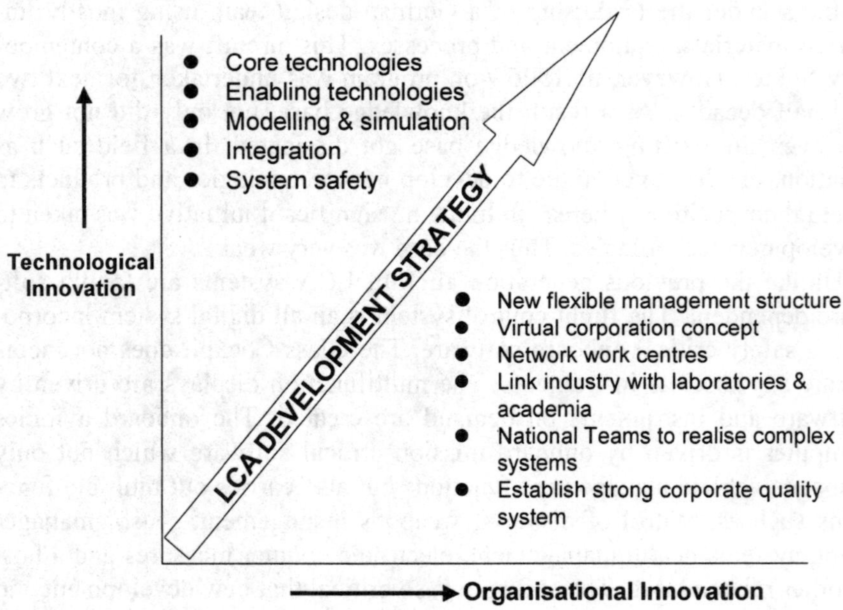

Fig. 4. LCA Development Strategy

The Knowledge Circuit

Following major tasks were accomplished within the program:

Knowledge Generation

The design team strength varied from 300 engineers/scientists at projected definition phase to almost 3000 at the peak of development. The knowledge generation work was done at more than 300 industries, 25 academic institutions and 40 research laboratories.

The Subsystem/System Knowledge Intensification

System teams integrated the various components/equipment/software/-processes developed by industry/R&D labs./academics and carried out testing extensively. The vehicle and system designers also had to build high fidelity simulators (both hardware and software) to test the vehicle behavior, to fine-tune the man machine interface and to carryout failure analysis. This data and knowledge base was consolidated for subsequent formal validation by independent agencies.

Knowledge Validation

The validation of system functioning under normal and failure modes are done by independent certification agencies based on extensive testing done on simulators, ground rigs and flight testing.

Knowledge Transfer

One of the big challenges is to consolidate and document the database and knowledge to enable smooth transfer to production agencies. This is a difficult task. However, new generation enabling technologies such as digital models, virtual prototyping tools, product data management tools, networking environment are helping in the smooth transfer of knowledge base. Fig. 5 presents the knowledge circuit of the LCA program.

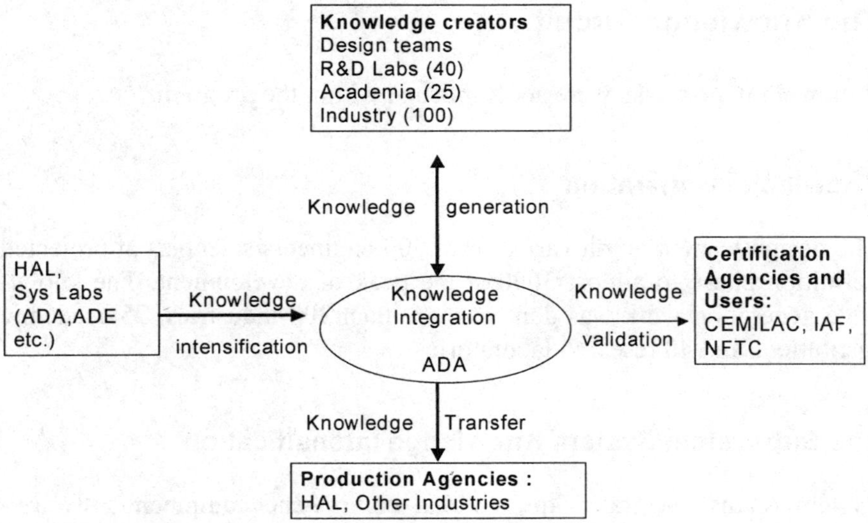

Fig. 5. The LCA Knowledge Circuit

Support System for Innovation

The most challenging task was establishment of culture that supports innovation and knowledge generation. Fig. 6 illustrates the support system established for innovation and knowledge generation. The key elements of this support system are the culture supportive of innovation and the culture of taking up challenges. This needed dismantling of all organizational and other barriers. Such a strong cultural base enabled ideas generation, facilities creation, technologies development and establishment and relevant systems to achieve the mission of developing the LCA.

Concluding Remarks

Development of Indian Light Combat Aircraft, the largest R&D Program undertaken in the country so far, is an extraordinary experience for the development team. It achieved a considerable degree of cultural and system changes. It enabled creation of a valuable knowledge base at the various work centers. This knowledge base is expected to have many spin-off benefits not only in the aviation but also in the non-aviation sector.

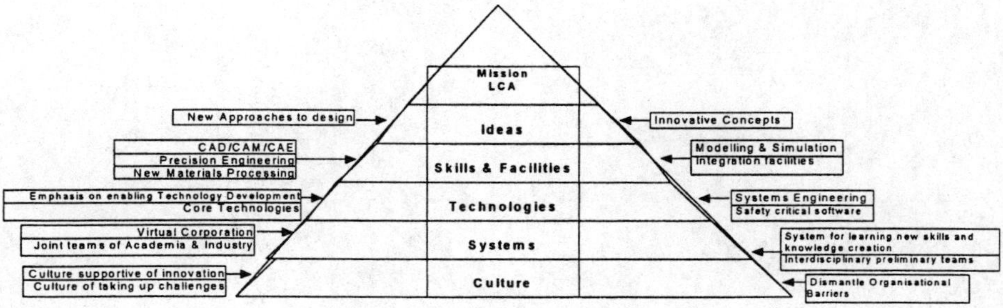

Fig. 6. Support System for Innovation & Knowledge Generation

Integrating eLearning and Knowledge Management

Larry G. Moyer

EDS Digital Learning, Dallas, TX, USA

Introduction

When we review actual implementations of knowledge management and eLearning, we often find that the goals and objectives of the organizations are tactical and highly pragmatic. Where thought leaders have imagined that these pursuits would transform organizations and lead to full realization of a knowledge-centric enterprise, business leaders have focused on the much shorter-term objectives of simply improving employee's performance. The usual goal is to improve the effectiveness and speed with which people think, analyze, react, decide and/or execute and in ways that benefit the organization, including:

- Better customer service
- Improved problem solving
- Improved sales of goods and services
- More effective analytical processes
- Better use of computer systems
- Better decision making at executive levels

Hence, it follows that unless we, the thought leaders, advocates and practitioners can build a compelling case for knowledge management and eLearning as a strategy for improving employee performance, few will invest in such initiatives. This paper further proposes that neither knowledge management nor training (digital or classroom) is, by itself, sufficient to generate the performance improvement sought by the typical organization. Rather, there must be a close coupling of what can be known, how one comes to know about it and how to do it. Knowledge management and eLearning must consider and promote both; and, the integration of the two must be highly focused on the questions that trouble most organizations today – how to operate faster and more effectively while selling more.

Are We Just Repeating Ourselves?

It should be emphasized that neither knowledge management nor eLearning are new business strategies, nor is the quest for faster and more effective operation. The U.S. Army has used integrated knowledge management and distance learning principles for at least the past 50 years to collect 'lessons learned' from the battlefield and convert to doctrine and revise training material through a constant feedback process. Over at least the past 25 years, the Laborers International Union of North America (LIUNA), a union of construction workers has regularly collected work site experiences during training events, then refined and updated the training and reference material. Both the U.S. Army and the LIUNA have long been involved with distance education, including the use of digital media such as VHS tapes and audio recordings.

What is new is that both knowledge management and distance learning are now considered to be within the domain of information technology. Moreover, both can be viewed as incarnations of an increasing list of technological 'point solutions' for enhancing organizational performance. Unfortunately, this list of isolated solutions for the highly complex human enterprises of learning, knowing and acting has a questionable history.

For example, during the 1970s and early 1980s the software industry attempted to both create a new genre of product and a solution to what some believed to be an impediment to better performing organizations – lack of decision support. The belief was that by improving the decision making process through access to increased information about an organization's operations, better decisions could be made and the organization's overall performance would improve.

Unfortunately, for the software industry, very few people in the typical United States organization actually make decisions. The majority of employees simply execute according to prescribed processes and procedures. Hence, even with considerable marketing emphasis and promotion by consultants and thought leaders, there were few actual purchases of such technology.

During the 1980s, the software industry suggested that the future of performance improvement was in the use of artificial intelligence, specifically in 'expert systems.' It was claimed that by capturing the knowledge of the experts in organizations that software technology could help organizations improve customer service, solve complex problems, anticipate opportunities and generally make better decisions.

Again, unfortunately for the software industry, we had to ultimately admit that there are very few actual experts in any organization. Rather, there are innumerable employees who have developed various ways by which to do their specific work and with an acceptable level of effectiveness if not efficiency. The degree of effectiveness and efficiency is usually debatable though the creativity people exercise in developing the solutions clearly evidences human ingenuity.

The 1990s saw the emergence of technology assisted knowledge management within software companies and business consultants. The belief was that by facilitating the creation, capture, use and reuse of knowledge, organizations could significantly improve their functioning, perhaps even assuring their survival in an ever increasingly competitive world. If nothing else, organizations could retain the corporate memory of processes, procedures and actions that were at risk of being lost through employee retirement, resignation and layoff. The success stories have been few and the results quite mixed.

While it would be unfair to claim that the paucity of success stories is a result of continued reliance on questionable assumptions, it is important to note that as before, the knowledge management initiatives have emphasized that:

- Organizations are increasingly composed of knowledge-workers, or those who make decisions about how they work and what actions are appropriate to achieve the corporate objectives
- Organizations are populated by people with useful expertise (tacit knowledge) that only need to be captured to benefit the organization and others

Finally, starting in the mid-1990s, Internet enabled training called 'eLearning' became the latest in the series of performance enhancements for organizations. Though learning 'at a distance' has been available for as long as remote communication has been available, recent software technologies made the creation and delivery of learning events via the Internet practical and desirable.

The expectation of vendor, consultant and consumer was that technologically delivered courseware is inexpensive, effective, efficient and available to any who choose to learn. Organizations can develop better-trained employees at less cost and thus improve the performance of the organization as a whole.

Cost savings for particular types of learning objectives (e.g., HR employee compliance matters) have indeed been significant when the content is moved to a digital format. However, measurable performance improvements have not been widely documented except in cases where specific types of knowledge workers were targeted, such as sales staff.

Taking these cases together and given the infrequent success story, it seems that: (a) our assumptions are no more valid than they were twenty-years ago, and (b) these 'point solutions' have not shown any significant effect on organizational performance. Still, few would argue against the value of knowledge transfer within an organization, whether through any of these technology initiatives for improving worker performance. So, why are there so few success stories?

What Is Not Working?

History suggests that an analysis of assumptions is usually a reasonable first step in reviewing outcomes. Some of the questionable assumptions motivating knowledge management and eLearning have already been identified. We can add to that list:

- Knowledge management and eLearning address different issues. The reality is that it is counterintuitive and counterproductive for training to be considered separate from knowing, collaborating and creating new knowledge.
- Organizations are sufficiently ready for and the need is present for knowledge management and eLearning. In reality, there are few organizations that are ready for and willing to commit to a comprehensive knowledge based initiative, whether knowledge management or online learning.
- Since knowledge management and eLearning address different issues, they need not be considered together. Unfortunately, neither knowledge management nor online learning has or will singly improve performance, at least as businesses try to use them today.

Disassociated Domains

The first point will not likely elicit debate although most discussions of knowledge management issues or eLearning matters fail to consider either as having more than a remote relationship to the other. Perhaps this is due to the separate focus of the various software products that serve the fields or separate organizational responsibilities, but it has not served the interests of the enterprise and does not assure the success of either initiative.

Disinterested Market

The second point considers the ideal world of organizations that, when shown the value of knowledge management and eLearning, are ready to move from pools of independent knowledge workers and structured process workers, each holding personal knowledge of something potentially important, to organizations of collaborators, knowledge creators and knowledge users. Ultimately, the ideal organization becomes one where knowledge is the principle product and all employees are involved in continually creating new and renewed knowledge. eLearning strives to add the employee as a continuous learner.

Such goals are admirable. They are also beyond reasonable near-term expectations for most U.S. organizations (commercial and governmental). The basis for this claim is the very history of science and workings of organizations. Individuals, science, or organizations do not change until they absolutely need to change.

Van Valen, a biologist, indirectly explained this phenomenon when, in 1973, he proposed that organisms evolve as quickly as possible just to survive in a highly threatening environment. This has become known as the Red Queen Hypothesis. The theory took its name from Lewis Carroll's book *Through the Looking Glass* wherein Alice noticed that no matter how fast she ran in this realm of the Red Queen, she could not make progress.

Likewise, it is almost axiomatic that organizations will not change until encountering a sufficiently difficult and threatening environment whereby survival depends on evolution. In such an environment, only those who learn to deal with the Red Queen can leave that realm. For the vast majority of organizations, that moment of extreme threat has yet to be acknowledged, if even suspected.

This then invites the question: Can we change before we need to? Perhaps, but the goals of knowledge management and eLearning need not wait for the occasional inspired leader and highly motivated worker. There are significant business problems and objectives that can be addressed and there are performance improvements that can be identified in most organizations as being likely targets for integrated knowledge management/eLearning concepts, technologies and methodologies. The challenge is to demonstrate how an integrated initiative addresses those specific problems and measurably improves performance.

Disconnected Solutions and Needs

For the third point, it is safe to claim that eLearning implementations have both ignored the knowledge management issues (e.g., digital library support, work-aids and subject matter expert access) and lacked emphasis on objectives that will yield measurable performance improvements. For example, the rush to comply with Federal requirements (e.g., harassment, abuse, OSHA and HIPPA) often takes precedence over the training of operating department employees to better perform their work. Adding to the problem, these compliance motivated initiatives and the lower priority training sessions are often driven by objectives such as employee tracking, fast content development and low cost rather than effectiveness.

Likewise, knowledge management programs often ignore online learning and too rarely deliver any measurable performance improvement. One reason is that the first intervention is usually to make documents available on some web site and with little or no consideration about who might use or find the content usable. Unfortunately, most often, organizations make no distinction between knowledge, information and data, leaving value judgments to the employee. Moreover, there is little attempt to qualify that which might be actual knowledge. Hence, the most useful content in the typical knowledge base is often the form one must submit for requesting a vacation.

Taken together, we have two fields attempting to: (a) address the same issue – transfer of knowledge, (b) avoid consideration of the other, and (c) miscalculate the need for focus on performance objectives. The position taken here is that this lack of focus is the single most important factor in the questionable results shown in both knowledge-based initiatives.

And, the Answer Is...

If we assume that this premise is correct, there are a few obvious remedies. Some of possible answers include position and commitment to:

- Knowledge is effectively transferred and performance potentially enhanced when there is an integrated context for learning and training, an opportunity for continuing development, support for one's work, use and reuse of what the organization knows and renewal of the knowledge considering what lessons people learn.

- The concepts with which we work (knowledge, information, training, etc.) must be defined and operationalized in ways that contribute to worker and organizational performance improvement.
- The knowledge of most immediate value focuses on what has value in addressing the performance objectives of an organization.

Tight Integration

At first reading, this set of statements might be taken as a traditional set of objectives for knowledge management. However, the introduction of training as a specific objective and medium for the transfer of organizational knowledge introduces the opportunity for new objectives, the challenge of new technologies, new change adaptation requirements and additional systems, processes and strategies. In particular, the inclusion of learning activities tends to refocus the initiative, lessoning the emphasis on knowledge capture and creation (e.g., collaboration facilities) and applying a greater emphasis on knowledge transfer and learner/worker support. This tightly integrated, refocused offering highlights attributes such as:

- Ability to take online training courses
- Ability to register for any organization sponsored learning event
- Ability to manage one's career objectives through learning activities
- Ability to access deeper knowledge about any subject of importance to the organization and using a digital library
- Access to online work-aids, processes and practices
- Access to those who know about and those who know how to do the subjects
- Ability to access and contribute to lessons learned about the subjects and the learning opportunities (training or other)
- Access to and ability to contribute to better practices
- Ability to share questions and insights with those of similar interests and/or responsibilities

This list makes a particular assumption about the nature of training, learning and knowledge, namely that they contribute to organizational performance. Depending on the definitions, this assumption might or might not be valid.

Pragmatic Definitions

What is this thing, this knowledge of which the organization must become aware? What is this thing called training that supposedly improves an individual's performance? If we cannot define it in ways that promote capture, how will know when we have it? If we cannot define it in ways that help the organization and the employees perform, what value does it have to either?

A multitude of possible definitions complicates any attempt to answer these questions. For example, the term 'tacit knowledge' has come to mean everything from deep understanding to all non-conscious cognitive processes and memories. Knowledge has been treated as everything from the form for requesting a vacation to the process by which aircraft engines are assembled. What is needed is business pragmatism grounded in science and philosophy. Some examples follow.

Knowledge

First, not everything of interest is valuable to the organization and to those who benefit from it. That which is central to a knowledge-aware organization has broad-based appeal, meaning and usefulness. It directly affects the operation of the enterprise and decisions to be made by individuals. It is neither data nor information.

To better understand what knowledge for the organization might be, it is necessary to clearly distinguish data, information and knowledge. For centuries, debates have raged among philosophers and scientists over the meaning of knowledge. It is not likely that this paper will resolve the issue. However, some definitions can be proposed that are consistent with received agreement and that are consistent with the goals and objectives of organizations attempting to leverage their member's knowledge.

Perhaps the best place to start is with a diagram offered by Gene Bellinger (1998):

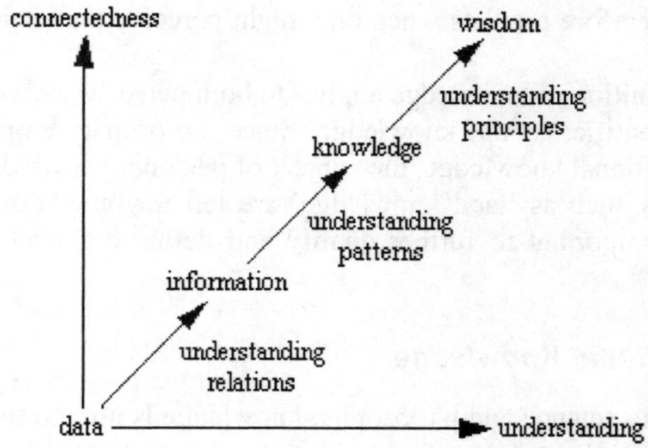

Fig. 1. A Relationship between Data, Information, Knowledge and Wisdom

This chart does not infer a smooth continuous progression from data to wisdom, nor should it be taken as the product of a single person. It is intended to show only the relationship between the components.

- Datum is an event out of context. Since it has no inherent context, it is without a meaningful relation to anything else.
- Information answers the questions: What? Who? It is not just a collection of datum.
- Knowledge provides answers to the questions: When? Where? How?
- Wisdom answers the question: Why?

Information is data that have meaning to someone. A Datum or a collection of datum might represent information but it depends on the understanding of the one perceiving the datum, the interpreter and his/her associations. For example, a statement such as 'there is a ring around the moon' can be called a datum or information depending upon the meaning assigned by the observer. In either case, the statement explains nothing, prescribes nothing and predicts nothing.

The next point in the chart includes a shift in the cognitive processes. Relationship between datum is no longer sufficient. Next, the individual must be able to identify patterns as well as relations (Bateson 1988) thereby developing understanding. The result is **knowledge – something that provides understanding; that is, it has explanatory, predictive and/or prescriptive power.** For example, returning to the informational statement about the moon having a ring, a knowledge statement explains why a ring appears to be about the moon, identifies the conditions necessary and therefore predicts when one might perceive that a ring surrounds the moon.

This definition of knowledge applies to both personal and organizational (social, scientific, group) knowledge. Since the primary emphasis here is on organizational knowledge, the subject of personal knowledge and views about terms such as 'tacit knowledge' are left for other discussions. For now, it is important to further qualify and define organizational knowledge.

Organizational Knowledge

According to science and philosophy, knowledge is not the sole product of an individual. Knowledge starts with the individual but it is only through testing, review and agreement among some larger group that the individual's knowledge claim can become accepted by the larger body of people, in this case the organization. Because of the process, it becomes the most reliable understanding the organization has of something. It has endured a test of time. This does not mean that organizational knowledge is certain truth. Things change and understanding evolves, sometimes even radically. Still, at any moment we can say that we have organizational knowledge of something when a claim meets particular criteria:

- It has explanatory, predictive and/or prescriptive power
- It has been shown to be reliable over time
- It has been subjected to organizational review and testing; thus it is generalizable to large populations of people, situations and/or things

For example, organizational knowledge might include: (a) business processes, (b) business practices, (c) algorithms for achieving certain ends (e.g., determining the most effective means of delivering technology projects), (d) demographic studies of a customer base, and (e) training courses on how to accomplish some task. **Organizational knowledge is explicit, measurable, inherently valuable (to some group) and transferable, whether through documents or training events.**

Training

Before suggesting a definition of training, it is useful to suggest a definition of learning. As used here, it is simply some cognitive change in a person. Change might occur in attitude, thinking, beliefs and/or behavior. Something will have changed; else learning did not occur. Perhaps experience or material is captured and retained in memory but remains merely mental dust that can be recalled upon appropriate neural stimulation. However, efficient recall is not learning.

So, how shall we understand training? First, training can be described as but one example of multi-modal delivery of organizational knowledge. It might be delivered as a 'required reading' document, an online course or a classroom event.

Second, regardless of the delivery method, training is a specific type of learning, one that develops or changes the level of an individual's competence. Training is not a matter of changing an attitude. It is a matter of changing behavior. While learning of all sorts (e.g. changes in attitudes, beliefs and thinking) is essential for the creation of new knowledge and the ultimate realization of knowledge management goals, training has the most immediate and measurable impact on organizational performance. In summary, it is a medium for communication of organizational knowledge, a measurable activity that specifically targets worker behavior and organizational performance.

Useful and Usable Knowledge

Given these definitions and the attributes of an integrated offering, it is possible for the technologies, processes and other interventions to emphasize that which is known by the organization and needs to be known by the worker. Whether communicated through a course or a document, this is the knowledge that provides the learner with opportunity, deeper understanding, support during and after the learning process and reference when memory fails. This is the knowledge that can be constantly reviewed and assessed considering lessons learned then fed back into training curriculum and content.

From a content perspective, this organizational knowledge, whether a document or a course is most useful, usable, and used when it is readily available in digital form, centrally managed, electronically accessible, and:

- Current
- Reliable
- Validated within context
- Relevant
- Searchable

Current

Knowledge evolves! Given this dictum, the question becomes – how do I know that the knowledge, including the training exercise upon which I am dependent is current? How do I know when a new version of this knowledge becomes available? If I, as a user, cannot satisfy myself that both conditions are addressed, I am unlikely to risk my job on what the organization calls knowledge. Moreover, if a user cannot immediately determine that an item has outlived its usefulness, it has questionable value to the user or organization.

Furthermore, if I carry a piece of knowledge, such as critical process, on my notebook computer, by whom and how will I be notified that: (a) a new version is available, (b) the knowledge item is no longer current, or (c) that the useful life of the item is about to expire. How will I become aware of the current experiences and/or adaptations of others? Such experiences might have a significant effect on how I use the knowledge. This is not just a bulletin-board matter or a course catalog matter.

Reliable

Organizational knowledge, including training opportunities are never ownerless. We navigate our lives using an abundance of received skills, information, myth and belief. Some of this is quite useful and some is quite dangerous. An organization cannot afford to base its future on such. Organizational knowledge is most reliable when it can be attributed to some person or group of people who will at least periodically assure the organization that the knowledge is valid and current. Without ownership, knowledge becomes merely a claim; thus, it is inherently unusable. Without a periodic review by an owner(s), it is inherently unreliable.

Valid within Context

Even if organizational knowledge is reliable, a questions remain about its scope of validation: Within what context might I rely on this knowledge without further research[1]? Typically the owner(s) is also a subject matter expert, or at least represents the findings of subject matter experts. As

---

[1] In an early knowledge management experiment within EDS, a single symbol (trust symbol, patent pending) was used to indicate currency, reliability and scope of validation. Unregistered – not current, not reliable, not validated; Registered – current, not validated; Silver – current, reliable, validated within a context; Gold – current, reliable, validated company wide.

such, the owner(s) can also warrant that the knowledge is usable without further research within particular contexts. The material might have been validated and deemed usable for a project, a team, department, division or even company wide. The scope might apply to languages or geographies. In any case, convenient indications of scope are important for users to be able to quickly determine to what degree the knowledge can be used without adaptation or research. Furthermore, changes in the scope of validation need to be communicated to those who are using the knowledge and/or those who have it stored locally on their computer.

Relevant

As the organizational knowledge base grows so does the need to make the knowledge relevant to an individual. If a user happens to be functioning as a 'business analyst' on some occasion and only needs to know about processes and practices of a business analyst, all existing search engines create burdensome steps in finding the relevant material. If the objective is to quickly find material relevant to a role one might play, a different mechanism and categorization scheme is necessary. Even a network of categorizations must be considered and designed. For example, a business analyst within one group likely has need for a different (and possibly overlapping) set of knowledge than a business analyst in another. Those in Germany likely have different sets than those in the U.S. From a training perspective, relevance also means that the content has implications for the way specific people and roles work.

Searchable

Just making knowledge relevant does not address all needs for finding answers. Eventually, each user will need to be able to perform complex searches of the organizational knowledge base, including all lessons within all training courses, and the collaborations of users. For example, "Find all instances of pricing models where the most important factor is delivery speed." Such a query might return items form a content repository, discussions about pricing models and lessons from a course on pricing.

Summary

If we objectively review the myriad of technology-based initiatives, including knowledge management and eLearning, that have successfully developed a following and repeatedly been introduced to organizations, we find few studies that show a significant impact on the way organizations perform. While there are numerous case studies of cost savings, little establishes the degree to which the performance of the organizations has actually improved. Is customer service better? Are the analytical processes more effective? Is there fewer product returns? Are we selling more products? Are the executives making better, more informed decisions?

Assuming the initiatives have value, we must then ask the question: Is the lack of evidence simply a function of inadequate baseline evaluations, poor measurements or is the problem with the organization, the technology or something else? The position taken here is that, aside from some cost savings, little performance change has occurred and the problem is a lack of a systemic approach, one that integrates knowledge management and eLearning, to the performance challenges that organizations face.

The remedy is to first understand the performance motivations and the opportunities within organizations, not just the desire for cost saving. Then it is possible to tackle those questions that are inherently difficult to answer and to do so from a human and organizational systems perspective, not just a computer system viewpoint. What will measurably improve the effectiveness, efficiency and/or results of the target groups in the organization? How can that best be achieved when incorporating knowledge-based initiatives? What has immediate value to an organization while also contributing to the other, less tangible objectives?

All theory, case studies and lessons learned from actual implementations point to a high potential for significantly improving an organization's performance when such questions are answered with an integrated, systemic solution. Failure to answer the questions continues to suggest that there is limited business case, hence limited interest.

References

Bateson, G. (1988), Mind and Nature: A Necessary Unity. New York: Bantam.

Bellinger, G. (1998), Knowledge Management. (Available from www.outsights.com/systems/kmgmt/kmgmt.htm).

Van Valen, L. (1973), Body size and numbers of plants and animals. Evolution 27: 27-35.

Printing: Strauss GmbH, Mörlenbach
Binding: Schäffer, Grünstadt